INDIGENOUS RIGHTS IN SCANDINAVIA

This book sets the standard for scholarship on Sami issues. It reveals what has long been hidden from English readers. The breadth of these chapters is impressive; nuances and subtleties are well-contextualized to readily enhance understanding of this field.

John Borrows, University of Victoria, Canada

This book provides a ground-breaking overview of the intersection of law, politics, morality, history and the Sami people. Helping to forge Sami Law as a distinct subject of inquiry, this thought-provoking collection draws from the expertise, experiences and novel insights of a diverse group of scholars.

S. James Anaya, The University of Arizona, USA, and Former United Nations Special Rapporteur on the Rights of Indigenous Peoples

Throughout the world, indigenous peoples have been confronted with exported European concepts of state sovereignty and land rights. Indigenous Rights in Scandinavia: Autonomous Sami Law *explores how the legal claims of an indigenous people are treated within Europe. This book is therefore an invaluable contribution not only to scholars interested in indigenous peoples, but for anybody interested in European ideas of law and justice.*

René Kuppe, University of Vienna, Austria

Juris Diversitas

Series Editors:
Seán Patrick Donlan, University of Limerick, Limerick, Ireland
Julian Sidoli del Ceno, Birmingham School of the Built Environment,
Birmingham City University, UK

Editorial Board:
Olivier Moréteau – Louisiana, US
Ignazio Castellucci – Trento, Italy/Macau, China
Lukas Heckendorn Urscheler – Swiss Institute of Comparative Law, Switzerland
Salvatore Mancuso – Cape Town, South Africa
Christa Rautenbach – North-West University, Potchefstroom, South Africa

Series Advisory Board:
Philip Bailhache – Jersey, UK
Sue Farran – Northumbria, UK
Patrick Glenn† – McGill, Canada
Marie Goré – Pantheon-Assas (Paris 2), France
Werner Menski – SOAS, London, UK
Esin Örücü – Glasgow, UK (Emeritus)
Vernon Valentine Palmer – Tulane, US
Rodolfo Sacco – Turin, Italy (Emeritus)
William Twining – University College London, UK (Emeritus) and Miami, US
Jacques Vanderlinden – Free University of Brussels, Belgium (Emeritus) and
Moncton, Canada (Emeritus)

Rooted in comparative law, the *Juris Diversitas* series focuses on the interdisciplinary study of legal and normative mixtures and movements. Our interest is in comparison broadly conceived, extending beyond law narrowly understood to related fields. Titles might be geographical or temporal comparisons. They could focus on theory and methodology, substantive law, or legal cultures. They could investigate official or unofficial 'legalities', past and present and around the world. And, to effectively cross spatial, temporal, and normative boundaries, inter- and multi-disciplinary research is particularly welcome.

Forthcoming titles in the series:

The Practice of a Mixed Pluralistic Legal System
State and Non-State Orderings in South Africa
Christa Rautenbach
ISBN 978-1-4724-3682-5

Law Between Buildings
Emergent Global Perspectives in Urban Law
Edited by Nestor Davidson and Nisha Mistry
ISBN 978-1-4724-7406-3

For more information on this series, visit www.ashgate.com

Indigenous Rights in Scandinavia
Autonomous Sami Law

Edited by

CHRISTINA ALLARD
Luleå University of Technology, Sweden and
UiT The Arctic University of Norway

SUSANN FUNDERUD SKOGVANG
UiT The Arctic University of Norway

ASHGATE

Published by
Ashgate Publishing Limited
Wey Court East
Union Road
Farnham
Surrey, GU9 7PT
England

Ashgate Publishing Company
110 Cherry Street
Suite 3-1
Burlington, VT 05401-3818
USA

www.ashgate.com

British Library Cataloguing in Publication Data
A catalogue record for this book is available from the British Library

The Library of Congress has cataloged the printed edition as follows:
Allard, Christina, author.
    Indigenous rights in Scandinavia : autonomous Sami law / by Christina Allard and Susann Funderud Skogvang.
        pages cm. -- (Series juris diversitas)
    Includes bibliographical references and index.
    ISBN 978-1-4724-2541-6 (hardback) -- ISBN 978-1-4724-2542-3 (ebook) -- ISBN 978-1-4724-2543-0 (epub) 1. Sami (European people)--Legal status, laws, etc.--Scandinavia. 2. Indigenous peoples--Legal status, laws, etc.--Scandinavia. 3. Minorities--Legal status, laws, etc.--Scandinavia. I. Allard, Christina. II. Skogvang, Susann Funderud, 1975- III. Title.
    KJC5144.M56A74 2015
    342.48508'72--dc23

2015014528

ISBN: 9781472425416 (hbk)
ISBN: 9781472425423 (ebk – PDF)
ISBN: 9781472425430 (ebk – ePUB)

Printed in the United Kingdom by Henry Ling Limited, at the Dorset Press, Dorchester, DT1 1HD

Contents

PART III: SAMI LAW AS A KNOWLEDGE FIELD

Notes on Contributors

Christina Allard (b 1971), LLD, Senior Lecturer at Luleå University of Technology, Sweden, and Associate Professor II at the Faculty of Law, UiT The Arctic University of Norway, is Project Leader of the Nordic Research Network for Sami and Indigenous Peoples Law (NORSIL, www.uit.no/jurfak/norsil). Allard's research interests centre on Sami and indigenous peoples' rights comparatively and within the context of the recognition of territorial rights, natural resource use and environmental protection. In her doctoral thesis Allard analysed and contrasted laws of Sweden, New Zealand and Canada. In 2015, Allard will publish the book *Renskötselrätt i nordisk belysning* [The reindeer-herding right from a Nordic perspective] (Makadam förlag). Currently she participates in two interdisciplinary research projects: 'Indigenous rights and nature conservation in Fenno-Scandinavia' and 'Indigenous rights and the global politics of resource extraction: The case of mining in Sapmi'.

Nigel Bankes (b 1956) is Professor of Law and Chair of Natural Resources Law at the University of Calgary. Bankes is also Adjunct Professor of Law at UiT The Arctic University of Norway and the K.G. Jebsen Centre for the Law of the Sea. He obtained his Law degree from Cambridge University (1978) and holds an LLM from the University of British Columbia (1980), as well as an honorary doctorate from the University of Akureyri, Iceland. Bankes is a former editor of the *Journal of Energy and Natural Resources Law*. His main research areas are oil and gas law, domestic and international water law (principally the Columbia River Treaty) and indigenous peoples' law.

Bertil Bengtsson (b 1926) is currently Guest Professor at Luleå University of Technology and Advisor to the Ministry of Justice, Sweden. He has previously served as a Professor in Private Law at the universities of Stockholm and Uppsala and as a Justice of the Swedish Supreme Court (1977–1993), as well as jur. Dr. h.c. at the universities of Copenhagen (1988), Helsinki (1990), Oslo (1991) and Bergen (1996). Bengtsson is a member of the Royal Swedish Academy of Sciences and the author of several books on tort law, insurance law, contract law, land law, public law, environment law, constitutional law and Sami law.

Kirsti Strøm Bull (b 1945) is Professor of Law at University of Oslo, Norway, and an Adjunct Professor at Sami University College, Guovdageaidnu/Kautokeino. For the past 20 years of her research, Strøm Bull's main interests have been in Sami law and natural resources law, as well as legal history regarding these topics, and she has written books and several articles in these fields. Strøm Bull chaired the committee that prepared the draft Norwegian Reindeer Herding Act (2007), was the main Secretary of the Group of Experts which created the draft Nordic Sami Convention (2005), and was a member of the second Sami Law Committee (2007). She was also an expert of legal history for the Coastal Fishing Committee for Finnmark (2008) and is Chair of the Research Group in Natural Resources Law at the Faculty of Law at University of Oslo. Since 2012 Strøm Bull has been a member of the Board of The Norwegian Academy of Science and Letters and, in 2013 and since 2015, the President of the Academy.

Leena Heinämäki (b 1974), LLD, is Senior Researcher at the Northern Institute for Environmental and Minority Law in the Arctic Centre, University of Lapland, Finland. Heinämäki is also Vice Leader of the University of Arctic Thematic Network on Arctic Law. Her research interests relate to indigenous peoples' human and environmental rights and the rights of Sami people. Heinämäki is currently co-authoring and editing a book on the protection of sacred sites of indigenous peoples in the Arctic. She is also coordinating an international network on indigenous peoples' sacred sites and teaches indigenous peoples' rights and Sami Law at the University of Lapland.

Tanja Joona (b 1975), Doctor of Social Sciences, is Senior Researcher at the Northern Institute for Environmental and Minority Law in the Arctic Centre, University of Lapland, Finland. Joona is currently working as the leader of a project addressing reindeer herding and other land uses in Finnish Lapland, with a special focus on ILO Convention No. 169. She is also a visiting researcher on the topic of Sami youth for a project with the Norwegian Institute for Urban and Regional Research (NIBR). Joona's main research interests focus on comparative legal and political aspects of Sami society and especially issues dealing with traditional livelihoods, international human rights law and identity questions. From 2012 to 2015 Joona was heard as an expert in the Finnish Parliament in connection with the renewal of the Finnish Sami Act and ratification of ILO Convention No. 169. She teaches Sami Rights at the University of Lapland and works as Vice Lead for the Thematic Network on Arctic Law, University of the Arctic. Joona is a member of the Sami Research Board and the Board of the Communities and Changing Work Doctoral Programme at the University of Lapland.

Kristina Labba (b 1976) is a PhD student at the Faculty of Law, UiT The Arctic University of Norway. In her doctoral thesis Labba analyses ways in which regulations in the Swedish and Norwegian Reindeer Herding Acts protect individual rights and minorities within Sami villages and reindeer herding districts, as well as to what extent Sami reindeer herding customs are incorporated into these legislations. She is a member of a Sami family which, since time immemorial, has pursued what is now considered Swedish-Norwegian border-crossing reindeer herding between the northernmost area of Norrbotten County in Sweden and Troms County in Norway.

Kjell Å Modéer (b 1939), is currently Guest Professor at Luleå University of Technology, Sweden and Senior Professor of Legal History at the Faculty of Law, Lund University, Sweden. He was formerly Professor of Legal History (1977–2007) at Lund University and holder of the Ragnar Söderberg Professorship in Honour of Samuel Pufendorf (2005–2007). Modéer's honorary degrees include: jur. Dr. h.c. Greifswald (2000), Teol. Dr. h.c. Lund (2004), and jur. Dr. h.c. Helsinki (2010). He was constituted Judge for the Swedish Lower Norrland Court of Appeal [Hovrätten för Nedre Norrland] in the so-called Härjedalen case concerning the right to winter pasture for reindeer. Modéer has also served as expert in a Swedish public commission regarding delimitation of reindeer herding areas (SOU 2006: 14 *Samernas sedvanemarker*). He was a member of the Theological Committee of the Swedish Church arranging the *Sagastallamat* regarding the Church's reconciliation with the Sami in 2011. In addition, Modéer is a corresponding member of the American Society of Legal History, former member of the Board of the Max Planck Institute for European Legal History, Frankfurt/Main, Germany, member of the Board of Olin Foundation of Legal History, Stockholm, Sweden, and member of the Advisory Board of the European Society of Comparative Legal History. Modéer's main research areas are legal profession, comparative legal cultures, legal traditions, law and development, and law and religion.

Jacinta Ruru (b 1974) is Associate Professor of Law at the University of Otago, New Zealand, Associate at the Indigenous Law Centre, University of New South Wales, Australia, and a member of the Research Leadership Team of Nga Pae o te Maramatanga (New Zealand's Centre of Maori Research Excellence). She holds a PhD from the University of Victoria, Canada, and is editor of *Resource Management Journal, Resource Management Theory & Practice*, and a consultative editor for *Maori Law Review*. Ruru's research explores indigenous peoples' legal interests to own, manage and govern land and water. She is co-author of *Discovering Indigenous Lands* (Oxford University Press 2010). Ruru is of Maori descent; her tribes include Raukawa and Ngati Ranginui.

Susann Funderud Skogvang (b 1975) is Professor of Law at Faculty of Law, UiT The Arctic University of Norway, where she also received her Law degree (2000) and later her PhD in Law (2012). In addition to her experience in teaching and research, Skogvang has practised as a lawyer and law clerk at the Supreme Court of Norway. Skogvang is an expert in Sami law and international indigenous peoples' law. She was the Secretary of the Group of Experts for the preparation of the Nordic Sami Convention, and member of the Coastal Fishing Committee for Finnmark. Skogvang is the author of the first text book on Sami law in Norway [*Samerett*] (first edition, 2002, second edition in 2009), as well as the author of the doctoral thesis 'Retten til fiske i fjorder og kystnære farvann' [The right to fish in the fjords and coastal waters]. She has also authored several articles on Sami law, international law regarding indigenous peoples, and fisheries law. Skogvang is coastal Sami from the North Sami language territory.

Johan Strömgren (b 1973), is an LLD student at the Faculty of Law, Uppsala University, Sweden and Assistant Professor in Sami Law at the Sami University College, Kautokeino, Norway. The topic of Strömgren's doctoral thesis addresses the understanding of the first acts of the Swedish State regarding Sami rights and the Swedish Reindeer Herding Acts of 1886 through1928. In particular the thesis addresses the ways in which questions and definitions of the applicable legislative and preparatory works were products of their time and yet still formative for present-day status of land rights for the Sami and reindeer herding in Sweden. He has worked as a researcher and lecturer on Sami Law since 2006 including, inter alia, reindeer herding rights, land rights, legal history and international law. He is Sami and from a mountain reindeer herding community in the South Sami area of Sweden.

Eva-Maria Svensson (b 1958), LLD, is Professor of Law at the Faculty of Law, UiT The Arctic University of Norway, and at the Department of Law, University of Gothenburg, Sweden. She is also Director for Centre for Interdisciplinary Gender Research (GIG), University of Gothenburg. Svensson's research focuses mainly on legal philosophy and theory, in particular within the field of feminist/gender legal studies, and to that end and more specifically within Studies of Academic Knowledge in Law (part of the field of Studies of Science and Technology, STS) in which she has published extensively. Her research is and has mainly been financed by the Faculty of Law at the University of Tromsø, the Department of Law at the University of Gothenburg, Swedish Research Council, Bank of Sweden Tercentenary Foundation, Alice and Knut Wallenberg Foundation, Swedish Governmental Agency for Innovation Systems, and the Ragnar Söderberg Foundation. Svensson has been a visiting professor at Melbourne Law School, Australia in 2010 and 2013, and at Queen's University, Kingston, Canada in 2014. She has written extensively and internationally on gender equality and theoretical aspects of law.

Eivind Torp (b 1956), is Associate Professor at Mid Sweden University and obtained his PhD (1987) from the Faculty of Social Science and LLD *dr juris* (2008) from the Faculty of Law at UiT The Arctic University of Norway. In his research Torp has focused partly on the conflict between environmental law and Sami law in Sweden, and partly on public law principles within Swedish Sami law. Within these topics, Torp has published a number of scientific articles in Sweden as well as internationally. He has received several scientific prizes, among them The Scientific Prize from Sami Center at Umeå University (Vaartoe/CeSam), Sweden.

Mattias Åhrén (b 1971), PhD, is Associate Professor at the Faculty of Law, UiT The Arctic University of Norway, where he received his PhD in 2010. Åhrén holds Master of Law (LLM) degrees from the University of Stockholm and the University of Chicago. He has written extensively on Sami and indigenous rights and lectures on indigenous peoples' rights at major universities around the world. Åhrén has extensive experience with applied, practical work within the sphere of indigenous peoples' rights, predominantly within the United Nations (UN) system. He was one of the lead indigenous negotiators in the process that resulted in the adoption of the UN Declaration on the Rights of Indigenous Peoples (UNDRIP) and has assisted the President of the UN Permanent Forum on Indigenous Issues (UNPFII) as well as the UN Special Rapporteur on the Rights of Indigenous Peoples. Åhrén was also a member of the Expert Group that negotiated the draft Nordic Sami Convention. He originates from the Ohredahke Sami reindeer herding community.

Acknowledgement

Finalizing this volume has included the contributions and involvement of several persons. The book represents an integral component of NORSIL, the Nordic Research Network for Sami and Indigenous Peoples Law, which is a network comprising scholars from Norway, Sweden and Finland and mostly affiliated with the northernmost universities in the respective countries.[1] Funding from *Tromso Forskningsstiftelse* (2011–2015) has facilitated annual NORSIL meetings and, in turn, a platform for working towards a joint collaboration within the network in the form of a book publication. Therefore, our deepest and sincerest gratitude goes to our treasured colleagues and members of NORSIL who have willingly contributed to the completion of this book, as well as to those who did not contribute through writing but have been helpful in other ways.

Early in the process of creating this compilation we engaged two well-regarded legal scholars from opposite corners of the world, Professor Nigel Bankes from the University of Calgary, Canada, and Associate Professor Jacinta Ruru from Otago University, New Zealand. They have, in very insightful and competent ways and from their respective positions, provided comments and reflections on both shared ground and different approaches of 'their' legal systems in contrast to Scandinavian experiences. Warmest gratitude to you both! In this light, writing the book has been a process for us all, and indeed an important one for the subject of Sami Law. The value of the process has also included shedding light on the contrasts between the three Scandinavian countries on the one hand, and between Scandinavia, Canada and New Zealand on the other. In many regards there is a shared history of colonization amongst these regions.

The result of the above collaborations is a compilation of chapters that contributes to the international literature on Indigenous Peoples Law, containing both in-depth research of Scandinavian historical and legal contexts with respect to the Sami and demonstrating current stances in Sami Law research.

We would also like to take the opportunity to give thanks to other key persons. The Steering Committee of NORSIL, comprising the editors and professors Kirsti Strom Bull, Juha Karhu, Timo Koivurova and Associate Professor Eivind Torp, have provided peer review of all articles. Writing in English has been a challenge

---

1   The project leader is Christina Allard. See the web page of the NORSIL, available at: http://www.uit.no/jurfak/norsil (accessed 18 January 2015). Allard has been the Lead Editor of this volume as the initiator and coordinator of the work from the very beginning, as well as through responsibility for overseeing the book's process through to the completion of the final editing.

for most of us; for instance, it has been difficult to translate certain national legal concepts whilst making them understandable for an international audience. In this regard we are, in particular, grateful for the second English language editing by and discussions with three skilled persons: India Reed Bowers, BA (Brown University) and LLM (Utrecht, Netherlands), now an independent freelance consultant living in Sweden and Founder and Director of the International Organization for Self-Determination and Equality (IOSDE); Anett Sasvari, MIA (Columbia University) and PhD candidate at the Department of Cultural Anthropology and Ethnology, Uppsala University, Sweden, and former professional journal editor in the USA and, last but not least, Professor Nigel Bankes of the Faculty of Law at the University of Calgary who, amongst many other qualifications, has been the editor of the *Journal of Energy and Natural Resources Law* for the past five years and was co-editor of 'The Proposed Nordic Saami Convention: National and international dimensions of indigenous property rights' (Hart 2013). Format editing has been skilfully managed by María José Belmonte Sánchez, licentiate and research assistant at the Erik Castrén Institute of International Law and Human Rights, within Faculty of Law at the University of Helsinki, Finland. Thank you all!

To the reader: we sincerely hope that you will enjoy the chapters within this book, and that they will deepen your knowledge and understanding of the complexities of Scandinavian settler societies and the Sami.

Abbreviations of Scandinavian Legal Sources

Preparatory Works (early stages)

KM: *Komiteanmietintö* – Finnish government official reports. Reports from committees appointed by the Finnish government with the task of investigating certain matters. The reports are delivered to the Finnish government, are usually subject to a hearing process, and provide the background for further preparatory work. Every KM has a unique identification number that consists of a year and serial number, e.g. KM 1990:32.

NOU: *Norges offentlige utredninger* – Norwegian government official reports. Reports published by a committee, panel or expert group appointed by the Norwegian government. The reports are delivered to the government, sometimes after request from the Parliament. The reports are usually subject to a hearing process and provide the background for further legal preparatory work. NOU are used as legal sources with significant weight. Every NOU has a unique identification number that consists of a year and serial number, e.g. NOU 2008:5.

SOU: *Sveriges offentliga utredningar* – Swedish government official reports. Reports from committees appointed by the Swedish government with the task of investigating certain matters. The reports are delivered to the Swedish government, are usually subject to a hearing process, and provide the background for further preparatory work. Every SOU has a unique identification number that consists of a year and serial number, e.g. SOU 2001:101.

Preparatory Works (later stages)

HE: *Hallituksen esitys* – Finnish government Bill. A proposition for legislation that the Finnish government presents to the Parliament (*Riksdagen*). HE are used as legal sources with significant weight. Every HE has a unique identification number that consists of a serial number and year, e.g. HE 167/2014.

Ot prp nr: *Odelstingsproposisjon nummer* – Older Norwegian government Bill, i.e. proposals to the *Odelstinget* (the branch of the Norwegian Parliament dealing with legislation). The *Odelstinget* was closed in 2009. References are made to Ot prp number (nr) along with reference to the respective Parliament years, e.g. Ot prp nr 20 (2007–2008).

Prop L: *Proposisjon til Stortinget*. From 2009 on; government Bills to the Norwegian Parliament (*Stortinget*) are referred to with Prop number and a reference to the respective Parliament years, e.g. Prop 70 L (2011–12).

Prop: *Proposition* – Swedish government Bill. A proposition for legislation that the government presents to the Parliament (*Riksdagen*). Prop are used as legal sources with significant weight. Every Prop has a unique identification number that consists of a year/s and serial number, e.g. Prop 1971:52 or Prop 1992/93:32.

Case Law

KHO: Case law from the Finnish Supreme Administrative Court. Reference is made to KHO year and page, e.g. KHO 1999:55.

NJA: *Nytt Juridiskt Arkiv* – Archives of Swedish Supreme Court case law. References are made to NJA, year and page on which the court decision begins, e.g. NJA 2011 p 109.

RG: *Rettens gang* – Decisions of Norwegian Courts of Appeal and some district court decisions. References are made to RG year and page, e.g. RG 1987 p 128.

Rt: *Norsk Rettstidende* – Archives of Norwegian Supreme Court case law. References are made to Rt year and the page on which the court decision begins, e.g. Rt. 2001 p 769.

PART I
Introducing and Contrasting

Chapter 1

Introduction

Christina Allard and Susann Funderud Skogvang

This book provides an in-depth source of scholarly work related to laws of the Scandinavian[1] states of Norway, Sweden and Finland that concern the Sami people. The book consists of a collection of chapters that address and compare contemporary issues regarding Sami rights within these Scandinavian nation states. All authors within this collection are nationally renowned legal scholars, and most are engaged in research that is either in or closely related to the field of Sami Law. However, the majority of these authors usually write in their respective Scandinavian languages. Therefore, an aim of this book is also to bridge the gap where there is a scarcity of English language literature addressing legal aspects regarding the Sami.

It has indeed been a challenge to describe and make the Scandinavian colonial history, legal traditions and concepts understandable for an international audience. Thus, the chapters by the Scandinavian authors within are complimented by two introductory chapters, serving to address legal issues comparatively in the context of the indigenous peoples of both Canada and New Zealand. Such introductory chapters are included so as to facilitate the international reader in better grasping specifics as they relate to the Scandinavian countries. We sincerely hope that this book helps to bring some clarity to the complex patterns of histories and laws related to the Sami as the indigenous people of *Sapmi*.[2]

The Field of Sami Law and History

Knowledge of historical events is important for the field of Sami Law in general, as present regulations echo much of the past. Due to a long coexistence between

---

1   In this book we use the term 'Scandinavia' to describe the geographic region consisting of the countries of Norway, Sweden and Finland. The term 'Scandinavia' is somewhat ambiguously used and sometimes refers to Denmark, Norway and Sweden. With respect to Finland, the proximity and historical connection to Sweden, as well as in regards to the Scandinavian Peninsula, it is still appropriate to include Finland for our purposes in this collection. The term 'Nordic' refers to five countries, including also Denmark and Iceland, and to use it would be misleading.

2   *Sapmi* is the Sami name for the traditional Sami homeland region, stretching across the state borders of the Scandinavian North through the Russian Kola Peninsula.

the Sami and migrant settlers, as well as various decrees and decisions by kings, a historical context is crucial for understanding how laws are currently expressed or not expressed. The formation of the nation states, the establishment of the state borders as well as various assimilation policies have all had major impacts on the Sami societies.

The formation of state borders and the resulting restriction of free movement of reindeer across those borders have had profound effects on the Sami. In short, with the establishment of the Norwegian-Swedish border in the far north in 1751 and through the so-called Lapp Codicil, Sami were allowed continuing free and customary migrations across the settled state border. However, such free movement was eventually put to an end for the Finnish Sami in 1852 and 1889, respectively, when the Finnish-Norwegian and Finnish-Swedish borders were closed. The Finnish Sami could no longer undergo their seasonal migrations for reindeer herding and fishing to northern Norway, nor could they use grazing areas on the Swedish side of the borders. This situation caused a domino effect throughout the Sami society; one result was the forced relocation of Sami from the northern to the southern reindeer herding areas due to a shortage of herding lands and overgrazing. Only the Swedish-Norwegian border is still open for Sami reindeer-herding migration, but governed via renewed and changing bilateral treaties.

The Sami were formerly called 'Lapps' (*lappar*) or 'Finns' (*finner*), which is still traceable in the colonial naming of some Sami traditional regions. Finnmark, for instance, is the northernmost county in Norway and also a core Sami area. Likewise, northern counties of Sweden and Finland are still called Lappland. In the same vein, old documents and maps refer to long-established Sami areas, such as Ume and Kemi lapplands (*lappmarker*), in present-day Sweden and Finland. The word 'Sami' originates from the word *Sapmi*, meaning both the Sami homeland and the Sami people.

The Field of Sami Law in Legal Discourse

The title of this collection, *Indigenous Rights in Scandinavia: Autonomous Sami Law*, relates to a claim that Sami Law as a legal discipline and related legal scholarship therein needs to be distinct as well as autonomous. As a legal field, Sami Law is young within Norway, Sweden and Finland and was first established in Norway during the late 1970s, and only in the last two decades or so with respect to Sweden and Finland. To some extent to acknowledge the field is, however, to pour old wine into new wineskins, because the legal questions relating to the Sami by far pre-date the field itself. Sami Law cuts across several conventional legal disciplines, such as Legal History, Constitutional Law, Public International Law, Property Law, Administrative Law and Environmental Law. However, it also has a specific Sami dimension, which is that it contains questions relating to Sami customs as well as Sami perceptions of law and legal norms.

Although Sami Law is not a well-established discipline – not even amongst Scandinavian universities in the north in the heart of *Sapmi* – much has happened in recent decades, and the field's scholarship is steadily increasing. Eva-Maria Svensson has, in the last chapter of this book, commented on the formation of Sami Law as a new field of knowledge, from her position and experience taking part in the forming of gender-based legal scholarship. Svensson emphasizes that the two formation processes exhibit many similarities. Both fields of knowledge represent critical perspectives regarding mainstream legal scholarship, challenging the ways in which law is comprehended. Likewise, both are also quite recent additions to Nordic legal scholarship, with several common challenges and obstacles in the process of being institutionalized.

Scandinavian Laws and Legal Sources

Within the context of this book 'Scandinavian laws' means national laws of those three countries. The Sami, as a transnational indigenous people with variations in language and traditions between different regions and groups, face a different legal situation in each state, where Norway can be interpreted as most favourable. In principle, there exist a 'Norwegian Sami Law', a 'Swedish Sami Law' and a 'Finnish Sami Law'.[3] State borders cut across *Sapmi* and state-based politics and interests have, over the years, established boundaries of various kinds. The emphasis of the Sami as one *people*, which, in fact, forms a part of an overall Sami political statement, has largely been ignored.

Although Norway, Sweden and Finland have distinct state jurisdictions, they also share common grounds. Not least they have a shared history of both wars and unions. Norway was a part of the Danish kingdom from the end of the fourteenth century until 1814, at which point Norway was submerged into a new union with Sweden until 1905 before it became independent. Finland was a part of the Swedish kingdom from the thirteenth century; however, as a result of war Finland was lost in 1809 and became a grand duchy in the Russian Empire. Nonetheless, Finland retained much of its former Swedish legislation and institutions, and thus kept its Swedish legal heritage. For this reason, it is natural to speak of a West Nordic (Denmark, Norway, Iceland) and East Nordic (Sweden, Finland) legal traditions. During the first half of the twentieth century, the Nordic countries were collaborating in the drafting of laws within the context of civil law, resulting, for example, in a common Contracts Act.

From a macro-comparative outlook there are general traits amongst the three states' legal systems, often referred to as Nordic Law, a name not least emphasizing

---

3 The Laws simply differ and the institutional settings differ, eg due to the facts that Norway is party to the ILO Convention No. 169, whereas Sweden and Finland are not, and Sweden and Finland are members of the European Union (EU) and bound by the EU law, and Norway is not a member of the EU.

shared concerns regarding social justice and social ethics of the countries. Nordic legal systems are also commonly considered to be of the same legal family.[4] Nordic Law is, moreover, known to use legislation as a vehicle for social reform and development, forming the Nordic welfare states. The pragmatic attitude of Nordic Law coincides with the lay character of its legal systems and the lack of grand codifications therein. The majority of regional legal scholarship has, in the same vein, avoided becoming overly theoretical, and in this way it has preserved its social relevance. Since here we can only provide glimpses of Nordic Law, we recommend the excellent anthology *Nordic Law: Between Traditional and Dynamism* edited by Jaakko Husa, Kimmo Nuotio and Heikki Pihlajamäki,[5] as well as text books on Norwegian, Swedish and Finnish laws for further reading.

Amongst the majority, mainstream legal sources – legislation, preparatory works, case law and legal literature – Nordic lawyers, in contrast to most other jurisdictions, consider the importance and weight of preparatory works to be unique. Preparatory works are used as an authoritative source for interpreting specific statutes and establishing the meaning behind them or certain provisions; there are various forms of preparatory works, ranging from government/commission reports and bills to parliamentary protocols. For a short explanation of such sources commonly used by the authors within this book, we provide a list with abbreviations of Scandinavian legal sources.

Authors and Structure of this Book

The authors of this collection represent an impressive mix of both new and seasoned scholars within the field of Sami Law from all three Scandinavian countries. The authors include four Sami legal scholars (Labba, Skogvang, Strömgren and Åhrén) and one Maori legal scholar (Ruru), which is significant. We are also particularly pleased that two senior professors, Kirsti Strøm Bull and Bertil Bengtsson, have contributed. Strøm Bull and Bengtsson have not only made substantial contributions to Sami Law in Norway and Sweden, respectively, through scholarly works, they have also encouraged and recruited younger colleagues to the field. Their importance to the development of Sami legal scholarship must be highlighted. Bengtsson was also one of the Supreme Court judges in the Taxed mountain case (*Skattefjällsmålet*) of 1981, which has been discussed by a couple of authors within this collection. Professors Kjell Åke Modéer and Eva-Maria Svensson also provide important insights from their respective positions in Legal History and Comparative Legal Cultures and Feminist/Gender Legal Studies.

---

4   See eg Zweigert and Kötz, *Introduction to Comparative Law* (Clarendon Press 1998).

5   Intersentia, Antwerp 2007. We also recommend Anna Nylund, 'Mixing Past and Future: The Making of a Nordic Legal Culture 1850–2050' in Jørn Øyrehagen Sunde and Knut Einar Skodvin (eds), *Rendezvous of European Legal Cultures* (Fagbokforlaget 2010).

An important methodological aspect one has to consider when working with Sami Law and Sami legal matters is that there are three different larger legal traditions that apply: state legislation, Sami customary law and applicable international law. Several of the chapters within this book discuss legal sources from all of these three realms.

The book is divided into three parts. Part I covers, in addition to this introduction, two chapters with a comparative purpose – one from a Canadian Law perspective and one from a Aotearoa New Zealand Law perspective. Via knowledge and experience from these diverse jurisdictions as a backdrop, the prominent legal scholars, Professor Nigel Bankes and Associate Professor Jacinta Ruru, comment on the legal situation of the Scandinavian Sami. Bankes discusses three themes therein: the interaction between different normative orders, the role of the state and settler-based law in constituting 'the other', and the significance and implications of separation of powers. Ruru focuses on indigenous ways of life, sovereignty and property, as well as politics, voting and identity and the rule and role of law from a Maori legal scholar perspective.

Part II of this book begins with chapters addressing more general legal questions. Kjell Åke Modéer skilfully presents a panoramic view of and significant reflections on Sami Law in late modern legal contexts. Christina Allard then discusses some characteristic features of Scandinavian laws and their influence on Sami matters, giving an impressive comparison of legal matters in the three Scandinavian countries. Bertil Bengtsson, with his deep experience with and knowledge of law, provides a more personal account and arguments concerning the discussion on Sami Law in his chapter 'Reforming Swedish Sami Legislation: A Survey of the Arguments'. The following chapters then address historical perspectives. Kirsti Strøm Bull has an undisputed role as the leading expert on reindeer-herding rights in Norway. Strøm Bull's contribution, 'Sami Reindeer Herders' Herding Rights in Norway from the Nineteenth Century to the Present Day', discusses the development of the rights of reindeer-herding communities in Norway. The chapter by Johan Strömgren focuses on historical aspects of law-making, namely the Swedish state's legacy of Sami rights codified in 1886. Strömgren analyses and questions development of the notion of the codification of reindeer-herding rights as usufruct rights in Swedish legislation.

Legal history is quite important in Sami legal scholarship; history can explain the reasoning behind legislation or the lack of a solid foundation for current legislation. Even though the following chapters discuss more specific, present-day legal questions in the three Scandinavian countries, in doing so they also focus on the historical development of such laws and questions. Eivind Torp draws attention to rights of non-reindeer-herding Sami, and he argues that Sami hunting and fishing rights in Sweden are still unresolved, in his chapter 'Sami Hunting and Fishing Rights in Swedish Law'. Susann Funderud Skogvang discusses the contested and topical question of coastal fishing rights for Norwegian Sami in her chapter 'Local Community Right to Fish: A Sami Perspective' and she also addresses the protection of Sami fishing rights in international law. Kristina

Labba analyses the important functions of ancient, still applicable Sami customs related to reindeer herding, the complex *siida*-system, in her chapter 'The Legal Organization of Sami Reindeer Herding and the Role of the Siida'. Tanja Joona focuses on a highly controversial matter in contemporary Finland: the right to a Sami identity. Joona's chapter, 'The Definition of a Sami Person in Finland and its Application', presents a both interesting and important perspective and analysis concerning an ongoing identity and rights discussion in Finland.

The two chapters following are concerned most with international laws relevant to the Sami. Mattias Åhrén asks, 'To What Extent Can Indigenous Territories be Expropriated?' Åhrén gives examples of the topical and complex question concerning mining extractions planned in the Swedish side of *Sapmi*. Then, Leena Heinämäki focuses on developments in international law and current implementation in Finnish Law in her chapter 'Indigenous Peoples' Rapidly Evolving International Status:The Sami People in Finland'.

Lastly, Part III of this book consists of insightful reflections from Eva-Maria Svensson in her chapter 'Sami Legal Scholarship: The Making of a Knowledge Field'. Svensson's chapter has the purpose of summarizing all of the contributions and the process leading up to the edited collection. Svensson has articulated the need for a continuous meta-reflection of Sami Law as a field of knowledge in-the-making, regarding, for instance, its basic presumptions, theories, methods and also concepts applied. If one wishes, Svensson's chapter could very well be read first, as well, because it also situates Sami Law within academia and addresses challenges therein for the future.

Chapter 2

Themes and Reflections: A Perspective from Canada

Nigel Bankes

This chapter identifies some of the themes that emerged for me during the discussion of Sami law and rights at the Sommarøya workshop and from my re-reading of the revised contributions for this volume. I also offer some reflection on those themes from the perspective of a Canadian academic.

The themes that I identified during the workshop and which continued to resonate as I re-read the papers were as follows: the interaction between different normative orders (i.e. between settler state norms, international law and the customary laws of the indigenous community); the role of the state and settler law in constituting 'the other'; and the significance and implications of the separation of powers for the development and enforcement of the land and resource rights of indigenous communities.

The Interaction between Different Normative Orders

Many of the chapters in this volume deal with the interaction between different normative orders – although perhaps not always using that precise terminology. Modéer for example refers to 'polycentric law', others refer more specifically to the conflict between state norms and custom,[1] while others might refer to legal pluralism.[2] But I think that we are all talking about the same thing which is the interaction in the post-modern world between positive state law and other sources of norms including in particular for present purposes, the customary laws of indigenous communities and international law. This is an significant theme in the context of indigenous rights because one of the important tools of the colonial state has been its hegemonic ability to use law, positive state law, to constitute the other. Recognition of the validity of other normative orders is an important tool in

---

1 See Tanja Joona's Chapter 12 in this volume.

2 For an extended review see Jonnette Watson Hamilton, 'Acknowledging and Accommodating Legal Pluralism: An Application to the Draft Nordic Saami Convention' in Nigel Bankes and Timo Koivurova (eds), *The Proposed Nordic Saami Convention: National and International Dimensions of Indigenous Property Rights* (Hart Publishing 2013) 45–77.

decolonizing the state and indeed law. Recognition of the other offers an example of resistance to the state's hegemonic power. It is therefore important to assess how open the different states (and groups of states perhaps in a Nordic context) are to these two important sources of normativity, international law on the one hand and the customary laws and norms of indigenous peoples on the other hand.

My overall sense is that Nordic states are relatively open to international law. This openness is reflected in both the constitutional instruments of the Nordic states especially in relation to human rights norms[3] and in actual practice. Two examples of the latter will have to suffice. The first example draws on the trilogy of the Länsman decisions[4] of the Human Rights Committee in response to a series of petitions from Sami reindeer herders in northern Finland. Each of those decisions involved resource development of some sort within the reindeer herding territory of the petitioner who argued that the state authorization of these activities breached Article 27 of the International Covenant on Civil and Political Rights (ICCPR).[5] In each case, the Human Rights Committee concluded that the interference with traditional activities was not so great as to amount to a denial of the right to culture and therefore that there was no breach of Article 27. But what interests me about these proceedings is the appreciation that the precise legal question had already been considered, not only by the Finnish courts, but also by various Finnish administrative decision-makers.[6] This is indicative of the degree to which international law has been internalized in the domestic laws of Finland.[7]

A second example which I have used before involves the Norwegian Storting's careful attention to Norway's international legal obligations as part of its

---

3　Norway, Constitution, Article 92, 'The authorities of the State shall respect and ensure human rights as they are expressed in this Constitution and in the treaties concerning human rights that are binding for Norway'; Sweden, Instrument of Government, Chapter 2, Article 19, 'No act of law or other provision may be adopted which contravenes Sweden's undertakings under the European Convention for the Protection of Human Rights and Fundamental Freedoms'; Finland, Constitution, Article 74, supervision by the Constitutional Committee of legislative enactments to ensure conformity with international human rights treaties. See also Susann Funderud Skogvang's contribution (Chapter 10) in this volume discussing the implications of a provision in Norwegian legislation that the statute be applied in 'in accordance with international law on indigenous peoples and minorities'.

4　*J Länsman* et al v *Finland*, Case No 511/1992, UN Doc CCPR/C/52/D/511/1992 (1994); *J Länsman* et al v *Finland*, Case No 671/1995, UN Doc CCPR/C/58/D/671/1995 (1996); *J Länsman* et al v *Finland*, Case No 1023/2001, UN Doc/CCPR//C/83D/1023/2001 (2005).

5　Adopted by the United Nations General Assembly 16 December 1966, 999 UNTS 172.

6　See in particular *Jouni Länsman*, 671/1995 (n 4) paras 2.8–2.9 and 10.5.

7　See Harold Koh, 'Bringing International Law Home' (1998–99) 35 Houston Law Review 623.

deliberations on the Finnmark Act.[8] Indeed as part of that process the Standing Committee on Justice of the Storting, through the Ministry of Justice, commissioned an expert opinion from two Norwegian public international lawyers[9] asking them to assess whether the proposed legislation would satisfy Norway's obligations under both the International Covenant on Civil and Political Rights[10] and ILO Convention 169 concerning indigenous and tribal peoples.[11]

International law does not play an important part in the indigenous rights jurisprudence of Canadian courts or more generally in Canadian administrative practice. This is true of both customary law and treaty law. Canada's Constitution contains no reference to the status of international law. While there have been some judicial references to the United Nations Declaration on the Rights of Indigenous Peoples in recent years,[12] there is, so far as I know, no court case or tribunal decision that reflects on the implications of Article 27 of the ICCPR in relation to resource activities within the traditional lands of indigenous communities.[13] My sense is that counsel rarely if ever considers bringing the ICCPR to bear in such a case. My conclusion therefore is that Canadian law, or at least this part of Canadian law, is not open to international law and is certainly far less open than are the legal systems of the Nordic states.[14]

One might expect the situation to be different with respect to customary law given the foundational importance of custom in common law jurisdictions such as Canada[15] but the position is not that clear cut. While customary international law does form part of the law of Canada[16] it is always difficult to establish the existence of a customary norm and especially one that is specific enough to help

---

8   Nigel Bankes, 'Land Claim Agreements in Arctic Canada in Light of International Human Rights Norms' (2009) 1 Yearbook of Polar Law 175.

9   The opinion was subsequently published as Hans Petter Graver and Geir Ulfstein, 'The Sami People's Right to Land in Norway' (2004) 11 International Journal on Minority and Group Rights 337.

10   ICCPR (n 5).

11   Adopted Geneva, 27 June 1989, entry into force 5 September 1991.

12   See, for example, *Smerek v Areva Resources Canada Inc* (2014) SKQB 282. The plaintiffs did refer to the Declaration as well as several treaties (but not ICCPR). The court struck the statement of claim on the basis that international instruments were not part of Canadian law (for other than interpretive purposes) unless implemented by statute. See also *Simon v Canada (Attorney General)* 2013 FC 1117 paras 53, 75, 121.

13   But see *Montana Band of Indians v Canada*, [1991] 2 FC 30 (FCA) discussed in Bankes (n 8) 187–88.

14   See more generally, Bankes (n 8).

15   See Christina Allard's comments in this volume on the distinction between the West and East Nordic traditions and further comments to the effect that the approach of the Norwegian courts is closer to the common law tradition and style of reasoning than is the approach of Swedish and Finnish courts.

16   *Foreign Legations Case*, [1943] SCR 208 and *Reference re Secession of Quebec*, [1998] 2 SCR 217.

resolve a particular legal claim. Furthermore, while Canadian courts are receptive to the use of indigenous customary laws in matters related to family law[17] they are less receptive to the use of indigenous customary norms relating to property – as illustrated by the three leading decisions of the Supreme Court of Canada on aboriginal title: *Delgamuukw* (1997),[18] *Marshall and Bernard* (2005),[19] and *Tsilhqot'in* (2014).[20] The customary law issue in each of these cases was the extent to which the indigenous community could rely upon proof of customary property norms as a way of establishing its aboriginal title to its traditional territory in addition to relying on proof of occupation at the time of the Crown's acquisition of sovereignty. While all three decisions refer to customary norms it is harder to see what work those norms actually perform in the court's reasons. This is particularly the case in *Marshall and Bernard*[21] but is also evident in the more recent *Tsilhqot'in* case. Thus, while the court indicates that the 'question of sufficient occupation must be approached from both the common law perspective and the Aboriginal perspective'[22] and that the 'Aboriginal perspective focuses on laws, practices, customs and traditions of the group'[23] the actual application of this perspective rests more on the physical use of land (facts) rather than the *normative* content of indigenous practice:[24]

> the kinds of acts necessary to indicate a permanent presence and intention to hold and use the land for the group's purposes are dependent on the manner of life of the people and the nature of the land. Cultivated fields, constructed dwelling houses, invested labour, and a consistent presence on parts of the land may be sufficient, but are not essential to establish occupation. The notion of occupation must also reflect the way of life of the Aboriginal people, including those who were nomadic or semi-nomadic.

Various authors in this volume speak to the importance of Sami customary norms in a Nordic context. Kristina Labba, for example, refers to the significant role that customs play in Sami society but suggests that customary norms may also

---

17   For an early and important Canadian decision on the role of indigenous customary norms in the context of marriage see *Connolly v Woolrich* (1867) 17 RJRQ 75 (Que Ct QB). For a more recent authority see *Casimel v Insurance Corp of British Columbia* [1994 2 CNLR 22 (BCCA).

18   *Delgamuukw v British Columbia* [1997] 3 SCR 1010.

19   *R v Marshall; R v Bernard* [2005] 2 SCR 320.

20   *Tsilhqot'in Nation v British Columbia* 2014 SCC 44. It is telling that there is no discussion of international law in any of these three leading cases dealing with aboriginal title.

21   Nigel Bankes, '*Marshall and Bernard*: Ignoring the Relevance of Customary Property Norms' (20006) 55 UNBLJ 120.

22   *Tsilhqot'in* (n 20) para 34.

23   ibid para 35.

24   ibid para 38.

be vulnerable and that thus it is necessary to legally acknowledge the custom in legislation.[25] Eivind Torp, however, notes that while customary law is still a fundamental source of law in matters concerning Sami land and water rights in a number of cases the courts have failed to apply relevant customary norms.

The Role of the State in Constituting the Other

Another important tool of the colonizing state is the ability to authoritatively constitute the other by such techniques as defining who is indigenous, who is entitled to membership and who has access to particular resources and livelihoods. Thus, while international law on the right of self-determination emphasizes that it is up to the people concerned to make decisions on these matters[26] it is clear that settler states in both Nordic countries and Canada have routinely made these decisions in the past. While these states may now be more reluctant to define the other it is equally clear that indigenous communities continue to live with the present consequences of those historical interventions, and that attempts to unravel some of those interventions are fraught with difficulty and may create new and equally invidious distinctions within indigenous communities.

Canada's Indian Act[27] contained, and to some degree still contains, a number of examples of such interventions in the lives and polities of indigenous communities. For example, the act arrogates to the federal executive (the Governor in Council) the authority to replace the customary governance structures of Indian bands and First Nations with elected forms of office.[28] And famously, or infamously, the Act used to provide that Indian women lost their Indian status (and therefore the right to live on reserve) when they 'married out' (i.e. married a non-Indian). Indian men, however, did not lose their status, a difference that the Human Rights Committee denounced in its views on the application of Sandra Lovelace.[29] Canada ultimately repealed the relevant section of the Indian Act but argument continues as to whether the amendments went far enough in unravelling the consequences of past discriminatory decisions.[30] There are also continuing questions as to the resourcing and economic implications (provision of housing, sharing of resource revenues etc.) of decisions to restore status to potentially large numbers of the disenfranchised.

---

25   Labba refers to Mikkel Nils Sara, 'Rules of Usage and Siida Autonomy' (2011) Arctic Review on Law and Politics 144.

26   See ILO 169 (n 11), Article 1(2) and Joona's chapter (12) in this volume.

27   RSC 1985, c I- 5.

28   ibid s 74, and see *Logan v Styres* (1959) 20 DLR (2d) 416 (Ont HCJ).

29   *Lovelace v Canada*, Communication No 24/1977: Canada 30/07/81, UN Doc CCPR/C/13/D/24/1977.

30   Jennifer Koshan, 'The Nordic Saami Convention and the Rights of Saami Women: Lessons from Canada' in Bankes and Koivurova (n 2) 379–98, especially 390–91.

Several of the chapters in this volume address similar interventions in the context of the Nordic states, particularly in the context of Sweden and Finland. Bertil Bengtsson, for example, refers to the provisions of the Swedish Reindeer Herding Act (RHA) which vests the reindeer herding right in the Sami people but provide that it is only exercisable by members of a Sami village.[31] Torp's contribution emphasizes that this restrictive eligibility rule extends to hunting and fishing rights.[32] By contrast and more positively, Labba suggests that the RHA rules in Norway for determining membership in the village correspond better to customary norms than do the RHA rules in Sweden. Joona addresses this issue in the context of Finland pointing to a number of difficult issues associated with Sami eligibility in that Nordic state. One particular difficulty is that Sami status in Finland today seems to depend upon a less than scientific survey carried out during the 1960s. Another difficulty she points to involves the role that the state's administrative courts play in reviewing decisions of the Sami Parliament on membership issues.

The courts also play a role in constituting the other and in this context the rules of evidence applied by the courts and the courts' cultural (in)sensitivity is especially important. Kirsti Strøm Bull's chapter discusses several aspects of this issue. For example, her chapter points to the fact that the Norwegian courts and administrative commissions for many years privileged some forms of evidence and some perspectives over others – indeed preferring the view of one historian to the effect that Norwegian settlement preceded Sami occupation in some parts of Norway. All of this was consistent with an ideology of Norwegianization and cultural supremacy.

Problems of admissibility of evidence and the weight to be accorded to indigenous oral evidence have also been significant in aboriginal title litigation in Canada. In the seminal *Delgamuukw*[33] case, for example, the Supreme Court of Canada sent the matter back to trial on the basis that the trial judge had erred in certain important aspects in his appreciation of the evidence. Thus the trial judge had concluded that 'territorial affidavits' sworn out by elders and clan chiefs[34] were inadmissible and that other forms of evidence (oral histories based on recitals during feast ceremonies, and declarations of witnesses' ancestors as to land use) should

---

31   See also Christina Allard on the same point, 'Who Holds the Reindeer-herding Rights in Sweden: A Key Issue in Legislation' in Bankes and Koivurova (eds) (n 2) 207–27.

32   And this notwithstanding the fact that it was recognized historically that not all Sami were involved in reindeer herding and who found themselves (as of amendments to the RHA in Sweden in 1928) with no rights at all. It also meant that persons who ceased to be able to herd reindeer also lost their hunting and fishing rights and became exposed to prosecution. And noting as well in a number of cases that the Swedish Court of Appeal overruled decisions of the local community as to membership in the Sameby.

33   *Delgamuukw* (n 18).

34   A territorial affidavit would be a sworn statement by the relevant person as to the territorial bounds of the clan or family territory.

not be accorded independent weight.[35] For Chief Justice Lamer this approach failed to accord with the court's overall objective of securing reconciliation between the 'prior occupation of North America by distinctive aboriginal societies' and 'the assertion of Crown sovereignty over Canadian territory'.[36]

The Separation of Powers

Several of the chapters in this volume and the discussion at the workshop reflect directly or indirectly on the implications of the separation of powers within the settler state for relations between indigenous communities and the state or settler society. The separation of powers refers to the distinctive roles of the three branches of government that typify Western liberal democracies, the judicial branch, the executive branch and the legislative branch. Allard's chapter addresses this topic most explicitly and she notes that the role of the judicial branch will be more pronounced where the law is unclear or where there are important interpretive issues to be resolved.

I discuss three different themes under this heading. The first is the 'leadership' role assumed by the different branches of government at different times when it comes to the recognition of indigenous land and resource rights. A second theme is the role of judicial review of legislation and decisions, and the third relates to the role of each branch in limiting the land and resource rights of indigenous communities.

Leadership

In the era of modernity (to use Modéer's terminology) it is often possible to point to particular events or tipping points that led to (or were themselves instrumental in bringing about) increased recognition of the rights of indigenous communities with the state. Some of these events include protest movements (e.g. the Alta project in Norway and the subsequent occupation outside the Storting in Oslo)[37] notable court cases (e.g.. the *Mabo* cases in Australia),[38] specific legislative

---

35 ie they had to be corroborated by something in the records of the settler society.

36 *Delgamuukw* (n 18) para 81.

37 Allard (Chapter 5 this volume) observes that 'Sweden and Finland have no "Alta cases" with such deep societal impact'.

38 Both are significant. In *Mabo v Queensland (No 1)* (1988) 63 ALJR 84. the Australian High Court used Australia's ratification of the Convention on the Elimination of All Forms of Racial Discrimination and its domestic implementation by the Commonwealth legislature as the basis for striking down state legislation purporting to extinguish aboriginal title in that state. In *Mabo v Queensland (No 2)* (1992) 107 ALR 1 the majority of the High Court found that the Meriam people of Murray Island had established an aboriginal title that was recognized under the law of Australia.

changes (perhaps the enactment of the Finnmark Estate legislation in Norway, and constitutional amendments (the 1982 amendment of Canada's Constitution to recognize and affirm existing aboriginal and treaty rights). Some key developments originating outside national legal systems (e.g. the adoption of the United Nations Declaration on the Rights of Indigenous Peoples or the recognition of indigenous property rights by the Inter American Court of Human Rights)[39] serve to emphasize the point made earlier with respect to the interaction between different normative orders. The significance of some of these triggering events is obvious at the outset, (*Mabo No. 2* for example) whereas in other cases the importance of the event is not immediately apparent.[40]

The key point that I wish to make here is that different branches of government assume different leadership roles at different times and to some degree there is a conversation of sorts between the different branches. Øyvind Ravna has written thoughtfully about this elsewhere in the context of Sami rights in Norway[41] carefully tracing the interaction between decisions of the Supreme Court of Norway, constitutional amendment, and amendments to the Reindeer Husbandry Act.[42] Agreeing with much of that, Strøm Bull in this volume emphasizes the time lag between judicial recognition of the distinctive juridical basis of Sami rights and the public acceptance of that view by the executive branch. Thus the first judicial recognition of Sami rights as something more than a permitted use that the state could change or abolish came in the early 1970s, but it was not until the RHA was amended in 1996 that the executive branch took the same position. A similar time lag is evident in Sweden. As both Bengtsson and Johan Strömgren note in this volume the Taxed mountain case came down in 1981 but it was not until 1993

---

39   The first decision is *Mayagna (Sumo) Awas Tingni Community v Nicaragua*, Judgment of 31 August 2001, Series C, No 79. For analysis of this and the subsequent indigenous property decisions of the court see Nigel Bankes, 'The Protection of the Rights of Indigenous Peoples to Territory through the Property Rights Provisions of International Regional Human Rights Instruments' (2011) 3 Yearbook of Polar Law 57.

40   See for example in Canada the decision of the Supreme Court in *Calder v British Columbia (Attorney General)*, [1973] SCR 313. The court split 3:3 on the question of whether pre-confederation legislation of the colony of British Columbia had extinguished aboriginal title. A seventh judge concluded that the plaintiffs were not eligible to bring the claim and as a result, in formal terms, the Nisga'a Nation lost its case. However, further reflection reveals that the decision also confirmed 6:0 that the common law recognized the concept of aboriginal title (prior to extinguishment). See also Bengtsson (Chapter 6 in this volume) observing that while the plaintiffs lost in Taxed mountain the decision has come to be regarded as a success for the Sami insofar as it suggested that Sami further north in Sweden might have a better case to title based on the use of land for reindeer herding.

41   Øyvind Ravna, 'The Draft Nordic Saami Convention and the Assessment of Evidence of Saami Land Use of Land' in Bankes and Koivurova (eds) (n 2) 177–205, especially 188–92.

42   And, one might add, the implications of Norway's ratification of ILO 169.

that the RHA was amended to recognize the private property roots of the reindeer herding right.

While it may often be the judicial branch that takes the leadership role we should not completely discount the possibility that the executive branch will take a leadership role or that it may be more responsive in some cases than Strøm Bull suggests in her essay. For example, the Norwegian executive must be credited with taking a leadership role in deciding to ratify ILO 169. Sweden and Finland have been much more reluctant to follow this lead although as some of the authors of the chapters in this volume suggest (see Leena Heinämäki for Finland and Strömgren for Sweden) this remains a live issue.[43] Furthermore, Heinämäki surely offers another positive example in the context of her discussion of the recent (2011) amendments to the Finnish Mining Act. In Canada the executive has rarely taken a leadership role (witness for example its reluctance to endorse the UN Declaration) but it did prove to be responsive in the mid 1970s to the Supreme Court's decision in *Calder*.[44] The then Liberal administration under Prime Minister Trudeau (who had once famously described aboriginal rights as historical 'might-have-beens') reversed itself and agreed to adopt a policy of negotiating modern land claim agreements.[45] The inclusion of aboriginal rights protection in the Constitution in 1982 was largely the result of the public's reaction to the initial exclusion of such protection.[46]

Judicial Review of Legislation

Perhaps the most crucial separation of powers issues in any jurisdiction is the constitutional authority of the courts to review and pass upon the validity of legislation. Until 1982 Canadian courts could, for the most part, only review the validity of legislation on federalism grounds.[47] The role of the courts expanded in 1982 with the adoption of Canada's Charter of Rights and Freedoms and a

---

43   But not in Canada for a variety of reasons; see Bankes (n 8).

44   Department of Indian Affairs and Northern Development, 'Statement Made by the Honourable Jean Chrétien, Minister of Indian Affairs and Northern Development on Claims of Indian and Inuit People' *Communiqué*, 8 August 1973.

45   While I have criticized such agreements as political settlements (see Bankes (n 8)) rather than as agreements that are designed to recognize, demit and title the full extent of aboriginal land and resource entitlements, the willingness of the government to negotiate is clearly a more forward looking approach than that of a policy of non-recognition.

46   Roy Romanow, John Whyte and Howard Leeson, *Canada ... Notwithstanding: The Making of the Constitution 1976–1982* (Carswell 1984).

47   Although the federal parliament adopted a statutory Bill of Rights in 1960 the Supreme Court of Canada in a number of decisions, some which involved indigenous peoples (*R v Drybones*, [1970] SCR 282 and *Canada (Attorney General) v Lavell*, [1974] SCR 1349 (this latter decision was the domestic precursor to the *Lovelace* decision (n 29)) the court declined the invitation to take a more activist role.

special section (outside the Charter) protecting aboriginal and treaty rights.[48] Allard (this volume) observes a similar trend in the Nordic countries although Finland continues to envisage a more restrained role for the judiciary permitting interventions only where there is a manifest contradiction between an enactment and the Constitution. While the Canadian courts will review the validity and applicability of both federal and provincial legislation on the basis of aboriginal rights protection provision of the Constitution, the courts have also emphasized that such rights are not absolute and in recognition of that have developed a doctrine of 'justifiable infringement'.[49]

Land and Resources

A crucial legal issue in every modern state with an indigenous community is the vindication of indigenous land and resource rights against the state. While the acquisition of sovereignty (imperium) by the settler state over indigenous communities remains contested and contestable, it is now broadly recognized in both international law[50] and the domestic laws of individual states, that the acquisition of sovereignty itself (however contestable) did not have any necessary consequences for the property interests of indigenous communities.[51] Such lands were not terra nullius because they were in fact occupied by communities who governed themselves in accordance with their laws, including land laws.[52] However, while benefiting from a presumption of continuity, the property interests of indigenous communities became legally vulnerable as a result of another's acquisition of sovereignty – at least within the legal system of that other. The

---

48   Section 35 of the Constitution Act, 1982 provides that 'The existing aboriginal and treaty rights of the aboriginal peoples of Canada are hereby recognized and affirmed'. Sections 1-34 of that act represent the Canadian Charter of Rights and Freedoms; s 35 is Part II of the Act.

49   The key authorities are *Sparrow v R*, [1990] 1 SCR 1075; *Delgamuukw* (n 18) paras 165–69; and *Tsilhqot'in* (n 20) paras 77–88, 118–27.

50   *Advisory Opinion re Western Sahara* [1975] ICJ Rep 12.

51   See generally PG McHugh, *Aboriginal Title: The Modern Jurisprudence of Tribal Rights* (OUP 2009).

52   See *Mabo No 2* (n 38). For Canada see *Tsilhqot'in* (n 20 para 69): 'The doctrine of terra nullius (...) never applied in Canada, as confirmed by the Royal Proclamation (1763)' but this may be a convenient ex post facto rationalization of the case law. Certainly lower court judges in *Calder v AGBC* (n 40) (the leading aboriginal title case in Canada before *Delgamuukw*) made statements consistent with the view that aboriginal communities lacked a sophisticated system of property law. See Justice Hall in the Supreme Court in *Calder* quoting Justice Davey from the British Columbia Court of Appeal to the effect that the Indians of the mainland of British Columbia 'were undoubtedly at the time of settlement a very primitive people with few of the institutions of civilized society, and none at all of our notions of private property'.

vulnerability lies in the legal power of the new sovereign to extinguish, regulate, or limit, the existing property interests of the indigenous community.

There are at least two types of questions that must be answered in each such settler state. One set of questions relates to the *legal* means by which the state may limit such interests. The separation of powers statement of this question is whether such limits can be imposed by executive act or only by the legislature. If the executive has this authority then it might mean that a land grant by the executive branch of government will, in and of itself, extinguish an inconsistent property claim of an indigenous community.[53] Another version of this argument which seems to have some resonance in Nordic states (for Norway prior to the Brekken and Altevann cases of 1968[54] and in Sweden prior to *Taxed mountain*)[55] to the effect that such interests as Sami had were mere statutory privileges rather than real property rights; and as such might be limited by executive or legislative act without compensation. Yet another variant on that argument is that the indigenous community only has such rights or privileges as are conferred by statute. Strömgren discusses a version of this argument in his chapter of this volume in the context of Swedish Reindeer Grazing Act[56] and Susann Skogvang alludes to this issue in the context of Sami fishing rights in near coastal waters which she argues are derived from property rather than statutory privilege.

On the other hand, if only the legislature is constitutionally competent to extinguish, regulate or limit the property rights of the indigenous community then it would follow that the indigenous community could only lose its property interest when the legislature expressly extinguishes that interest[57] – assuming that there are no other constitutional impediments to such legislative action.[58]

The answers to these questions are of course contingent on the specific substantive rules within each jurisdiction and generally require reference to both constitutional law and property law. There is, however, one important norm that should produce a degree of uniformity in response and that is the requirement of equality before the law. This standard serves to ensure that if the property rights of settler interests are protected from executive taking

---

53   This seems to be the position in Australia. See *Mabo No 2* (n 38).

54   See Strøm Bull (Chapter 7 this volume).

55   See Bengsston (Chapter 6 this volume).

56   A Canadian version of this argument is that the indigenous communities have such rights as are conferred by executive act such as the Royal Proclamation, 1763. That argument is now thoroughly discredited and the Proclamation interpreted as recognizing pre-existing rights. See, inter alia, *Tsilhqot'in* (n 20) para 69.

57   See Torp, (Chapter 9 this volume) referring to the Taxed mountain case.

58   For example in a federal system the sub-unit of the federation may well lack the legal authority to do so for a variety of reasons. In *Mabo No 1* (n 38) the Queensland legislation was struck down because it was discriminatory and as such inconsistent with Commonwealth legislation implementing CERD. In Canada, while it appears *post-Tsilhqot'in* (n 20) that a provincial legislature might impair an aboriginal title interest, provincial legislation aimed at extinguishing an aboriginal title would still be ultra vires.

(which they typically will be), then such a rule should also apply to indigenous land and resource rights.[59] Certainly such interests cannot be singled out for special treatment as they were by the State of Queensland in the legislation that was at issue in *Mabo (No. 1)*.[60]

Mattias Åhrén's contribution to this volume takes that logic one step further emphasizing the need for substantive equality and not just formal equality. Substantive equality requires differential treatment of those that are culturally different. Thus states must take account of cultural differences when designing property rights regimes and that differential treatment should extend to the application of state expropriation laws including those associated with natural resource projects such as mining projects. This should require the state (including its judicial branch) to take account of the fact that indigenous communities such as reindeer herding communities value their lands for cultural reasons and not for economic reasons. The role of the judicial branch in all of this is thus to insist upon the non-discriminatory application of the law but in doing so to recognize a thicker and more substantive notion of equality which respects cultural differences.[61] This may be reflected in both the substantive protections accorded indigenous property rights and in procedural matters.[62]

A second type of question focuses, as just noted, on procedural matters such as the burden of proof of indigenous property rights. If we take seriously the proposition that sovereignty does not erase property then it must follow that the state cannot establish its title merely by proving that it exercised sovereignty in a particular area. It might further follow from this that the state (and indeed private property owners who claim title from the state) should have the burden of showing how it acquired its title in any given area following its acquisition of sovereignty where those lands were occupied by indigenous communities. However, the leading cases generally all proceed on the assumption that the burden of establishing title falls on the indigenous community whether through sui generis rules specifically developed in response to the challenges posed by aboriginal title claims

---

59   See Bengtsson's contribution (Chapter 6 this volume) discussing s 30 of the RHA and compensation as a result of mineral activities.

60   *Mabo No 1* (n 38).

61   *Mabo No 1* (n 38) only had to apply a formal version of equality. For another decision of the Australian High Court which discusses the need for special measures in protecting aboriginal lands see *Gerhardy v Brown* [1985] HCA 11, (1985) 159 CLR 70.

62   Skogvang's Chapter 10 in this volume also contains reflections on the implications of the protection of property rights in international law for the fishing rights of Sami in coastal waters.

(the Canadian model)[63] or through the application of doctrines of adverse possession, prescription or immemorial usage.[64]

One Nordic jurisdiction (Norway) has responded to the evident challenges faced by indigenous communities in establishing title by relaxing both the procedural rules and the substantive rules but this example has yet to be fully followed in Sweden and Finland.[65] Allard (this volume) suggests that the variety of proprietary concepts dealing with the issue of protracted use in Norwegian law has given the Norwegian courts more room to manoeuver in adapting the Norwegian tests to the particular circumstances of the Sami, but to a Canadian observer it is still remarkable how much the debate is framed in terms of mainstream property law norms drawing on ideas of immemorial usage rather than some sui generis ideas that recognize that indigenous title in a settler state must inevitably be a cross-cultural or inter-societal concept.[66]

Conclusions

Settler states and their indigenous communities face the common challenge of reconciliation notwithstanding their different histories of colonization, whether as blue\saltwater colonies or as colonies that slowly, and over time, encroached on the contiguous territories of indigenous communities. There is still much to learn from the project of reconciliation at a comparative level. In this chapter I have identified a number of themes that emerged for me in our discussions and from the chapters in this volume: interaction between different normative orders; the role of the state and settler law in constituting 'the other'; and some reflections

---

63   Canadian courts have by and large articulated a conceptualization of 'aboriginal title' as a sui generis concept without regard to ideas of prescription, immemorial usage or adverse possession. Thus the principal test for establishing an aboriginal title is exclusive possession of sufficient quality or intensity at the time of the Crown's acquisition of sovereignty. Possession may be established by proof of physical occupation and by the application of indigenous property norms: see *Tsilhqot'in* (n 20) paras 33–44.

64   This is evident in Sweden (*Taxed mountain* discussed here by Bengsston and *Handölsdalen Sami Village and Others v Sweden* (ECtHR, Third Section) 30 March 2100) and in Norway (*Selbu*, discussed here by Strøm Bull).

65   In this context it is important to refer to the dissenting judgment of Judge Ziemele in *Handölsdalen Sami Village* ibid. in which she suggested that the majority of the chamber had based its reasoning on two false premises: (1) the assumption that the non-Sami landholders had good title, and (2) the assumption that the traditional rules on the burden of proof were adequate to deal with the issue.

66   For academic discussion of the need to establish an inter-societal concept of indigenous title see Brian Slattery, 'The Metamorphosis of Aboriginal Title' (2006) 85 Canadian Bar Review 255; and see also other references in Nigel Bankes 'Recognizing the Property Interests of Indigenous Peoples within Settler Societies: Some Different Conceptual Approaches' in Bankes and Koivurova (eds) (n 2) 21–43, 28–30.

on the implications of the separation of powers for the project of reconciliation. This also suggests avenues for further research. For example, while all three Nordic constitutions as well as Canada's offer some form of recognition of the rights of indigenous communities, the texts differ and the countries have different traditions of constitutional and judicial review. Similarly it might be important to have a clearer understanding of the different approaches to the recognition of indigenous property and resource rights both at a procedural level (rules of evidence and burden of proof) and at a substantive level (sui generis approaches versus approaches rooted in general property doctrine).

Chapter 3

A Comparative Gaze with Aotearoa New Zealand

Jacinta Ruru

In the summer sunlight of June 2014, my family and I spent several magical days on the island of Sommaroy in the Norway Arctic Circle joining a research workshop of Nordic legal scholars in Sami law. In this chapter I attempt to capture some of the richness of this cultural and academic exchange by providing a comparative glimpse into how the Sami colonial legal experiences share similarities (or not) with Māori – the Indigenous peoples of islands on the other side of the world, Aotearoa New Zealand. The voices of Canadian Indigenous Law Professors Sakej Henderson and John Borrows are loud in my ears as I write this work for both encourage comparative dialogue. As Henderson has stated: 'This methodology not only allows others to learn from the Indigenous experience, but also offers greater legitimacy for Indigenous peoples. The relevance of the "Indigenous Humanities" to the postcolonial consciousness and law can provide teachings and lessons learned by Indigenous peoples around the world'.[1] Likewise, Borrows has recognized: 'Our intellectual, emotional, social, physical, and spiritual insights can simultaneously be compared, contrasted, rejected, embraced, and intermingled with those of others. In fact, this process has been operative since before the time that Indigenous peoples first encountered others on their shores'.[2] Much activity is done in the comparative space especially in forums such as the United Nations Permanent Forum on Indigenous Peoples and the World Indigenous Peoples Conferences on Education. The workshop held on Sommaroy Island was a small but significant event for the opportunities it afforded me to think comparatively. This chapter thus provides a discussion of some of the themes captured in this book from an Indigenous Māori legal scholar comparative perspective. The four themes that have resonated for me in thinking about the similarities and differences between Sami and Māori legal experiences are: Indigenous ways of life; sovereignty and property; politics, voting and identity; and, rule and role of law. But first, a brief insight into Aotearoa New Zealand.

---

1   James (Sakej) Youngblood Henderson, 'Postcolonial Indigenous Legal Consciousness' (2002) 1 Indigenous Law Journal 1, 4.

2   John Borrows, *Recovering Canada: The Resurgence of Indigenous Law* (University of Toronto Press 2002) 147.

Aotearoa New Zealand – A Brief Insight

Māori first discovered and settled the lands and waters of Aotearoa New Zealand sometime after AD 800.[3] Grouped into distinct peoples, the Māori tribes became, literally, the people of the land (*tangata whenua*), living upon *Papatuanuku*, the earth mother, with *Ranginui*, the sky father, above. The common language (with regional dialectal differences) captured this worldview. For instance, *hapu* means 'sub-tribe' and 'to be pregnant'; *whanau* means 'family' and 'to give birth'; and *whenua* means 'land' and 'afterbirth'.[4] Of some 40 distinct *iwi* (tribes), and hundreds of *hapu*, each derived their identity from the mountains, rivers, and lakes.[5] Today, Māori are visibly present throughout the country (currently constituting over 15 per cent of the population), integrated into all parts of society and share a long history of intermarriage with *Pakeha* (the Māori word for Europeans) and others.[6] Since 1950s, Māori began a noticeable drift from rural to urban living to the point that now more than 80 per cent of Māori live in cities, notably Auckland and Hamilton. Many Māori have retained strong cultural links to their tribal areas, in particular visiting *marae* (traditional meeting houses) for family celebrations and funerals. There is nonetheless a small but significant group of Māori who no longer know their tribal backgrounds and instead identify and participate as 'urban Māori'.[7]

In 1840, many Māori chiefs officially consented to Europeans living in Aotearoa New Zealand by signing the bilingual Treaty of Waitangi with the Queen of England. The Māori language version, which contains the most signatures, records that Māori would retain *tino rangatiratanga* (sovereignty) over their lands and treasures but otherwise gave *kawanatanga* (governance) rights to the British Crown. The English version has some significant translational differences where it states that Māori ceded sovereignty to the British Crown but Māori retained full exclusive and undisturbed possession of their lands, estates, forests, fisheries and other properties.[8] However, the future did not eventuate as Māori had expected. In 1840, with the British assuming formal sovereignty, Aotearoa New Zealand

---

3   Ranginui Walker, *Ka Whawhai Tonu Matou: Struggle without End* (2nd edn, Penguin Books 2004) 24 but note others put it at about AD 1200. See Michael King, *The Penguin History of New Zealand* (Penguin Books 2003) 48.

4   For an introduction to the Māori language see HW Williams, *Dictionary of the Māori Language* (GP Publications 1992); and HM Ngata, *English-Māori Dictionary* (Learning Media 1993).

5   For an introduction to Māori mythology see Ross Calman and AW Reed, *Reed Book of Māori Mythology* (2nd edn, Reed Books, 2004).

6   Paul Callister, Robert Didham and Anna Kivi, 'Who are We? The Conceptualisation and Expression of Ethnicity' (2009) 4 Official Statistics Research Series 1.

7   As an example, see the Te Whanau o Waipareira Māori Urban Authority in Auckland 'Home' Te Whānau o Waipareira < http://www.waipareira.com/> accessed 20 November 2014.

8   To view a copy of the Treaty see schedule 1 of the Treaty of Waitangi Act 1975.

became a British colony. In 1852, the New Zealand Constitution Act created provincial councils throughout the country and a central General Assembly, that constituted the Governor-in-Chief of New Zealand, a Legislative Council and a House of Representatives modelled on the United Kingdom.[9] Many Māori tribes were unhappy with the colonial government regime. Some protest action was peaceful (travelling to England to petition Queen Victoria) and some was violent. By the 1860s, the violence had escalated into the New Zealand Land Wars.[10] By the 1870s, European settlers outnumbered Māori.

Today, Māori own an unknown quantity of general freehold land and own in fee simple about 6 per cent of the country's landmass in Māori freehold land title. There are no like reserves as in North America (Māori were not forcibly removed from lands to live within the borders of colonially defined reserves). Initially, the colonial government accepted that Māori owned most of the land. Following the signing of the Treaty of Waitangi, the British Crown set about acquiring land from Māori and by the early 1860s had become the owner of most of the land in the South Island and the lower part of the North Island (constituting about 60 per cent of New Zealand's land mass and where about 10 per cent of Māori lived).[11] The Crown then on sold this land as general freehold land to the new European settlers. In the 1860s, legislation enabled the Crown acquisition of most of the remaining lands in the North Island through outright confiscation and the more subtle but equally successful waiver of the British Crown's right of pre-emption in favour of the creation of Māori freehold land titles.[12] The Native Land Court was established with the primary purpose to encourage Māori land owners to transfer their customary holdings into a freehold title that would then enable them to alienate their lands as they wished. In reality, many owners were forced to sell their lands to pay for financial debt incurred in the transaction process. Today, there is said to be virtually no Māori customary land remaining. The 6 per cent that is held in Māori freehold titles is mostly: held in multiple in common titles, not inhabited, and in rural areas but with little arable value. Māori freehold land can be alienated, but legislation enacted in 1993 – Te Ture Whenua Māori Act / the Māori Land Act – has emphasized new twin principles to ensure that it is retained in Māori ownership and that it is utilized and developed. There are some remarkable financial success stories mostly concerning forestry on Māori freehold land where the Māori trusts or Māori incorporations are returning million plus dollar profits.

---

9   This historical revoked act can be viewed online at Victoria University of Wellington Library <http://nzetc.victoria.ac.nz/tm/scholarly/tei-GovCons.html> accessed 20 November 2014.

10   See James Belich's books *The New Zealand Wars and the Victorian Interpretation of Racial Conflict* (Penguin 1998) and *Making Peoples: A History of the New Zealanders from Polynesian Settlement to the End of the Nineteenth Century* (Penguin Press 1996).

11   An excellent source of this history is the Waitangi Tribunal reports <http://www.waitangi-tribunal.govt.nz/> accessed 20 November 2014.

12   Native Lands Act 1865 (now repealed).

Māori are regaining control of their affairs boosted by Treaty of Waitangi claim settlements. Since the mid 1980s, the Crown has sought to engage in a 'fair and final' settlement process of claimed historical breaches of the principles of the Treaty of Waitangi.[13] The settlements aim to provide the foundation for a new and continuing relationship between the Crown and the claimant group based on the Treaty of Waitangi principles. Settlements thus contain Crown apologies of wrongs done, financial and commercial redress, and redress recognizing the claimant group's spiritual, cultural, historical or traditional associations with the natural environment. Some significant cultural redress examples include the return of pounamu ownership to Ngai Tahu[14] and the new co-management of the Waikato River.[15] More than 20 tribal groups have now received redress.[16] In addition, there have been financially notable pan-tribal settlements regarding commercial fisheries, commercial aquaculture and forestry.[17] The increased wealth of the tribes has enabled Māori to have more national political clout,[18] and the means to work with their tribal members to grow their tribal assets and provide many social benefits.

Since 1975, Māori have had the opportunity to present arguments to the specially created permanent commission of inquiry – the Waitangi Tribunal – on alleged Crown contemporary breaches of the principles of the Treaty of Waitangi.[19] From 1985 to 2010, Māori were able to lodge arguments that the Crown actions, policies or laws between 1840 and 1992 breached the Treaty principles.[20] The Waitangi Tribunal consists of Māori Land Court judges and other notable Māori and non-Māori appointed persons. It is a powerful bicultural place where hearings

---

13 See Office of Treaty Settlements, *Ka tika a muri, ka tika a mua: Healing the Past, Building a Future* (2nd edn, Office of Treaty Settlements 2002); and R Joseph, 'Contemporary Māori Governance: New Era or New Error?' (2007) 22 NZULR 628.

14 Ngai Tahu (Pounamu Vesting) Act, No 81 1997 (NZ).

15 Waikato-Tainui Raupatu Claims (Waikato River) Settlement Act, No 24 2010 (NZ).

16 See the Office of Treaty Settlements website 'Progress of Claims' online for a current list of negotiated settlements: Office of Treaty Settlements. Available at: <http://nz01.terabyte.co.nz/ots/fb.asp?url=livearticle.asp?ArtID=-1243035403> (accessed 20 November 2014).

17 Treaty of Waitangi (Fisheries Claims) Settlement Act, No 121 1992 (NZ); Māori Fisheries Act, No 78 2004 (NZ), Māori Commercial Aquaculture Claims Settlement Act, No 107 2004 (NZ), Central North Island Forests Land Collective Settlement Act, No 99 2008 (NZ).

18 For example, in 2005 the Iwi Chairs Forum was established, see 'Kaupapa' (2008) Iwi Chairs Forum <http://www.iwichairs.Māori.nz/Kaupapa/> accessed 20 November 2014.

19 Paul Hamer, 'A Quarter-century of the Waitangi Tribunal: Responding to the Challenge' in Janine Hayward and Nicola Wheen (eds), *The Waitangi Tribunal: Te Roopu Whakamana i te Tiriti Waitangi* (Bridget Williams Books 2004).

20 Treaty of Waitangi Amendment Act, No 148 1985 (NZ) s 3(1).

are often heard on *marae* with Māori protocols and Māori language often utilized. The Tribunal has released numerous reports on tribe-region specific claims alleging historical breaches throughout the country and has reported on an array of generic issues ranging from the use of the Māori language, customary fishing, the allocation of radio frequencies, petroleum, aquaculture, and water. In some instances the government has accepted the Tribunal's recommendations for redress and enacted appropriate legislation (for example, the Māori Language Act 1987 and the Māori Commercial Aquaculture Claims Settlement Act 2004), but denied several others (for example, the reports on petroleum, and the foreshore and seabed).[21]

The law today recognizes the Māori language as an official language of the country.[22] Many statutes recognize Māori cultural values including *kaitiakitanga*,[23] and *taonga*.[24] Numerous statutes across a wide spectrum from environmental management, to family property division, to land transport require decision-makers to have some level of regard to the principles of the Treaty of Waitangi. Nonetheless, Māori still constitute all the wrong side of the statistics, for example, for health, education, imprisonment, and unemployment.[25] Past legislation legitimated horrendous actions against Māori including taking their lands and treasures, and encouraging the demise of the Māori language and Māori culture. While the country is reconfiguring towards reconciliation, the relationship between Māori and government and society generally is still tense at times. In 2003 and 2004 the country's race relations erupted concerning the issue of possible Māori ownership of the foreshore and seabed.[26] In 2012, disquiet emerged about possible Māori ownership of freshwater.[27]

This overall account of Māori and the law aligns with many Indigenous peoples experiences of colonization. Indigenous peoples throughout the world have been dispossessed of much of their lands and treasures, lost many of their languages and much of their cultural knowledge but have retained collective strength in who they are and what they desire. There are of course differences arising in part from the different colonial tools utilized. This chapter now turns to consider more closely some similarities and differences between Māori and Sami experiences.

---

21 Waitangi Tribunal, *The Petroleum Report*, Wai 796 (Wellington: Legislation Direct 2003); Waitangi Tribunal, *Report on the Crown's Foreshore and Seabed Policy*, Wai 1071 (Legislation Direct 2004).

22 Māori Language Act, No 176 1987.

23 For example, Resource Management Act, No 69 1991 (NZ) s 7(a) [RMA].

24 For example, Property (Relationships) Act, No 166 1976 (NZ) s 2.

25 See 'Browse for Statistics'. Available at: <http://www.stats.govt.nz/browse_for_stats.aspx> (accessed 20 November 2014).

26 See Abby Suszko, 'The Marine and Coastal Area (Takutai Moana) Act 2011: A Just and Durable Resolution to the Foreshore and Seabed Debate?' (2012) 25 NZULR 148.

27 See Jacinta Ruru, 'Indigenous Restitution in Settling Water Claims: The Developing Cultural and Commercial Redress Opportunities in Aotearoa New Zealand' (2013) 22(2) Pacific Rim Law & Policy Journal 311.

Indigenous Ways of Life

As many contributors discuss in this book, including Labba, Bull, Bengtsson, Torp and Allard, reindeer were, and remain for some, central to many Sami lifestyles and identity. In Aotearoa New Zealand, because it was a country with no terrestrial mammals except for bats and seals, there is no similar history of Māori herding animals. Māori were hunters and gatherers of predominantly fish and birds. *Tītī* (sooty shearwater birds) are perhaps comparative to reindeer in the sense of cultural importance. The prominent home for *tītī* is on small islands to the east, south and west of Stewart Island that lie below the South Island. *Tītī* have always been a central component of diet, trading and thus identity for Ngai Tahu (the tribe in the lower two-thirds of the South Island). In 1864, the Crown and Ngai Tahu negotiated the sale and purchase of Stewart Island. As part of this deed of cession, 21 of the islands surrounding Stewart Island were exclusively reserved for certain Ngai Tahu individuals and their descendants. These islands became known as the Beneficial Titi Islands. The remainder became known as the Crown Titi Islands. Pursuant to the Ngai Tahu Claims Settlement Act 1998 the latter were renamed the Rakiura Titi Islands and ownership vested in Te Runanga o Ngai Tahu (the legal body/entity of Ngai Tahu). Historically and still today, those Māori who are permitted to enter the Titi Islands, will travel to these islands in April and May each year to harvest the chicks. This annual travel is important for cultural identity and sustenance. The law strictly defines that only those descendants of the original Māori owners of the islands are entitled to enter the islands and harvest titi chicks.[28] In this context, blood descendant membership is important like with reindeer herding as is discussed by many in this collection including Labba and Joona. While spouses can accompany those entitled to go to the *tītī* islands, there is current controversy about whether legally adopted in children can do so when they are adults.[29]

Another cultural lifestyle resource is *pounamu* (nephrite jade mineral). Regarded as a treasure in the Māori world, for centuries Māori have traded pounamu for use historically to be turned into chisels, adzes, fishing hooks, weapons and pendants. The stone is found in the mountains and rivers on the west coast of the South Island. Ngai Tahu travelled in certain seasons to collect pounamu for use including for trading purposes with other tribes. In 1997, the Crown recognized the paramount value of pounamu for Ngai Tahu in the enactment of the Ngai Tahu (Pounamu Vesting) Act 1997. Section 3 states clearly that all pounamu occurring in its natural condition ceases to be the property of the Crown and becomes the property of Te Runanga o Ngai Tahu. This means that if anyone or any company wishes to mine

---

28   See Titi (Muttonbird) Islands Regulations 1978. See Michael J Stevens, 'Kāi Tahu *me te* Hopu Tītī *ki* Rakiura: An Exception to the 'Colonial Rule'?' (2006) 41(3) The Journal of Pacific History 273.

29   *Re Coote* (2013) NZMLC Judges MB 1018.

for pounamu, they must first obtain the permission from Te Runanga o Ngai Tahu. The Crown has prosecuted people who fail to obtain this permission.[30]

The chapters by Skogvang and Torp in this collection that discuss Sami fishing resonate well with Māori because fishing (inland and coastal) is of central importance to Māori and their communities. Māori customary and commercial interests in fishing are now recognized in law.[31] Fishing cases are often at the forefront of cases in the courts. For instance, one of Aotearoa New Zealand's seminal cases concerned whether a Māori person had a customary right to collect legislatively prohibited undersized paua (abalone). The High Court, in 1986, held yes, this customary right was protected as part of the inherited English common law doctrine of native title.[32] But, while this case was a significant win for Māori, there are many other instances where Māori have been prevented from hunting and gathering flora and fauna. This is probably similar to Sami too, as Torp and Allard, for instance, explain in their chapters, where a reindeer-herding Sami man was prosecuted for having gathered reindeer lichen within a nature reserve. Unfortunately similar strict rules are operative for national parks in Aotearoa New Zealand that prevent Māori from accessing native plants and birds.[33] Moreover, many of the country's native birds are protected where ever they may live irrespective of whether they are within a national park or reserve or not. There are several instances where Māori have been prosecuted for killing native birds for food, for example, *kererū* (wood pigeon).[34]

Sovereignty and Property

All of the contributions in this book bring to life the Sami experiences of European assumptions of sovereignty and ownership of property. Many of these experiences correlate with Māori in Aotearoa New Zealand. Ahren's strong opening lines in his chapter are particularly illustrative of what has happened with Indigenous peoples around the world, essentially that 'classical international law largely emerged to justify the European realms placing territories and natural resources in other continents under their hegemony and control'. Another poignant example is Heinamaki's opening lines in her chapter that similarly acknowledge the power of international law to legitimate European expansion into the Sami lands now known as Finland. Some of this legal magic endorsed in international and Nordic domestic

---

30   *R v Saxton* (2009) 3 NZLR 29; *R v Hutton* (2008) NZCA 126. Also see Meredith Gibbs Ngai Tahu (Pounamu Vesting) Act 1997 (2000) 4 NZJEL; and Nicola R Wheen, 'Legislating for Indigenous Peoples' Ownership and Management of Minerals: A New Zealand Case Study on Pounamu' (2009) 20 *Management of Environmental Quality – An International Journal* 551.

31   Māori Fisheries Act 2004.

32   *Te Weehi v Regional Fisheries Officer* (1986) 1 NZLR 643.

33   See National Parks Act 1980 s5.

34   *Police v Mareikura* (1990) DCR 1.

law was prevalent in Aotearoa New Zealand too. In Aotearoa New Zealand, in 1840, British sovereignty was in part derived from a treaty of cession – the Treaty of Waitangi – and the applied English common law doctrine of discovery that has its roots in international law.[35] While Māori have often protested the Crown's assumption of sovereignty including by petitioning the Queen and King in England throughout the eighteenth century and in contemporary recent claims taken to the Waitangi Tribunal,[36] Parliament, government and the courts have had little interest in the disputed sovereignty issues. In comparison on the property front there is a long contested history of judicial and parliamentary pronouncements.

In the first court case to consider the issue of property, in *R v Symonds*, a case decided in 1847, the court asserted that Māori property is entitled to be respected at least in times of peace.[37] But, just as Bull writes in her chapter, despite some initial recognition of Sami rights in Norway, in 1889 there was an abrupt change in attitude. Interestingly, this similar retreat occurred in Aotearoa New Zealand too. The famous case that captures this backlash is *Wi Parata* decided in 1876.[38] This case asserted that there was no body politik in the Māori world capable of holding or ceding sovereignty and that Māori had no property tenure that was recognizable to the Europeans. The Court of Appeal finally overruled this case in 2003 in its *Ngati Apa* decision.[39] This case contains the test for proving continuing rights to property in accordance with the common law doctrine of native title that shares some similarities with the property tests developed in the Nordic countries that is discussed in many of the chapters in this collection, particularly Allard's chapter. In Aotearoa New Zealand, Māori would need to prove in accordance with Māori law that they continue to own the property in question. While the test does not use the language of time immemorial as is common in the Nordic countries, the sentiment is the same as is the need to rely on oral evidence of connection to place. If Māori can prove this, and the Crown cannot identify any legislation that clearly and plainly extinguishes this right in property, then the courts could recognize Māori customary ownership of the lands.

But this is mostly a theoretical exploration as Māori mostly seek to settle property issues in Treaty of Waitangi claim settlement negotiations directly with the government. The one area where Māori might pursue a common law doctrine of native title claim in the courts is freshwater. It was interesting to learn in reading Skogvang's work that in Norway freshwater is capable of being privately owned

---

35   See Jacinta Ruru, 'Asserting the Doctrine of Discovery in Aotearoa New Zealand: 1840-1960s' in Robert J Miller et al (eds), *Discovering Indigenous Lands: The Doctrine of Discovery in the English Colonies* (OUP 2010).

36   See Waitangi Tribunal, *He Whakaputanga me te Tiriti. The Declaration and the Treaty The Report on Stage 1 of the Te Paparahi o Te Raki Inquiry* (Waitangi Tribunal, Wai 1040 2014).

37   *R v Symonds* (1847) NZPCC 387.

38   *Wi Parata v Bishop of Wellington* (1877) 3 NZLR (NS) 72.

39   *Ngati Apa v Attorney-General* (2003) NZLR 643.

in contrast to the ocean which is considered common property. In Aotearoa New Zealand there is a Crown assumption, supported in law, that water cannot be owned (but could be challenged by Māori in the future).

As Bankes discusses in his comparative chapter, the importance of international law is by contrast in Canada less dominant than in the Nordic countries as discussed by various authors including Skogvang, Heinamaki and Ahren. This is true too in Aotearoa New Zealand. In fact, in regard to the United Nations Declaration on the Rights of Indigenous Peoples, article 26, that is cited by Skogvang in full, states Indigenous peoples have the rights to the lands, territories and resources which they have traditionally owned, occupied or otherwise used or acquired was not supported by New Zealand's government. New Zealand's support of UNDRIP has several caveats and one is non-support of article 26.[40] This is an interesting area of comparison between the countries.

Politics, Voting and Identity

It was fascinating to read in this collection of the intense issues surrounding politics, voting and identity, all linked in with fraught issues of membership. There is a similar long history of issues in Aotearoa New Zealand. It was remarkable to learn, as Bull writes, that as early as 1818 a proposal was considered to amend the constitution in Norway to secure voting rights for the Sami in Finmark – a right that became effective in 1821. Some decades later, in 1867, on the other side of the world, Māori men were given the right to vote in New Zealand's House of Representatives[41] but only within four electoral seats that were set aside for Māori male adult voters.[42] Later, in 1893 Māori women were also given the right to vote within these four seats. It was not until 1975 that Māori had the choice to enrol in either the Māori or the General electoral roll.[43] Since the 1990s, when the country moved from a first past the post to a mixed member proportional voting system, the Māori seats have been adjusted to reflect the number of the persons enrolled in the Māori seats. There are currently seven Māori seats, and an increasing number of Māori being elected to Parliament on party lists, representing the spectrum of political ideologies. The Māori Party (first established in 2004) has a confidence and supply agreement with the National Party that currently leads government.

---

40   See Jacinta Ruru, 'Finding Support for a Changed Property Discourse for Aotearoa New Zealand in the United Nations Declaration on the Rights of Indigenous Peoples' (2011) 15 Lewis & Clark L Rev 951.

41   The Parliament of New Zealand has two parts. One is the head of state, Queen Elizabeth II who is represented by the Governor-General. The other part is the House of Representatives. This comprises members of Parliament who are elected every third year.

42   Māori Representation Act, No 47 1867, (NZ). See Andrew Geddis, 'A Dual Track Democracy? The Symbolic Role of the Māori Seats in New Zealand's Electoral System' (2006) 5 ELJ 347.

43   Electoral Amendment Act, No 28 1975 (NZ).

One of the benefits of this arrangement is that the co-leader of the Māori Party is the Minister of Māori Development.[44]

But how has the legislation defined who are Māori and is it comparable to the Sami experiences? Who constitutes an Indigenous person appears to be a colonial minefield in many countries. In the Nordic context, several of the contributions in this collection discuss Sami membership. Joona's chapter in particular is revealing for what has happened in Finland. In regard to who are Māori, contemporary legislation simply defines Māori as 'Māori means a person of the Māori race of New Zealand; and includes a descendant of any such person'.[45] There has never been a language requirement to identify as Māori. Historically though the definition of Māori was linked in with blood quantum that used notions of 'half-caste'.[46] The contemporary definition of Māori is perceptibly different to the detailed legal definitions used to define the Aboriginal peoples in, for example, Canada and Finland. The contemporary descent definition, rather than the historically utilized legal blood quantum classification, is much more aligned to a Māori perspective of identification – 'When children are born with whakapapa [genealogy] they are grandchildren or "mokopuna of the iwi". They are Māori'.[47] However, for Māori, while descent from a Māori ancestor is a minimum requirement, being Māori is primarily a matter of subjective, social identification with other Māori and within that wider group with particular tribes and sub-tribes.[48] Thus, any Māori can choose to go on the Māori electoral roll to vote for a candidate in the Māori electoral seat where he or she resides. The membership issue in this context is not controversial. However, there is certainly increasing contestation about who qualifies as being Māori in regard to benefiting from tribal Treaty of Waitangi claim settlements[49] and whether newly formed urban tribal entities that bring together those Māori who no longer know their tribal affiliations can benefit from pan-tribal Treaty settlements.[50]

---

44   See the Māori Party website. Available at: <http://www.Māoriparty.org/index. php> (accessed 20 November 2014).

45   Section 4 of Te Ture Whenua Māori Act 1993/ Māori Land Act, No 4 1993 (NZ).

46   (Half caste bit).

47   Moana Jackson, 'The Part-Māori Syndrome' (2003) June-July Mana Magazine 52 at 62. For a past example of how Māori were historically defined in legislation sees 2 of the Native Land Court Act, 1894.

48   See Natalie Coates, *Kia tū ko taikakā: Let the heartwood of Māori identity stand – An investigation into the appropriateness of the legal definition of 'Māori' for Māori* (Oct. 2008 unpublished BA (Hons dissertation), online 'Te Tumu: School of Māori, Pacific and Indigenous Studies' <http://eprintstetumu.otago.ac.nz/67/> accessed 20 November 2014.

49   See Kirsty Gover, 'Tribal Constitutionalism and Membership Governance in Australia and New Zealand: Emerging Normative Frictions' (2009) 7 NZJPIL 191.

50   For example, see the Māori Fisheries settlement saga that included appeals to the then top court for New Zealand, the Privy Council, about the definition of 'iwi' (tribe), *Tainui Māori Trust Board & Ors v Treaty of Waitangi Fisheries Commission & Ors* [1997] 1 NZLR 513 (PC); *Manukau Urban Māori Authority & Ors v Treaty of Waitangi Fisheries Commission & Ors* [2000] 1 NZLR 285 (HC); 331 (CA); (2002) 2 NZLR 17 (PC).

It is worthwhile to note here that while there is no like Sami Parliament in Aotearoa New Zealand, there was certainly an historical attempt by many Māori to create a Māori Parliament in the late eighteenth century.[51] The recently created Iwi Leaders Forum that brings together some of the tribal leaders in a formal manner that provides advice to New Zealand's government is perhaps an initiative that might grow in time to resemble not necessarily an alternative Māori Parliament but a 'parliament within a parliament' type model.[52]

Role and Rule of Law

Many of the contributions in this book strike a common theme that conveys the dominance of the role and rule of law, including Ahren, Stromgren and Modeer's chapters. Parliament is supreme and can legislate in a manner that overrules Indigenous' rights and relationships with the land, animals and resources, and court decisions can contain bias against Indigenous peoples. These observations are true too for Aotearoa New Zealand. For example, in Ahren's chapter he illustrates the compensation issue – while monetary compensation may work for Swedish property holders when the government acquires their land for mining activity, it does not work for Sami where continuous access to their land for reindeer herding is essential for the survival of cultural identity. Monetary compensation is of little value. This issue arises in Aotearoa New Zealand with similar emotion especially in the context with how the government has often used public works legislation to compulsorily acquire Māori freehold land. However, the courts have in 2014 highlighted the significance of this issue and in a rare instance found in favour of the Māori applicant.[53] Here, Māori freehold land was sought for a national road project but the courts agreed with the applicant that this land was of historical and cultural significance to her family and it would be repugnant to the principle of retention contained in Te Ture Whenua Māori Land Act/Māori Land Act 1993 to permit this land to be compulsory acquired under other legislation for roading purposes.

Whether Parliament recognizes (or not) Indigenous laws is a critical issue. As Labba writes, as long as Sami customs do not receive legal recognition they are in a vulnerable situation. In Labba's chapter, she discusses the Sami siida custom as rich and complex. As she writes, decisions in a siida are made at four levels: the individual, the household, the siida and the siida-leader. This was fascinating and reminds me of a Māori decision-making cultural legal context with the different roles of *whanau* (family), *hapu* (sub-tribe) and leaders having different but complimentary roles in this process. But as Labba states, 'for a long time national authorities, especially in Sweden, have undermined the role of the siida'. But the

---

51   Richard S Hill, 'Māori and State Policy' in Giselle Byrnes (ed), *The New Oxford History of New Zealand* (OUP 2009).

52   See (n18).

53   See *Grace – Ngarara West A25B2A* Maori Land Court (2014) 317 Aotea MB 268.

Reindeer Herding Act 2007 in Norway is a breakthrough legislative enactment that now recognizes the siida. In Aotearoa New Zealand there is a like long history of government mostly undermining the practice of Māori law,[54] although since the 1980s there have been some legislative enactments that seek to recognize components of Māori law. The Resource Management Act 1991, for example, requires decision-makers to have regard to *kaitiakitanga* (guardianship).[55] Te Ture Whenua Māori Act 1993, for example, permits owners to devise their interests in Māori freehold land to persons who have been adopted according to the Māori legal practice of *whangai*.[56]

Legislative recognition of Sami rights and customs is occurring across the Nordic countries that indicate a positive progression towards reconciliation (in particular see Allard's comparative chapter). A significant legislative moment is captured in Heinamaki's chapter with the reformed Mining Act 2011 in Finland that now recognizes Sami as having substantive and participatory rights in the mining permission procedure. This is true in New Zealand too with recent amendments to mining legislation.[57] And of course as Skogvang's writes of in her chapter there is in Norway new legislation in 2012 that recognizes Sami fishing rights.

Conclusion

Opportunities to gaze comparatively provide intense considerations of one's own legal situation. This comparative gaze with countries at opposite sides of the world demonstrates (a) the Indigenous strength in surviving colonization, (b) the shared long journeys for reconciliation and justice, and (c) thankfully glimmers of real hope and inspiration for some contemporary reconciliation. I hope the comparative gazing continues strongly into the future for there is much rich knowledge, institutions, laws and experiences to dialogue comparatively with to better understand our own journeys towards reconciliation. For example, the questions raised in many parts of the book, including prominently in Svensson's chapter, deserve close attention. While I conclude here now I wish to reinforce how special this research exchange has been and the honour it has been to contribute towards this special collection of writing.

---

54   The most notable example is the Tohunga Suppression Act 1907.

55   See section 7(a).

56   See section 108(2)(e).

57   Such as the declining of a request for the disclosure of information on a submission as to avoid serious offence to *tikanga* Māori and to avoid the disclosure of *wahi tapu* locations, see section Crown Minerals Amendment Act 2013 18(5)(a).

PART II
The Legal Situation for the Sami

Chapter 4
Sami Law in Late Modern Legal Contexts

Kjell Å Modéer

Prologue: Sami Law in the Transition from Modernity to Late Modernity

This chapter will review the different and important contexts of *late modernity* in relation to Sami law. Due to the new geopolitical situation after 1990, *late modernity* – or *The second modernity*[1] – has continuously succeeded the *modernity* of the twentieth century, very much dominated by the *strong state* or the *welfare state*, characterized by state regulation and social security.[2] The strong nation state of the post-Second World War period based its identity on a homogeneous population who had assimilated to the values of the social state of the early twentieth century and its democratic device: *equal justice under law*. This legal paradigm has since the late 1980s successively changed into the legal paradigm of the twenty-first century, the late modernity within law. Today, lawyers experience a legal culture that is in transition. This chapter will demonstrate the dynamics within current Nordic legal cultures; that is the oppositional struggle between ideological and legal forces and their influences in societal development. It's a struggle between dominating forces and upcoming contra-forces, which to a great extent are trends in development; a struggle wherein the winner in one societal context could be the loser in another context in the future and vice versa.[3]

One of the most important developments within this late modern paradigm has been the creation of the European Union (EU) and its constitutional framework. In the Maastricht Treaty of 1992, a new article 128 (today article 151) on culture was introduced. It established a legal basis for EU cultural policy. It states that community action within the EU is an aim for encouraging cooperation between member states and support and supplementary action in the fields of cultural heritage, non-commercial exchanges and artistic and literary work. The

---

1 Ulrich Beck and Christoph Lau (eds), *Entgrenzung und Entscheidung: Was ist neu an der Theorie reflexiver Modernisierung?* (Edition Zweite Moderne, Suhrkamp 2004).

2 Lotta Vahlne Westerhäll, *Den starka statens fall?* (Norstedts Juridik 2002); Bo Rothstein and Lotta Vahlne Westerhäll (eds), *Bortom den starka statens politik?* (SNS Förlag 2005).

3 Kjell Å Modéer, 'Der Verlierer als Sieger? Rechtsgeschichte und Rechtsvergleichung in einer neuen Schulstreit' in Kjell Å Modéer (ed), *Europäische Rechtsgeschichte und europäische Integration* (Festskrift till Heinz Mohnhaupt, Rättshistoriska skrifter Vol 4 2002) 93.

original article introduced a legal basis for the EU policy on cultural activities in encouraging, supporting and supplementing the actions of the member states 'while respecting their national and regional diversity and at the same time bringing the common cultural heritage to the fore'.[4] National language, history and culture contribute to the identities of the member states of the union. Even if converging into a common European identity is a common aim of the treaty, the article on culture, however, is supporting divergence in relation to the construct of a European cultural identity.

During late modernity, a more differentiated concept of democracy evolved. With the democratic breakthrough after the Great War majority rule was introduced in parliamentarian democracies. Since the civil rights movement in the 1960s, however, democracy has developed a second dimension, incorporating respect for minorities and legal actions against discrimination. The concept of human dignity has since the Middle Ages been an important part of Catholic social ethics, but after the Second World War it became a common and secular concept. The Nazi-regime's disrespect for minorities resulted e.g. in paragraph one in the West-German Basic Law 1949 stating the inviolability of the human dignity.[5] Respect for human dignity also encouraged new legal statements on ethnic minorities and indigenous people in different parts of the world. International public law has also adopted this new minority doctrine. The ILO Convention No 169, today ratified by 22 nations, has also in the Scandinavian countries contributed to an integration process instead of assimilation of the ethnic minorities.[6] The case law of the European Court for Human Rights has also upheld the doctrine of respect for diversity and heterogeneity among the populations in the European nation states. The features of anti-discrimination and respect for diversity – also manifested in the EU law – have resulted in a shift in the legal attitudes to the Sami people. This transition of the legal cultures and the legal cognitive structures during the last three decades is a remarkable part of late modern legal culture. The Romani people, on the other hand, are a current example of how ethnic minorities in European countries still are met with disrespect for human dignity and non-discrimination.

Sami law has been affected by this transition. During the past three decades, Sami law has been increasingly visible in Scandinavian legal cultures. Today (2015), Sami law is considerably established not only in Scandinavian case law but also in discourses within legal scholarship and legal politics. No doubt, the contexts for the Scandinavian legal professionals have changed significantly since

---

4   Maastricht Treaty 1992, article 128 para 1.

5   Basic Law 1949, s 1: 'Human dignity shall be inviolable. To respect and protect it shall be the duty of all state authority'.

6   ILO Convention 169 - Indigenous and Tribal Peoples Convention, 1989 (No 169). Convention concerning Indigenous and Tribal Peoples in Independent Countries (Entry into force 5 September 1991).

1981, when the ruling in the Taxed mountain case by the Swedish Supreme Court was published.[7]

In two landmark cases – the Selbu case[8] and the Svartskogen case[9] – the Norwegian Supreme Court upheld the user rights to land of the Sami with reference to the historical context of the arguments presented. Similarly, the Swedish Supreme Court followed similar argumentation in the 2011 Nordmaling case ruling.[10]

In sum, in late modern legal culture, we have not only seen a codification or acceptance of Sami rights, but can also observe general trends and changes concerning the view of state models as well as societal attitudes concerning the rights of ethnic minorities. In this chapter, I will specifically analyse the different, especially Swedish, contexts, which has created this new late modern legal culture regarding the Sami and Sami law.

Historical Argumentation

One of the trends within the late modern legal paradigm is that it upholds a historic turn, that is, it uses historical perspectives and historical argumentation. This trend is particularly interesting in the context of real estate law, a legal discipline traditionally related to history and traditions.[11] One example from the Swedish legal culture can exemplify this new trend. Since the early modern period, the concept of entailed estates, *fidei commissum*, has been established in Swedish real estate law. In 1963, during the peak of the strong Swedish welfare state and the nation state's principle of equal justice under law, a law on dismantling of the *fidei commissum* contracts in Swedish law was adopted.[12] Such family contracts from the seventeenth and eighteenth centuries were common amongst the nobility and representative of the society of privileges and of the *suum cuique* principle, which later became obsolete in the modern welfare state post-Second World War. The 1963 statute stated that the presumed holder of the entailed estate in the first generation should receive half of the real estate as a *fidei commissum*, while the other half should be parted among the heirs in accordance with the law of inheritance. Concerning the second generation of heirs, however, the inheritance law should be fully implied.[13] This

---

7   NJA 1981 p 1 (*Skattefjällsmålet*).

8   Rt 2001 p 769.

9   Rt 2001 p 1229.

10   NJA 2011 p 109.

11   James Whitman, 'The Neo-romantic Turn' in Pierre Legrand and Roderick Munday (eds), *Comparative Legal Studies: Traditions and Transitions* (CUP 2003) 312.

12   Act on dismantling of entailed estates, 1963 (*Lag (1963:583) om avveckling av fideikommiss*).

13   Kjell Å Modéer, 'Fideikommissinstitutet i svensk rätt: en rättshistorisk skiss' in *Vetenskapssocieteten i Lund Årsbok* (1978) 50–73.

statute has been implemented for about 50 years, and most of the entailed real estates have applied this law, which emanated from the strong social state of the twentieth century. Today the legal contexts to this law are quite different. Privatization and the market economy have dismantled legislation from the legal paradigm of the strong welfare state, and in Sweden the immensely devastating inheritance tax (which created significant problems for several of the large real estates of the nobility) has been abolished. In 1995, a governmental investigation proposed a more arbitrary interpretation of the legislation from 1963 and suggested that a cautious extension of the possibility of prolonging the original wills should be accepted. Such a voluntary prolonging of the *fidei commissum* contract was to be facilitated by the government.[14] Recently, families within the nobility, who were hostile to the 1963 legislation but eager to uphold the cultural heritage of the estates and the traditions of the family, got their new family contracts confirmed, and thereby accepting the principles of the original one and letting the current eldest son inherit the entailed estate. The Swedish government has also confirmed such contracts.[15] By upholding the *suum cuique* principle from the context of the original contracts, the *freedom of contract* principle was given priority over the modern principle of *equal justice under law*. More could be elaborated on this creation of a synthesis of the law in late modern society. For the purposes of this chapter, however, the trend to argue historically and to emphasize the cultural heritage is an important legal context to the current state of the art also within Sami law.

The late modern legal paradigm has identified Sami law as a new field of law, which is visible in the legal culture, and the late modern nation state identifies minorities and new hierarchies, and introduces reconciliation as a new conflict resolution method. Reconciliation is today a part of the Swedish society's dialogue with the Roma people[16] as well as with the Sami population.

Sami Case Law as Practical Legal History

In Scandinavian late modern legal culture, Sami case law conflicts in an interesting way, demonstrating a new legal argumentation with historical references. James Q. Whitman has identified a contemporary 'neo-romantic turn' within the comparative law discourses that emphasizes the historical perspectives.[17] The interpretation of the 'original meaning' of the Constitution by the conservative

---

14   SOU   1995:128   *Kulturegendomar   och   kulturföremål.   Betänkande   av Kulturarvsutredningen*, 212.

15   In 1995, the entailed estates of Fullerö, Erstavik, Svenstorp and Björnstorp. See Björn af Kleen, *Jorden de ärvde* (Weyler 2009) 26–28.

16   SOU 2010:55 *Romers rätt - en strategi för romer i Sverige.*

17   James Q Whitman, 'The Neo-romantic Turn' in Pierre Legrand and Roderick Munday (eds), *Comparative Legal Studies: Traditions and Transitions* (CUP 2011) 312.

majority of the US Supreme Court is another example of this historical 'turn',[18] even if the interpretation of the 'original meaning' itself can be a problematic comparison due to the very different historical contexts.[19]

After his time and experiences as a Danish Supreme Court Justice, the Danish law professor Henrik Zahle (1943–2006) introduced the concept of 'practical legal philosophy', in which he argued for taking judicial jurisprudence seriously and thus identified it as an important part of the academic field of jurisprudence.[20] In his last works, he also tentatively argued for what he called a 'practical legal history', a concept both of us also elaborated on in an email exchange just a couple of months before he passed away.[21]

Zahle's point is that legal history during the dogmatic period (of modernity) turned to the non-current (*det uaktuelle*). In other words, legal history has turned away from the applicability of the law, and the legal historian no longer has the ambition to contribute to the identification of valid law. The autonomy of the discipline has resulted in its inability to act as an instrument for legal practice. Zahle made a 'neo-romantic' turn and argued for the practical use of legal history. In fact, a historical deliberation is necessary in resolving every legal problem in practice. Therefore, it is necessary to integrate legal history as a natural argument in the legal paradigm. Since the legal historians often chose the autonomy of their discipline, it is according to Zahle not certain whether it will be the legal historians who shall develop practical legal history. His view of the professional tasks of legal historians in 2006 was based on his Danish experiences. In the last decade, however, changes within the legal paradigm have not only altered the perspectives of legal historians but also the judicial jurisprudence and its relation to history, as predicted by Henrik Zahle.

Sami law is a good example of how practical legal history works in practice. As representatives of the Historical School of Law claimed in the early nineteenth century, history is an argument for legal claims. The lawyers in the Nordmaling case have also confirmed this in a recent article.[22] 'We early realized that we had

---

18   Antonin Scalia and Bryan A Garner, *Reading Law: The Interpreting of Legal Texts* (Thomson/West 2012) 78 et seq; Steven G Calabresi (ed), *Originalism: A Quarter-Century of Debate* (Regnery Publishing Inc. 2007); Kevin A Ring (ed), *Scalia Dissents: Writings of the Supreme Court's Wittiest, Most Outspoken Justice* (Regnery Publishing 2004).

19   Justice Scalia writing for the court in *District of Columbia v Heller* (2008); Jeffrey Toobin, *The Oath: The Obama White House and the Supreme Court* (Doubleday 2012) 113–14; H Jefferson Powell, 'The Original Understanding of Original Intent' (1984) Harvard Law Review 885, 903.

20   Henrik Zahle, *Praktisk retsfilosofi* (Christian Ejlers 2005).

21   Henrik Zahle, 'Taking Legal History Seriously – En praktisk retshistorie' in Bernhard Diestelkamp et al, *Liber Amicorum Kjell Å Modéer* (Juristförlaget 2007) 725. See also Zahle's posthumous work: *At forske ret: Essays om juridisk forskningspraksis* (Gyldendal 2007) chapter 12.

22   Lars Melin and Camilla Wikland, 'Nordmalingsmålet – några erfarenheter back stage' (2014) 4 Advokaten, 36.

to acquaint ourselves with Sami circumstances and especially with the historical conditions of the reindeer husbandry. We read literature associated to the Sami people, and during the extensive lawsuit, we took a class in Sami history and politics at Gothenburg University.'[23] In the Nordmaling case, the introductory presentation was filled with supporting facts, and non-legal circumstances of importance for 'the context of the case, but facts we were anxious that the court lacked knowledge about. It could be, for example, Sami culture, the specifics of the reindeer as an animal, the effect of modern society on reindeer husbandry, the importance of climate and weather for the reindeer husbandry and much more.' This introductory presentation took several days and became 'a sort of seminar in Sami culture'.[24] In other words, the lawyers presented historical arguments in the case. Presenting a historical context to the claims has been increasingly important for Sami people in their case law. The same historical argument has recently been articulated in the discourse regarding the court decision in the so called Härjedal case 2002.[25] In a critical analysis of the decisions in this case the Swedish historian Lars Rumar criticizes the lack of historical interpretation regarding historical facts.[26]

The Polycentric Argument in Sami Law

One of the main characteristics in late modern law is the break with the traditional monolithic theory of legal sources as defined both in theory as well as in practice, and a renaissance of multiple legal systems. Today, the parliamentarian *travaux préparatoires* as dominant legal sources for the Swedish judiciary are (again) in competition not only with customary law but also with international law. The application of several legal sources has been elaborated as a 'polycentric law' defined as 'a generic label for non-state law, including both customary and privately produced law'.[27]

---

23   ibid.

24   ibid 38.

25   The Court of Appeal for Southern Norrland, Case No. T 58-96, decided 2002-02-15.

26   Lars Rumar, *Historien och Härjedalsdomen: En kritisk analys* (Vaartoe/Centrum för samisk forskning 2014). See also Bertil Bengtsson, *Samerätt: En översikt* (Institutet för rättsvetenskaplig forskning/Norstedts Juridik 2004) 80-89.

27   Hanne Petersen and Henrik Zahle (eds), *Legal Polycentricity: Consequences of Pluralism in Law* (Dartmouth 1995). See also Tom W Bell, 'Polycentric Law in the New Millennium' (1999) Policy Autumn, 34; quoting Lon L Fuller's definition of the term: '[L]aw is the enterprise of subjecting human conduct to the governance of rules'. Lon L Fuller, *The Morality of Law* (Yale University Press 1964) 106. In defending his definition, Fuller admitted that it left ample room for non-statist legal systems. 'A possible objection … is that it permits the existence of more than one legal system governing the same population. The answer, of course, is that such multiple systems do exist and have in the history been more common than unitary systems', ibid 123.

This theory of polycentricity has been of great importance for the Sami law, because the main problem for Sami law to gain validity in judicial jurisprudence has been a general unwillingness of the courts and their judiciaries to expand the concept of modern legal sources outside that of legal positivism and legal dogma. From a formal perspective, it is easy to criticize an extensive contextual approach to the legal argumentation, which for example was used by the Sami's lawyer in the Taxed mountain case, who, with his unconventional presentation bothered not only the courts but also many of those who supported the Sami position.[28] However, Sami law cannot be applied without accepting references to a substantial historical context. In the Nordmaling case the lawyers emphasized that the case turned into an extensive historical and cultural history project. The use of the legal concept immemorial prescription (*urminnes hävd*) in the 1734 law book became important for them:

> An extremely important part of the trials was our introductory presentation of supporting facts and circumstances, which did not belong to the legal core but was important for the context of the case, of which we were feared the court didn't have the necessary knowledge. For example, the Sami culture, the peculiar nature of the reindeer as an animal, the impact of modern society, reindeer husbandry today, the importance of climate and weather for the reindeer husbandry and much, much more.[29]

The acceptance of an extensive context and a polycentric attitude to the legal sources used demonstrates the necessity of a historical argument for late modern judges' understanding of Sami law cases.

Contemporary late modern legal paradigm offers a wider interpretation of legal sources than the modern one from the twentieth century. The representatives of critical positivism argue that there are deep structures of law that must be considered in identifying a legal culture.[30] Sami law today represents not only a part of Scandinavian legal culture; it's also connected to transnational deep structures of law. That is, Sami law has to be interpreted in relation to the pre-modern concept of law, in which customary law and international public law (including collective human rights) were included.

In East Scandinavian legal cultures, customary law has been continuously diminished as a legal source throughout the modernity. The tolerated position of modernity in that respect holds that customary law has to be confirmed by

---

28   Tomas Cramér (ed), *Samernas vita bok* (vols 1–32, Stockholm 1972–2010).

29   Melin and Wikland (n 21) 38.

30   Kaarlo Tuori, 'Towards a Multi-layered View of Modern Law' in Aulis Aarnio, Robert Alexy and Gunnar Bergholtz (eds), *Justice, Morality and Society: A Tribute to Aleksander Peczenik*, (Juristförlaget i Lund 1997) 432.

the Parliament to be valid as a legal source.[31] This narrow interpretation has been devastating in the case law regarding Sami law for decades before the Nordmaling case.

Even if minority rights have been in focus globally since the human and civil rights movements in the 1950s and 1960s, the Swedish position in that respect has been very reluctant. The ILO Convention No 169 has since 1990 been of great importance for the identification of the legal position of indigenous people.[32] Norway has ratified the Convention; however, Sweden and Finland have not. In the Selbu case in 2001, the Norwegian Supreme Court decided in favour of the Sami reindeer herding districts.[33] The court,however, did not quote the ILO Convention. The first voting judge argued regarding the question whether ILO Convention No 169 article 14 nr 1 should be used in this case:

> Historians are in disagreement about whether the Sami came to the inner parts of Sør-Trøndelag before or after the farmers had cleared the land for their farms there. This discussion has no relevance to the question of whether the Sami can invoke the provision concerned also in Selbu.[34]

He ended his argumentation with the following statement:

> I do not find it necessary to go any further into the two conventions, the relationship between them and their application in disputes between private parties. As I see it, the Norwegian rules of law concerning use from time immemorial, based on traditional Norwegian sources of law and with the adaptation that must be allowed for reindeer husbandry, are sufficient to provide grounds for common of pasture in the disputed areas.[35]

Even if the court did not use the ILO Convention in its argumentation, it is, of course, an open question if the judges took this position regarding the Convention

---

31   Kjell Å Modéer, 'Legal Autonomy Versus Regulatory Law: Customary Law in East Nordic Countries' (2013) Texas International Law Journal, 393.

32   C169 - Indigenous and Tribal Peoples Convention, 1989 (No 169). Convention Concerning Indigenous and Tribal Peoples in Independent Countries (Entry into force 5 September 1991).

33   Rt 2001 p 769.

34   'Historikerne er uenige om samene kom til de indre delene av Sør-Trøndelag før eller etter at bøndene hadde ryddet sine gardsbruk der. Denne diskusjonen har ingen betydning for spørsmålet om samene kan påberope seg den aktuelle bestemmelsen i Selbu'. See Rt 2001 p 769, 790.

35   'Jeg finner det ikke nødvendig å gå nærmere inn på de konvensjonene, forholdet mellom dem og anvendelsen i tvister mellom private parter. Slik jeg ser det, er de norske rettsreglene om alders tids bruk, basert på tradisjonelle norske rettskilder og med den tilpasningen som må gjøres for reindriften, tilstrekkelige til å begrunne beiterett i tvisteområdene'. See Rt 2001 p 769, 791.

as an important immanent part of the Norwegian legal culture as a consequence of the ratification.

As Sami law is so closely connected to local living law as well as transnational legal concepts, the renaissance of customary law and 'natural law' – like concepts in the international public law – legitimate the importance of their minority law.

Sami Law Included in the Discourses Regarding the Concepts of Rights and Civil Religion

Discourses in late modern legal scholarship demonstrate the importance of upholding the rights of indigenous people and their legal position in (comparative) constitutional law and the role of minorities in late modern democracies. These discourses are related to the increasing role of the transnational European courts (*judicialization*) for a transition from the nation state to the conglomerate state.

The late modern nation state is no longer identified by sociological facts but by constitutional values. In this regard the discourse on civil religion introduced by the political scientist Robert N Bellah in the late 1960s is of great importance.[36] Bellah identified the essentials of an American Creed or a secular civil religion articulated in the presidential addresses, with its concepts of equality, liberty and popular consent. In 1998 John E Semonche went further, and argued that American civil religion is embedded in the Constitution and is continuously articulated by the opinions its 'High Priests', the justices in the Supreme Court.[37] Such fundamental values of the society have been of great importance not only for the identification of the American legal culture[38] but also for the European Union.[39]

In a later article Bellah returned to the civil religion discourse from a global perspective. Also within comparative constitutional law the civil religion discourse is of importance, for example in the preambles of (new or revised) constitutions, where minority rights are in focus.[40]

Post-apartheid South Africa also represents an interesting example of polycentric and diversified law, where colonial law is mixed with traditional deep structures of law. Albie Sachs describes the visibility of *Ubuntu-botho* in the contemporary South African constitutional and judicial

---

36   Robert N Bellah, 'Civil Religion in America' (1967) 1 Daedalus 1–21.

37   John E Semonche, *Keeping the Faith: A Cultural History of the U.S. Supreme Court* (Rowman & Littlefield 1998), 15.

38   John E Simonche, (n. 35), 35–36, 405–06.

39   Kjell Å Modéer, 'Den svenska och nordiska samhällsreligionen. Om författningskultur och samhällsreligion i ett komparativt perspektiv' in Anders Mellbourn (ed), *Författningskulturer och politiska system i Europa, USA och Asien* (Sekel Bokförlag 2009) 175.

40   Kjell Å Modéer, 'The Deep Structures of European Normativity in a Global Context' (2014) Rechtsgeschichte – Legal History 275–81.

culture. *Ubunthu-botho* is a concept that he finds 'intrinsic to and constitutive' of the South African constitutional culture.[41]

> Historically it was foundational to the spirit of reconciliation and bridge-building that enabled our deeply traumatized society to overcome and transcend the divisions of the past. In present-day terms it has an enduring and creative character, representing the element of human solidarity that binds together liberty and equality to create an affirmative and mutually supportive triad of central constitutional values. It feeds pervasively into and enriches the fundamental rights enshrined in the Constitution[42]

Sachs compares the original concept of *ubunthu-botho* with the concept of the *amende honorable* in the traditional Roman-Dutch law. Both share the same underlying philosophy and goal of restorative justice: 'Both are directed towards promoting a face-to face encounter between the parties so as to facilitate resolution in public of their differences and the restoration of harmony in the community. In both legal cultures, the centerpiece of the process is to create conditions to facilitate the achievement, if at all possible, of an apology honestly offered and generously accepted'.[43]

Ubuntuism represents a philosophy in contemporary South Africa with deep roots in history and defined as 'humanity towards others' – an immanent civil religion. A colleague of Albie Sachs, Justice Yvonne Mokgoro, has explained the meaning of *ubuntu* as 'it envelopes the key values of group solidarity, compassion, respect, human dignity, conformity to basic norms and collective unity, in its fundamental sense, it denotes humanity and morality'.[44]

In a setting of global normativity, the South African Ubuntuism and the Chinese Confucianism represent different forms of deep structures, which, like a civil religion, are embedded in constitutional cultures.[45]

The new constitutionalism is an increasingly important context for minority rights. The preamble of the Lisbon Treaty and the recent amendments to the Swedish Instrument of Government in 2010,[46] in which the Sami is defined as an indigenous people, support the upholding of the societal norms for minorities.

---

41 Albie Sachs, *The Strange Alchemy of Life and Law* (OUP 2011) 100.

42 ibid 102.

43 ibid.

44 ibid 107.

45 Kjell Å Modéer, (n.38), 278. Hans Joas, 'A Conversation with Robert Bellah', The Hedgehog Review (Summer 2012), 78.

46 Instrument of Government ch 1 s 2: 'Samiska folkets och etniska, språkliga och religiösa minoriteters möjligheter att behålla och utveckla ett eget kultur- och samfundsliv ska främjas'. Swedish Code of Statutes 2010:1408.

Sami Law and Religion as a Deep Structure in Sami Legal Culture

One important part of late modern legal culture is the alternative to public dispute resolutions in the courts, the so-called Alternative Dispute Resolutions (ADR). Reconciliation has in that respect been an effective instrument for conflict resolution not only in South Africa but also in the Scandinavian countries. One contribution to a new and better relationship between the Sami minority and the majority religious communities (*Den norske kirke, Svenska kyrkan*) is the contemporary ongoing reconciliation process. The Swedish Church is today a quasi-public/private religious community, which has inherited a bad relationship with the Sami population. However, it has started a reconciliation process, which can be compared with that of the Norwegian state Church and with post-colonial experiences elsewhere (e.g. in South Africa and Viet Nàm).

In Sami culture, law and religion have important contextual parallels. Historically, the disregard of Sami law and culture in the Swedish courts can be compared with the relationship between the Sami population and the representatives of the Swedish Church. Historically, the Swedish state Church since the seventeenth century aimed to convert or assimilate the Sami population. In the nineteenth century Social Darwinism became a specific feature of this project. There was no tolerance for the nature-inspired religion which dominated Sami culture. Since 2000, the Swedish Church has been an autonomous entity, and its synod has recently (2014) declined to support the Sami regarding the ratification of the ILO Convention No 169.[47]

The Board of the Swedish Church, however, has initiated a reconciliation strategy for the relationship between the Church and the Sami. As a part of this strategy a *Ságastallamat*, a reconciliation meeting, was held in Kiruna in October 2011.[48] One of the most important contributions to this meeting was delivered by a Norwegian clergyman, Thore Johnsen, from the Sami Church Council in Oslo. He introduced the audience to how the Latin American liberation theology since the 1970s introduced the post-colonial power perspective on the relationship between the colonial powers and the indigenous people. In the globalized world, Christianity is no longer primarily a majority religion for Westerners. Within the Nordic context contextual readings of the gospels have helped to understand the immanent conflicts between the majority Church and the ethnic minorities and between the Swedish Church and the Sami. Johnsen's talk demonstrated that the Norwegian Church is far ahead of the Swedish Church as far as the reconciliation process and the impact of contextual theology are concerned.

The meeting turned out to be a very emotional one, during which several of the Sami representatives gave testimony about how the former Swedish state Church

---

47   Swedish Church (*Kyrkomötet*), Kyrkolivsutskottets betänkande 2014:1, Stöd samernas rättigheter.

48   Swedish Church (*Kyrkokansliet*): Report from *Ságastallamat*, a conference on the Sami and the Swedish Church, in Kiruna (11–13 October 2011).

oppressed them over the years. Although the Swedish state Church earlier had argued for reconciliation, they had neglected Sami elements of religion and thus upheld an assimilation strategy. Today, however, the Swedish Church has made an effort to integrate Sami spiritual elements into their religious life. Historically both religious norms and legal norms have been used in the conflicts between the Swedish state institutions (parliament, courts and churches) and the Sami. In that respect, there are important parallels regarding the different attitudes of the parties in the conflicts within the concepts of law, religion and culture.

The meeting as a whole was concerned with how to combine reconciliation with justice. Justice has to be restored to the Sami, and the Swedish Church should not retaliate but reconcile. There is a need for discourse and reflection on the concept of justice in an ecclesiastical cognitive structure dominated by the concepts of grace and faith.[49]

Concluding Remarks

This chapter has explored how Sami law can be identified only with the help of history, contexts, civil religion and even religious concepts. The extensive doctrine on polycentricity – legal sources within late modern law – has supported a more favourable legal position for the law of minorities. Ethnic minorities have also been successful in claiming acceptance of their concepts of family law and law of inheritance in European countries. In Sami law, it is an ongoing process of making the courts conscious of the special character of Sami law and Sami religion.

Many parallels can be drawn between colonial deep structures and experiences of feudal relations that exist in post-colonial discourses (We and The Other) and globalization discourses to that of Sami law. Historically, the Sami population has been forced to assimilate into the Swedish, Norwegian and Finnish majority societies. The neglect of Sami cultural elements has suppressed the identity not only for the Sami culture in general but also for the Sami legal culture specifically.

One of the paradoxes of the late modern legal culture is that it has similarities with the early modern legal concept *suum cuique tribuere*, that is to give to each what belongs to her/him. The doctrine legitimating privileges in the natural law concepts of the seventeenth and eighteenth centuries has in the late modern legal culture experienced a renaissance for upholding the rights of minorities. Even if there are great differences as well in the contexts and the interpretations, the concept *suum cuique tribuere* is still vivid. In early modern times, it protected the privileged groups in the society; in the late modernity, however, the concept instead upholds the protection of vulnerable minorities in the contemporary society, such as indigenous peoples.

---

49   ibid 52.

Chapter 5

Some Characteristic Features of Scandinavian Laws and their Influence on Sami Matters

Christina Allard

Introduction

This chapter focuses on the less obvious aspects of the differences between the laws[1] of the Scandinavian countries Norway, Sweden and Finland with respect to Sami legal issues. In many instances legislation related to the Sami is characterized by its complexity and by the absence of clear statutory provisions and incompatible or silent legal sources. These matters are intertwined with the colonial roots of these three countries and the long-standing marginalization of the Sami as a group. Sami traditions and customary laws have generally not been codified because of the oral traditions of the Sami language and the lack of state interest. Uncertainty in the interpretation and application of the law serves to enhance the role of the courts.

This chapter aims to illustrate how general national characteristics within law play a role in how Sami legal matters are defined and resolved, and thus helps to explain the differences in the treatment of these issues in the three countries. The chapter is structured around three topics: judicial review and law-making functions of the Supreme Courts, the recognition of Sami land rights, and the acceptance of customary law. These observations are based on my own comparative work in the three countries conducted over past years, particularly regarding reindeer-herding rights.[2] My argument is that the law, broadly conceived, cooperates to define how Sami rights and interests are articulated, recognized and ultimately solved nationally.[3] The legal status of the Sami is not merely defined through present

---

1 I make a distinction between 'the law' and 'the legislation'. The former is understood as a broad concept, including case law and unwritten concepts and legal sources, such as legal principles and value-based balancing. Legislation, the primary source of law in the Scandinavian countries, refers to the enactments of the legislature, including preparatory works, and any delegated legislation.

2 Christina Allard, 'The Nordic countries' law on Sami territorial rights' (2011) 2 Arctic Review on Law and Politics 159.

3 Despite the increasing role of supranational courts, core Sami matters are still solved nationally. The EU law (Sweden and Finland are members) does indirectly affect

legislation and ratification of human rights conventions, such as ILO Convention No 169.[4] The differences go deeper than that. Some of these differences came to the surface within the work of the expert group drafting the text to the Nordic Sami Convention.[5]

Mindful of the multifaceted and complex pattern of factors – historical, cultural, economic, political and social – that shape and reshape each country's law and legal system,[6] my intention here is to highlight only a few of these underlying factors within national law itself. The study also has some limitations with respect to the Finnish law due to my linguistic shortcomings.[7] An analysis of differences in procedural law is also outside this study. The constitutional shielding of Sami culture is likewise not addressed. Although all three constitutions offer some degree of protection for Sami culture (Sweden's has the weakest), these provisions do not have a significant role.[8]

Scandinavian Laws and Historical Traits

How much do the Scandinavian countries' laws have in common? Undeniably they share a long-standing history of wars and unions. Finland for over 600 years was part of the Swedish kingdom, until 1809 when it came under the Russian Empire. Finland obtained independence in 1917. Norway belonged to the kingdom of Denmark from the 1400s till 1814, when Norway as a state was formed by the adoption of a new, independent constitution. Between 1814 and 1905 Norway was, however, in union with Sweden, and only gained full sovereignty in 1905. Because of shared history it is common to make a distinction between a West

---

the Sami in numerous ways, eg resource exploitations and the conservation of predators. 'Pure' property law issues are not part of EU law as such; and the European Court of Human Rights has so far refrained from substantive assessments of Sami land rights.

4   The Convention concerning indigenous and tribal peoples in independent countries, 1989. Hereinafter the ILO Convention 169.

5   Carsten Smith, 'Samiske rettigheter i nordisk perspektiv' in Carsten Smith (ed), *Dommersyn utenfor dommen: foredrag, artikler, taler* (Universitetsforlaget 2012) 183, 186, 206. The draft convention text is currently under negotiation in the three countries.

6   One example is the resurrection of Sami rights that occurred in Norway in the aftermath of the Alta crisis, ie the resistance of the building of a power station in the Alta River in a core Sami area, which culminated in the *Alta case* (Rt 1982 p 241). Sweden and Finland have no 'Alta cases' with such deep societal impact.

7   Legislation and old preparatory works are found in Swedish, but cases and legal literature are normally not. I have relied here on scholarly literature where available.

8   Norway: Constitution Act, 1814 s 108; Sweden: Instrument of Government 1974, ch 1 s 2; Finland: Constitution Act, 1999 s 17. The Scandinavian constitutions are traditionally weak compared to those of common law systems, and their provisions are seldom evoked before the courts. See also NOU 2007:13 *Den nye sameretten*, 190–91; Jaako Husa, *The Constitution of Finland: A Contextual Analysis* (Hart Publishing 2011) 193-94.

Nordic (Denmark, Norway, Island) and an East Nordic (Sweden, Finland) legal tradition, assuming shared characteristics.[9] Indeed, there is a closer resemblance between the Swedish and Finnish legal systems than the Norwegian; and even after 1809 and 1917 Finland kept much of the former Swedish legal system and legislation. Today, however, the Finnish law seem to becoming more distinct.[10] Whether or not there exists a separate Nordic Law, the general resemblance is built on a community of values, a specific shared social ethos, rather than on uniformity of political structure, history, language, et cetera, which are clearly diverse.[11]

There are uncomplicated explanations for many of the differences between these three states when it comes to Sami relations. For example, Norway is party to ILO Convention 169 whereas Sweden and Finland are not. As a result Norway in recent years has started to come to terms with its colonial past. In 2005 the Norwegian government and the Sami Parliament signed a Consultation Agreement, which in practice accords Norwegian Sami substantial influence in the drafting of legislation affecting them.[12] The Finnmark Act 2005 is a milestone in Norway as it partly aims to implement the ILO Convention 169 in Finnmark, a core Sami area.[13]

As a distinct Scandinavian trait, Scandinavian governments have generally sought to address Sami rights issues through government commissions and bills. But increasingly Sami land and resource rights are also being pursued through national and international courts. Norway's Sami Rights Commissions (SRC) I and II, have, beginning in the mid 1980s produced several important reports of a high quality dealing with Sami legal matters.[14] Sweden has also produced a number of commission reports investigating Sami matters,[15] but these have not resulted in new legislation or significant amendments. Finland has established a Sami homeland region in the far north with some cultural and linguistic autonomy, but struggles with defining who is to be regarded Sami.[16]

---

9   Jaakko Husa, *Nordic Law: Between Tradition and Dynamism* (Intersentia 2007) 5.

10   Johanna Niemi, *Sverige och Finland – lika eller olika?* (2010) 33 Retfærd 95, 96.

11   Husa, *Nordic Law* (n 9) 21-22, 38-39.

12   NOU 2007:13 *Den nye sameretten*, 824.

13   See further eg Oyvind Ravna, *Finnmarksloven og retten til jorden i Finnmark* (Gyldendal 2013).

14   In a national competition the two reports by the SRC II (NOU 2007:13; NOU 2007:14) was recently selected as the second-best commission reports in Norwegian law-drafting history.

15   See among others SOU 1999:25 *Samerna – ett ursprungsfolk i Sverige*; SOU 2001:101 *En ny rennäringspolitik*; SOU 2005:116 *Jakt och fiske i samverkan*; SOU 2006:14 *Samernas sedvanemarker*.

16   cf Tanja Joona's Chapter 12 in this volume. See also Juha Joona, 'The draft Nordic Saami Convention and the indigenous population in Finland' in Nigel Bankes and Timo Koivurova (eds) *The proposed Nordic Saami Convention* (Hart Publishing 2013) 246–50.

Separation of Powers and Judge-Made Law

As stated in the introduction, the role of courts expands where there is a lot of room for interpretation. This is the case for Sami legal matters which are not only complex but also involve unclear legal sources. This section seeks to explain in a comparative context the relative independence of the national Supreme Courts principally by considering if they are entrusted with judicial review functions and by examining their ability to develop the law. The differences are rooted in the national constitutional history,[17] where the Norwegian legal system stands out – also in a West Nordic perspective.[18]

The difference in style of Norwegian Supreme Court judgments is striking. Stylistically they are closer to a common law traditions of judgment writing; a first-voting judge argues openly with respect to the matter at hand and other judges agree or dissent.[19] Judgments are normally also quite lengthy. Swedish and Finnish cases are written as a common verdict, with a possibility of writing a dissenting opinion. These differences signify a distinction between the judge as merely applying the law and the judge as law-maker, where the latter needs to explain and develop his or her arguments more thoroughly.[20] Indeed, juxtaposed to the traditional Swedish and Finnish position, it is generally accepted that the Norwegian Supreme Court plays a role in developing the law, even if judge-made law is not as important a source in the Scandinavian tradition as it is in England and the USA.[21]

The relative autonomy of the Norwegian Supreme Court has long roots. Despite the fact that all power vested in the Danish-Norwegian king though the King's Act of 1665, by the late 1700s the Supreme Court had become rather independent; the judges had their own seals and the verdict was not made in the king's name.[22] As a result, by 1814, when the new independent Constitution was adopted, it furthered the functional distinction between executive and judicial powers along with the independence of the Supreme Court. The Constitution Act 1814 was thus not only a consequence of foreign constitutional ideas at the time, the American and French in particular, but as much a result of internal legal development.[23] The Constitution Act 1814 not only emphasized the division of powers between the legislative,

---

17   As being part of 'comparative constitutional law' there is no room here for deeper analyses.

18   Martin Sunnqvist, 'Konstitutionellt kritiskt dömande. Förändringen av nordiska domares attityder under två sekel' (doctoral dissertation, Jure 2014) 73, 761–64.

19   As a curiosity, since 1925 it has been obligatory for Norwegian judges to wear cloaks, which is not the case for Swedish and Finnish judges.

20   cf Sunnqvist (n 18) 758.

21   Torstein Eckhoff and Jan E Helgesen, *Rettskildelære* (5th edn, Universitetsforlaget 2001) 192, 209, 211.

22   Eirik Holmøyvik, *Maktfordeling og 1814* (Fagbokforlaget 2012) 247, 262; Peter Lødrup, *Norges høyesterett* (Universitetsforlaget 2011) 10, 16.

23   Holmøyvik (n 22) 477–78.

executive and judicial, but uniquely for the time guaranteed individual rights and freedoms.[24] As the oldest constitution in Europe the Constitution Act contains remarkably unchanged provisions, which still function well in modern-day society[25] and forms a strong national symbol. The union with Sweden did not bring about any significant changes in law and, despite constant quarrels between the Swedish king and the Norwegian Parliament, Norway enjoyed internal autonomy.

Since 1814 the Supreme Court has shouldered the legal development of the country, especially because of lack of new legislation, and has constantly guarded its power in relation to the legislature.[26] Its control functions, as constitutional custom, are threefold: judicial review, safeguarding implemented human rights conventions and control over the administration.[27] It is expected that the Supreme Court has both a right and a duty to try the constitutionality of legislation in its cases.[28] The court's functions are, moreover, said to be the declaration of law, and to ensure the uniformity of law and development of law.[29] This stands in contrast to the Swedish and Finnish experiences. The reasons for the more reluctant attitude towards judge-made law exhibited in these two countries can be found in constitutional history and the present constitutional acts.[30] In principle the courts in Sweden and Finland are only to apply the law.

Over the years both Sweden and Finland have had several constitutional documents, titled Instruments of government, as well as other documents forming part of the county's Constitution. Since 1634 Sweden has had five Instruments of government. The present Instrument dating from 1974 is one of four constitutional acts.[31] The constitutional acts from 1809 and 1974 have been remarkably untouched by preceding constitutional ideas and establish a strong sense of continuity. Judicial review adopted by amendment in 1979 has played only a minor role.[32]

In Finland the Instrument of government adopted in 1772 following separation from the Swedish kingdom, applied until 1919 when Finland adopted its first

---

24   Sunnqvist (n 18) 351.

25   In early summer 2014, in concurrence with its 200 years celebration, amendments of the Constitution took place, primarily to strengthen the human rights in the Constitution, and such provisions are now placed under chapter E. See FOR-2014-06-20-778.

26   Lødrup (n 22) 18.

27   The Human Rights Act, 1999 has directly implemented five central conventions.

28   Tore Schei, 'Domstolenes og dommernes uavhengighet og forholdet til de øvrige statsmakter' in Nils Asbjørn Engstad et al (eds), *Dommernes uavhengighet. Den norske dommerforening 100 år* (Bergen 2012) 21–22; Lødrup (n 22) 23.

29   Schei (n 28) 21.

30   Sweden: the Instrument of Government, 1974 (revised 2010); Finland: the Constitution of Finland, 1999.

31   Fredrik Sterzel, *Författning i utveckling. Tjugo studier kring Sveriges författning* (Iustus 2009) 93–96.

32   Joakim Nergelius, *Komparativ statsrätt* (Juristförlaget 2012) 61.

independent Constitution.[33] With the present Constitution Act of 1999 Finland revoked not only the former name (instrument of government) and the tradition of several constitutional acts but also left a part of the country's constitutional continuity behind with the emphasis on human rights and the possibility of judicial review.[34] The constitutional system of Finland displays a unique mix of a strong parliamentary system and presidential power not shared by Norway and Sweden as monarchies.[35]

With a tradition of strong royal power, Swedish-Finnish judges were conventionally loyal towards the king as head of the court, and later, after adoption of a parliamentary system allegiance shifted to the legislator. As a result, the independence of the courts has been different, visible even today as the constitutional position of the courts is less clear than in Norway. The division of power in the constitutions is not fully implemented. This is particularly the case for Sweden where the paramount principle of public sovereignty means that *all* power vests in the people.[36] This also means that judicial review by the courts is weaker.

Finland's Instrument of government of 1919 accepted that judges could not set aside legislation contradictory to the Constitution.[37] As a result, fundamental rights, whether based in constitutional or international human rights, did not appear in Finnish case law until 1988, which was consistent with the traditional view that courts could not invoke such rights at all.[38] Instead, the constitutional review of legislation happens before enactment through the Constitutional Law Committee, the recommendations of which are customarily thought of as binding.[39] The Finnish Constitutional Act of 1999 introduced a restrained provision on judicial review which permits the court to intervene only in the case of a 'manifest' contradiction with the Constitution. This suggests a degree of distrust of the judiciary.[40] This is practically identical to the former Swedish provision which was amended in 2010 removing the requirement of a 'manifest' contradiction.[41]

---

33 A draft text existed at the time of the declaration of independence in 1917 but because of civil war in 1918 the Constitution was adopted in 1919.

34 Jaakko Husa, *The Constitution of Finland* (n 8) 11. See further ibid 13–27. The partly new constitutional structure in Finland, in force 2000, will undeniably take some time to settle.

35 Nergelius (n 32) 52. It should be noted that Sweden and Finland have two courts in apex: the Supreme Court and the Supreme Administrative Court.

36 Instrument of Government, 1974 ch 1 s 1; Nergelius (n 32) 50, 59.

37 Sunnqvist (n 18) 131, 221; Nergelius (n 32) 52–53.

38 Juha Lavapuro, 'Constitutional Review in Finland' in Kimmo Nuotio et al (eds), *Introduction to Finnish Law and Legal Culture* (Forum Iuris 2012) 129–30.

39 ibid 132–33.

40 Constitution of Finland, 1999 s 106.

41 Instrument of Government, 1974 ch 11 s 14. This provision was applied in the Taxed mountain case (NJA 1981 p 1). The majority held, on the basis of statements in older preparatory works, that the administrative granting system for small game hunting

To summarize, Norway has a long tradition of strong, independent judges and a unique history of judicial review going back to the 1820s. Norway is also the Nordic country where judicial review has had a real influence.[42] Moreover, the Norwegian Constitution Act 1814 has evolved through reinterpretation, a legacy from the King's Act 1665 where interpretation emerged as the solution when theoretical and ideological ideas shifted. By contrast the traditional solution in Sweden has been written changes and new constitutional acts. Naturally, room for interpretation and 'judicial activism' declines where the legislator assumes an active responsibility for amending the Constitution.

Rights to Land and Resources

Traits in Property Law

This section discusses general differences in the property laws of Norway, Sweden and Finland and the implications of those laws for the recognition of Sami rights to land and resources, based upon age-old uses. Over time protracted use of land and natural resources may establish corresponding rights, which the property laws of all three countries in principle acknowledge. Protracted use may establish ownership rights or lesser rights. Written and unwritten proprietary concepts help to analyse and qualify the actual use, and to assess whether such use is sufficiently intensive and continuous in character to create rights, subject to the specific requirements inherent in each concept. It should be noted that not so long ago both Norwegian and Swedish law held that reindeer herding was insufficiently intensive to establish rights.[43]

The recognition of Sami land and resource rights differs in the three Scandinavian states and the question is why. In my view it is because the property laws of the three states embody distinct national characteristics and solutions. These laws are intermingled with each country's economic and social development. Each country's topography also influences the kind of land and water uses developed. Distinct national solutions tend to continue or repeat themselves in new forms because of a certain path dependency.[44] Legal reforms and applications are seldom completely new but build on national traditions. One example is the establishment

---

was not discriminatory towards the Sami; one dissenting judge (Bertil Bengtsson) found it discriminatory, but not 'manifestly' discriminatory, meaning that the provision was still applicable.

42 cf Lødrup (n 22) 10; Nergelius (n 32) 47.

43 Kirsti Strom Bull, *Studier i reindriftsrett* (Tano Aschehoug 1997) 42; NOU 2007:13, 309–311; SOU 2006:14, 400.

44 See new institutional theory, eg Douglass C North, *Institutions, Institutional Change and Economic Performance* (Cambridge University Press 1990).

of the Finnmark Commission with the task of investigating the existence of Sami land rights under the Finnmark Act 2005.[45] This is consistent with Norway's tradition of setting up ad hoc law commissions for investigating unsettled land rights and land boundaries.[46] The Act partly implements the land rights provisions of ILO Convention 169 and it was thus natural to appoint a commission for such an assignment.[47]

Norway, as quite a remote part of the Danish-Norwegian kingdom, was largely left alone to deal with its own property law affairs. In contrast the Swedish kings early developed a central administration with a land register and the National Land Survey in 1628 (1633 in Finland) with educated surveyors to make maps and measurements over Sweden-Finland. Hence, organized land divisions, both on paper and in reality, has been a cornerstone of the Swedish-Finnish bureaucracy.[48] During the twentieth century there was less need for primary land partition in Sweden and thus it was possible to focus on the division of existing titles for agricultural and housing needs.[49]

Norway's land survey unit has been active since 1773 but did not adopt educated surveyors until the end of 1800s, with the result that clear and demarcated boundaries, physically and on maps, did not come until the latter half of the 1800s.[50] But still by the mid 1900s Norway had large areas not subject to primary land partition, especially in more remote areas.[51] Consequently, Norway has had many disputes over real property, regarding the content of rights and land boundaries – thereby triggering the need for investigating commissions to resolve these issues. Common lands and co-ownership are also common in remote areas. Evidently, Norway has required several proprietary concepts and courts to settle disputes, which is helpful when considering Sami rights questions today.

Protracted Uses

Norwegian law recognizes a number of different proprietary concepts related to protracted uses, including immemorial usage (*alders tids bruk*), prescription (*hevd*), 'established privileges' (*festnede rettsforhold*) and local customary law.

---

45   Section 5 para 1 reads 'Through prolonged use of land and water areas, the Sami have collectively and individually acquired rights to land in Finnmark'.

46   There were several commissions during nineteenth and twenties centuries. See eg Øyvind Ravna and Magne Reiten, 'Grensegang og rettsavklaring i utmark og høyfjell' in Øyvind Ravna (ed) *Areal og eiendomsrett* (Universitetsforlaget 2007) 487; Thor Falkanger and Aage Thor Falkanger, *Tingsrett* (6th edn, Universitetsforlaget 2007) 113.

47   The SRC II has suggested a similar regime for Nordland and Troms Counties, the area south of Finnmark, see NOU 2007:13.

48   Jan-Olof Sundell, *Svensk fastighetsrättshistoria* (Iustus 2007) 60–66.

49   Olof Bagger-Jörgensen, 'Lantmäteriets organisation' in *Svenska lantmäteriet 1628–1928, Del I* (Sällskapet för utgivande av lantmäteriets historia 1928) 78.

50   Olaf Olafsen, *Jordfællesskab og sameie* (1914) 39–40.

51   Sjur Brækhus and Axel Hærem, *Norsk tingsrett* (Universitetsforlaget 1964) 22.

Most of them are unwritten and thus upheld and developed by courts. It is not always clear which concept applies as there is overlaps among them.[52] It is common for claimants to refer to more than one concept and thus the courts have several possibilities examine the actual usage taken place, and match it to the relevant concept thereby balancing the interests of the different parties.

Acquisition through prescription is codified in the Prescription Act of 1966 and both ownership and user rights can be acquired. A specific provision in the Act recognizes that collective uses in a district may serve as a means for acquiring collective user rights with a prescriptive time of 50 years. While there is some overlap between the different concepts, for instance between prescription and immemorial usage, each concept has its core area of application. The actual use and the evidence will normally determine which concept applied, resulting in a spectrum of rights ranging from weaker (collective) rights, such as public access to land, to ownership at the other end of the spectrum.

By contrast, Swedish and Finnish laws have essentially two main concepts, immemorial prescription (*urminnes hävd*) and customary law, as means for acquiring rights based on protracted uses, but neither is much used and the absence of case law is profound.[53] Immemorial prescription was annulled by the new Land Codes in Sweden as in Finland in 1972 and 1996 respectively as an outdated concept, but transitional rules allow for the recognition of rights already acquired rights. Any trial with respect to immemorial prescription is complicated not only due to the evidence but also because of the ancient provisions of the Land Code of 1734 which contains the provisions on immemorial prescription. In sum, while Norwegian law has a long tradition of using a range of different proprietary concepts, in courts and law commissions, there is no similar tradition in Sweden or Finland.

Disputes over protracted uses and Sami land rights most often arise in the context of reindeer-herding rights, coastal fishing and ownership. Reindeer herding has long been recognized and codified by the three states, but the way in which reindeer-herding rights are recognized differs between the countries. For example, in Norway and Sweden reindeer herding can only be practised by those of Sami heritage.[54] Although the normal procedural rules apply to these disputes, in the

---

52   Borgar Høgetveit Berg, *Hevd. Lov om hevd 9. desember 1966 nr. 1 med kommentarer* (Cappelen akademisk forlag 2005) 46; Thor Falkanger, *Fast eiendoms rettsforhold* (4th edn, Universitetsforlaget 2002) 131, 133; Kirsti Strøm Bull and Nikolai K Winge, *Fast eiendoms rettsforhold. Kort og godt* (Universitetsforlaget 2009) 90. See also the Tysfjord case, Rt 1996 p 1232, where a number of small farmers claimed ownership in an area of varied topography with forests, agricultural lands and mountain ranges.

53   There are rules on prescription in the Swedish and Finnish Land Codes but they only apply where a title deed (*lagfart*) already exists. Note that after the Swedish Nordmaling case (NJA 2011 p 109) customary law may be considered as a means for acquisition of user right with respect to the Sami reindeer-herding right.

54   In Finland reindeer herding may also be carried out by non-Sami residing in Finland. See also Allard, 'The Nordic countries' law on Sami territorial rights' (n 2).

assessment of the evidence some cultural adjustments are made. These include the recognition of the nature of reindeer herding in respect of the land use, adjustments to accommodate the lack of written proof from the Sami's side as Sami was an unwritten language, and the recognition of the potential for misunderstanding because of different language and culture. This cultural adjustment is more pronounced in Norwegian case law but is evident in the most recent Swedish case as well. There are no Finnish cases concerning recognition of Sami rights. The following section canvasses the main cases in Norway and Sweden.

Case Law

Most Norwegian cases on Sami rights are resolved under the concept of immemorial usage even though other concepts, such as prescription, may have been invoked before the courts. As a long-standing unwritten concept moulded by the courts, immemorial usage's flexibility and the interrelationship between the three conditions for proof facilitates a balanced, overall assessment of facts.[55] The concept's three basic conditions are: a certain use, over a long time-period that has occurred in good faith. Cultural adjustments have been adopted in two landmark cases.

The Svartskog case[56] dealt with whether the state or the local community (with a Sami majority) was the rightful owner of the land area. The Supreme Court held that the locals were the owners because their usage historically and presently was all-embracing, intensive and flexible, even if the land use as such was not distinctly Sami. In so holding the Court accepted that communal uses may establish collective ownership. The Court was attentive to the Sami culture in its assessment of the criteria of 'good faith'. At times the state tried to regulate the land use (as the formal title holder), but did not pursue those efforts, and there were risks of misunderstandings due to different language and culture. This is the only case to recognize 'Sami' ownership in any of the three countries and this decision along with the Selbu case, has meant a paradigm shift concerning Sami land rights and has revitalized interest in immemorial usage as applied to collective uses and as a source of title.[57]

In the Selbu case[58] the dispute concerned alleged reindeer-herding rights on privately owned lands. The Court found that such rights did indeed exist. The decision was reached in *plenum* by a total of 15 judges and offers a strong judgment which alters the course of previous decisions. The majority of the judges emphasized at the outset the cultural merits of the case:

---

55   Gunnar K Eriksen, *Alders tids bruk* (Fagbokforlaget 2008) 83, 325; Falkanger and Falkanger (n 46) 325.

56   Rt 2001 p 1229.

57   Eriksen (n 55) 324, 363.

58   Rt 2001 p 769.

Since our case regards pasture rights concerning reindeer, the specific conditions within this livelihood must be considered ... The conditions must be adjusted to the land uses of the area by the Sami and the reindeer. Regard must also be taken of the nomadic lifestyle of the Sami. Circumstances that have been significant for other grazing animals cannot without consideration be transferred to reindeer herding. These circumstances must be a part of the overall assessment.[59]

In doing so the Court emphasized the need for vast pasturage and thus accepted a lower intensity of use in outer zones. The Court also relaxed the 'good faith' condition in favour of the Sami by recognizing that the Sami at the time had limited knowledge of Norwegian written language. All in all, the interesting parts of the verdict are the Court's emphasis on the particular features of reindeer herding, the 'actual' land use, and the importance of taking these features into account when applying and balancing the conditions for immemorial usage.

The Swedish Nordmaling case[60] has many similarities with the Selbu case since it also dealt with reindeer-herding rights on private lands. This case is also the first successful case for Swedish Sami. Instead of applying immemorial prescription, as normal in these cases, the Supreme Court turned to customary law, and used its unwritten character to make a flexible overall assessment. As in the Selbu case the Court held that the specific Sami land use must be taken into account. For instance, in this case the Court emphasized weather conditions as directly determinative of the reindeer's migration and the herders' need for spare areas. It should be noted that a provision in the Reindeer Herding Act declares that herding on winter/spring-areas can be carried out on areas used 'of age' (*av ålder*), thus giving a statutory recognition to custom. Interestingly, customary law has not been applied in the context of real property for quite some time.

The emphasis on 'the actual use' in the two reindeer herding cases is fundamental in balancing the evidence in light of the conditions of proof, otherwise there is the risk that the semi-nomadic usage of vast pasture areas will be deemed not to be sufficiently intensive to establish rights. This was indeed the case during most of the twentieth century. The flexibility of proprietary concepts is paramount. It is no accident that the Norwegian courts prefer the flexibility of immemorial usage to the stricter written conditions of prescription when it comes to recognizing reindeer-herding rights or other Sami territorial rights.

---

59   Rt 2001 p 769, 789.

60   NJA 2011 p 109. See also Christina Allard, 'Case Review: The Swedish Nordmaling Case' (2011) 2 Arctic Review on Law and Politics 225.

Rights of Traditional Custom and Practice

Sami Customary Rights

Custom can be understood as a certain way of conduct followed by people due to a sense of duty.[61] Even if customary norms played a more prominent role in private law historically they are still important in some areas of the law notably with respect to Sami customs and traditions. In Norwegian law generally, local customs, especially in the remote and mountainous areas, may establish various forms of user rights, such as fishing rights, logging rights and pasture rights.[62] Customs, above all the actual uses, may thus be used as a primary legal source.

The Sami are a minority in all three countries and lack any formal law-making authority although they have some means to influence legislation. Previous and lingering assimilation policies in all three countries have strained the Sami culture and language, including the Sami legal culture. Much has been lost over the years although there is greater potential for finding living customs within the reindeer herding and coastal fishing cultures.[63] With this as a backdrop it is easy to understand the importance of Sami customs, at least from a Sami perspective.

The matter of Sami customs as an autonomous legal source raises crucial questions as to what counts as a source of law, questions that have echoed throughout history. The Sami legal culture has been, and still is, a marginalized part of the Norwegian, Swedish and Finnish dominant laws. The recognition of custom may come in two ways: either through recognition of customary law as a legal source by national law and/or through international human rights law. Of particular interest in this context is Article 8 of ILO Convention 169 which requires in Article 8.1 that '[i]n applying national laws and regulations to the [indigenous] peoples concerned, due regard shall be had to their customs and customary laws.' Norway, as party to this Convention, is obliged to address Sami customs and the relationship of those customs to Norwegian legislation.

Norwegian property law applies customary law and similar concepts quite actively in relation to the protracted use of land – at least by comparison with the Swedish and Finnish laws. Those legal systems recognize the role of custom in business and commercial law (*handelskutymer*) but are more reluctant to do so in the area of property law. In Swedish law, going back as far as the Swedish Code of 1734, specific statutory authorization is required to make use of customary law. As guidance for the judge the Procedural Code of 1734 stated that national custom

---

61   Eckhoff and Helgesen (n 21) 244.

62   Smith (n 5) 173–74; Nils Nygaard, *Rettsgrunnlag og standpunkt* (2nd edn, Universitetsforlaget 2004) 308–9. See also Rt 1995 p 644, the Westerbotn case.

63   Elina Helander-Renvall, 'On customary law among the Saami people' in Nigel Bankes and Timo Koivurova (eds), *The Proposed Nordic Saami Convention: National and International Dimensions of Indigenous Property Rights* (Hart 2013).

(*landssed*) could be used as positive law only where legislation was lacking.[64] As far as I know, the situation regarding customs is the same in Finnish law.

Norwegian law, on the other hand, accepts that customary law can be established before the courts regardless of statutory recognition. Nowadays, a custom will seldom be the only legal source to be evaluated; written provisions are balanced in the overall judgment and the quality of the custom is examined. Not surprisingly Norway has many more cases concerning customary issues brought before the courts. In Sami matters there is a growing body of case law, especially criminal law cases, in which Sami claim customary rights or traditions by way of defence, a few of them at the Supreme Court level. Nonetheless, there are too few precedents to be definitive about the status of Sami customs within Norwegian law. So far, most cases demonstrate that Sami custom must give way in the face of inconsistent Norwegian legislation.[65]

The subsections below present a few cases from Norwegian and Swedish courts. To my knowledge there are no cases on Sami customary law from the Finnish Supreme Courts.

Norwegian Cases and Customs in Legislation

The Dog leash case[66] from 2001 was the first time the Norwegian Supreme Court applied Article 8 of ILO Convention 169. The case examined whether a provision in the Wildlife Act, 1981 to hold dogs on leash during April to August could be interpreted in light of Sami custom in Finnmark. During a fishing trip a Sami man let his dog run free and this was observed by a state official. Before the court the man claimed that the provision was not applicable to him due to Sami custom. The majority of the Supreme Court held that Article 8 could not set aside the provision. The majority concluded that an indigenous custom could only have such an effect over written law if it had a clear content and was of particular quality. Here the custom to let dogs run free was imprecise on several points. The Court concluded that the custom was not necessary to maintain Sami culture or livelihoods as required by the ILO Convention 169.

In the Heart-stab case,[67] decided in 2008 a reindeer herder was seen to stick a knife through the heart of a reindeer without anaesthetic. The court examined whether this type of slaughter was protected by Article 8 preventing criminalization

---

64   Ch 1 s 11.

65   Øyvind Ravna, 'Sami Legal Culture: and its Place in Norwegian Law' in Jørn Øyrehagen Sunde and Knut Einar Skodvin (eds), *Rendezvous of European Legal Cultures* (Fagbokforlaget 2010) 161, 163; Susann F Skogvang, *Samerett* (2nd edn, Universitetsforlaget 2009) Ch 3.

66   Rt 2001 p 1116.

67   Rt 2008 p 1789. See also Rt 2006 p 957 on slaughter of reindeer. This case was, however, dismissed by the Supreme Court due to lack of sufficient facts.

under the Animal Protection Act. The majority (3 of 5)[68] held that it could if the herder had used a 'bent knife' (*krumkniv*) to sedate the reindeer before the heart-stab. The use of a *krumkniv* was also a Sami custom which had been codified by regulation since 2008.

The 2011 Inheritance case[69] concerned inheritance of reindeer, the reindeer ear mark and the leader position, and thus an application of a Sami custom internally within the reindeer herding community. One daughter claimed, against her brothers and sisters, that she was the rightful inheritor for their parents. The applicable reindeer herding and inheritance legislation allows the application of Sami custom where there are several possible inheritors. Although there was a relevant Sami custom the Supreme Court held that the daughter had not established a priority right against her siblings in accordance with that custom.[70] The case was instead resolved under Norwegian inheritance rules.

Many of the 'Sami cases' have originated in the Inner Finnmark district court, a bilingual court established in 2004, but still part of the normal Norwegian court structure. Its task is to investigate Sami customs in court practice.[71] Many cases concerning Sami customs that have gone to appeal from this court have, however, been altered by the appellate court or the Supreme Court. An equivalent to this court does not exist in either Sweden or Finland.

Sami customs have been increasingly acknowledged in Norwegian legislation in the last two decades.[72] One example is the Reindeer Herding Act of 2007 which rests on Sami traditions and the *siida*. It is now also possible to use mediation as a means for solving internal conflicts in the reindeer herding community. Another example is the legislation on spring hunting of duck in Kautokeino Municipality, Finnmark. After a general prohibition in 1951, a criminal case in the Supreme Court in 1988[73] and refusal by the local people – especially the Sami – to respect the prohibition on spring duck hunting the Ministry for Environment established a test period for hunting in 1999. The customary hunt has been regulated through government enactment from 2013. The Norwegian Consultation Agreement of 2005 makes it likely that discussions of Sami customs will continue to be essential in the law-making process.

---

68   The court was unanimous in the result but had different reasoning with respect to Article 8. See further Susann F Skogvang, 'Hjertesukk om hjertestikk' (2009) Tidsskrift for Strafferett 373.

69   Rt 2011 p 1180.

70   Rt 2011 p 1180, 52.

71   Smith (n 5).

72   Skogvang, *Samerett* (n 65) 81–83.

73   Rt 1988 p 377.

Swedish Cases

Very few Swedish cases deal explicitly with Sami customs, and of these cases relate solely to reindeer herding practises, including also hunting and fishing rights.[74] None has reached the Supreme Court. All of these cases are criminal law cases, in which the Sami claim to exercise their reindeer-herding right as a defence to the charge.[75] The Lichen case discussed below and decided by the Court of appeal, is the clearest example of this pattern.[76]

In the Lichen case,[77] Mr Spiik, a member of a Sami reindeer herding community, was charged with taking lichen on a nature reserve, which formed a part of the community's pasture area, without first obtaining a permit from the County Administrative Board. In essence the case concerned whether the custom to pick lichen was part of the reindeer-herding right even though it was not codified in the Reindeer Herding Act, and whether the alleged right could trump the environmental restrictions which would otherwise apply in the reserve. Mr Spiik claimed that he was exercising a right inherent in the reindeer-herding right and, therefore, did not need a permit. He intended to use the lichen to feed the reindeer when enclosed in a corral. In a very short opinion, the Court held that the custom to gather lichen to the extent exercised was part of the reindeer-herding right and, moreover, that the permit requirement for the picking of lichen could not limit this right and therefore Mr Spiik was not bound to the permit requirement.

Short Conclusions

By and large, law is a path-dependent enterprise. New solutions are nearly always built on existing experiences and, therefore, profound changes in law are slow. Legal history survives among us, whether we are aware of it or not.[78] Despite shared characteristics, Norway, Sweden and Finland have developed into somewhat different twigs. These differences are noticeable at a comparative micro-level

---

74 See also Eivind Torp, 'Betydelsen av samiska traditioner i svensk rätt' (2011) 1 Arctic Review on Law and Politics 77.

75 In a recent case from the Court of Appeal for Upper Norrland (Case No. B 564-13, decided 2014-09-23) a Sami reindeer herder was accused of a hunting crime which he self-defended by claiming that he was exercising his hunting right inherent in the reindeer-herding right and that the by-laws was infringing his right unduly. The Court of Appeal held, in a well-balanced judgment, that the County Administrative Board's by-laws, restricting the reindeer herder's enjoyment of his hunting right, was unlawful.

76 The case holds no precedent. See also Case No. B 855-11, decided 2013-05-31, Court of Appeal for Upper Norrland. The case concerned bear hunting in a nature reserve.

77 Case No. B 69-04, decided 2005-12-21, Court of Appeal for Upper Norrland. The case was not appealed to the Supreme Court.

78 Husa, *Nordic Law* (n 9) 10–12.

analysis and legal historical knowledge is crucial if we wish to understand the trunk and roots that inform the twigs.

This chapter has illustrated that there are hidden national characteristics within Norwegian, Swedish and Finnish laws which also govern the way Sami rights claims are and can be resolved within the three states. Legislation concerning Sami rights and interests represents only a part of the total puzzle. As indicated in the introduction, a distinction between law and legislation is helpful since it allows us to focus on aspects of the national laws other than legislation. Many Sami legal matters are complex, and in resolving these complexities, the flexibility of the law is important as is responsiveness towards Sami customs and views. It is the role of courts to flesh out the uncertain terrain and increasingly so today to guard basic human rights. Hence, a critical and autonomous interpretation of relevant legal sources is required and significant legal developments have been made – and can be made – through case law, especially when the national legislator refrains from resolving long-standing grievances.

It is not only differences in legislation that explain why Sami land rights and Sami customs seems easier to recognize within Norwegian law. The contrast between Norway, on the one hand, and Sweden and Finland, on the other, is apparent. The Norwegian Supreme Court enjoys a greater relative independence than the Supreme Courts of the East Nordic countries and Norway has a more flexible system of property law.

The role of judicial interpretation seems a touchy subject in Finnish constitutional law which explains the dominance of the literal legal-positivistic approach.[79] Finnish law is commonly considered to be more legalistic and positivistic than other Nordic countries and thus the room for recognizing custom as law absent statutory approval is minimal. Surely, despite the lack of case law, Sami customs exist in Finland too. The situation in Sweden is similar but perhaps not as strict as that of Finland as the recent Nordmaling case from 2011 seems to confirm.

Undoubtedly, Sami customs and customary laws exist in many areas of life. In some cases they may conflict with the national, written legislation or at least impose a challenge to the application of those laws. In Norway it is obvious that the courts are willing to consider Sami land rights and Sami customs and take their task of conformity with ILO Convention 169 seriously, but where a custom is not considered 'good' the threshold for maintaining the custom is high, especially if it contravenes Norwegian legislation. In any case, disputes must be solved on a case by case basis with profound understanding of the Sami culture and way of life.

---

79   Husa, *The Constitution of Finland* (n 8) 222.

Chapter 6

Reforming Swedish Sami Legislation: A Survey of the Arguments

Bertil Bengtsson

Introduction

The legal position of the Swedish Sami is primarily regulated by the Reindeer Herding Act of 1971 (RHA). The RHA provides specific regulation of Sami reindeer herding practices as well as general prescriptions concerning Sami peoples' right to land and water on so established year round pastures in the mountain regions, and to the extended northern areas of the country.[1] The reindeer herding right is a special type of usufruct right granted by law (not by contract) for an unlimited amount of time; and as such it is not tied to any fee nor can it be terminated on the initiative of the landowner. This legislation has long been considered ripe for reform. Apart from certain technical shortcomings, it has been mainly criticized for not paying due regard to the status of the Sami as an indigenous peoples and also for having failed to address their historical rights to territory. This chapter will deal with some examples of this critique, although a more detailed account of the present state of the law cannot be given here.[2]

The call for a reform is well founded. Nevertheless, it has been met with a number of challenges the most significant being that it is controversial from a political standpoint. Therefore, one central question is whether sufficient legal arguments are enough to convince a hesitant government to present a proposition to this effect. This chapter will aim to outline the arguments for and against a reform.

---

1 Other legislation also concerns the Sami. For instance, ch 1 s 2 para 6 in the Instrument of Government, 1974 prescribes that the possibilities of the Sami people to keep and develop a cultural and social life of their own should be furthered. However, this general description of one aim of the constitution has until now had small practical importance.

2 Concerning the present state of law, see above all Christina Allard, 'Two Sides of the Coin: Rights and Duties. The Interface between Environmental Law and Saami Law Based on a Comparison with Aoteoaroa/New Zealand and Canada' (doctoral thesis, Luleå University of Technology 2006); Eivind Torp, 'Renskötselrätten och rätten till naturresurserna. Om rättslig reglering av mark- och resursanvändningsrätt på renbetesmarkerna i Sverige' (doctoral thesis, University of Tromso 2008). For a short survey see Bertil Bengtsson, *Samerätt. En översikt* (Norstedts juridik 2004).

The politicians, in general, seem to be doubtful about a reform since the question at stake is considered to be of a delicate character. The Sami are also a comparatively small group (about 20,000 in Sweden), and there are certain traditional conflicts of interest with the other local groups that would have to be dealt with. No government, regardless of party colour, has been willing to risk losing votes by improving the position of the Sami. It has been emphasized in the party programme by nationalistic Sweden democrats (*Sverigedemokraterna*), that no particular advantages should be granted to the Sami, and similar views have also been expressed by political representatives from other parties, most prominently from northern Sweden. The governments have apparently feared that such currents may increase if the Sami question is handled without due consideration for the local opinion. Thus, a report proposing accession to the ILO convention (No 169) concerning indigenous and tribal peoples[3] has not led to any legislation, nor other proposals that aim at strengthening Sami rights.[4]

However, the government has been subjected to international pressure concerning the position of the indigenous Sami, and, in due time, it may be necessary to address the question of a legislative change. Here, a proposal concerning a Nordic Sami Convention has been of particular interest, as it implies that Sami indigenous rights are recognized in a more explicit way than they are at the present, and, to an extent, in accordance with the content of ILO 169.[5] To a considerable degree, the proposal has been inspired by Norwegian law. Norway has acceded to that convention and also in other ways improved the legal situation of the Sami. No corresponding development has taken place in Sweden. The Swedish Ministry for Rural Affairs has been working with the project although without any visible enthusiasm. The intention is that, at some future point in time, the government will make a decision about the proposal. In any case, the work with the convention will be a valuable excuse for the government's passivity when dealing with other reform proposals in this field.

Two Supreme Court Decisions

An essential background to the legislative discussion is that the courts have shown a more favourable attitude to the issue of Sami rights than the legislature has. Two decisions by the Supreme Court are preeminent: the Taxed mountain case, NJA 1981 p. 1, and the Nordmaling case, NJA 2011 p. 109.

---

3   SOU 1999:25, *Ursprungsfolk i Sverige. Frågan om Sveriges anslutning till ILO:s konvention nr 169.*

4   SOU 2001:101, *En ny rennäringspolitik - öppna samebyar och samverkan med andra markanvändare.*

5   See further Nigel Bankes and Timo Koivurova (eds), *The Proposed Nordic Saami Convention: National and International Dimensions of Indigenous Property Rights* (Hart 2013).

The Taxed mountain case dealt, above all, with the claims of certain Sami villages against the state[6] concerning the ownership of areas known as taxed mountains in the northern part of the province of Jämtland, in support of which they invoked various historical grounds. In addition, the Sami parties claimed several types of limited rights, mostly to the natural resources in the same areas. The Supreme Court affirmed the dismissal by the lower courts.[7] Notwithstanding the outcome, the Taxed mountain case has been regarded a partial success for the Sami to the extent that the court declared that it was possible, in older times, to acquire land rights through reindeer herding, hunting and fishing practices, and without either cultivating or permanently residing in the area. By this declaration, the court disclaimed the statement often made that 'nomads cannot acquire ownership rights'. However, the detailed prerequisite for this type of land acquisition by the Sami was not considered to have existed in Jämtland. Consequently, the court sided with the state and argued that, with reference to a certain decree of 1683 concerning the right to the northern wilds,[8] the land should fall under the ownership of the state. This decision suggested that the possibilities for the Sami to acquire ownership rights might have been better in the north of Sweden, where their use of mountain lands was more intensive and less disturbed by competing interests. As it was, the court had no reason to consider whether these factors could be considered a valid basis for ownership rights, since the litigation did not include any northern areas. As for the dispute over limited rights in the taxed mountains, the Sami claims were dismissed as unfounded to the extent that they exceeded the rights to natural resources already awarded to them by the RHA. The Supreme Court also declared that these rights, being based on civil law (immemorial prescription), were protected by the Constitution in the same way as ownership rights; as long as they were exercised, they could not be taken from the holder, either by legislation or otherwise, without compensation in accordance with the rules of the Instrument of Government, 1974.

One result of the Taxed mountain case was an amendment to the RHA, which stated that Sami rights to land and water are founded on immemorial prescription, and as such a civil right.

In the Nordmaling case, the reindeer herding right of three Sami villages, specifically concerning winter herding pastures, was acknowledged on private lands close to the Baltic Sea coast. The ruling has been regarded, especially by the Sami, as a landmark decision concerning the recognition of herding rights based on customary law. Whether this may be the case or not, the ruling will certainly have repercussions not only on other land disputes concerning winter pastures,

---

6 A Sami village is a particular type of legal person exercising the reindeer herding rights on behalf of its members, the nearest equivalent of which is a co-operative.

7 A translation of the Supreme Court judgment is given in *The Saami National Minority of Sweden* (Rättsfonden/The Legal Rights Foundation 1982) 146–247.

8 'Kongl. May:tz Nådigste Förordning och Påbyd Angående Skogarne och hwad därwid i acht tagas bör' (19.12.1683).

but probably also on the general legal position of the Sami. However, neither the government nor the Parliament has reacted in any way to this ruling.

The Game of Politics: Two Alternative Lines of Argument

Assuming that the government will agree to strengthen the rights of the Sami in accordance with the Nordic Sami Convention, there are two alternative lines of argument to follow.

The first is to emphasize the particular position of the Sami people as an indigenous minority, which should motivate that they be granted certain advantages before other Swedish citizens (the *minority argument*). As will be shown in this article, the draft Nordic Sami Convention proposal contains several rules that support this line of reasoning. Such arguments also find support in the ILO Convention 169. Taking this political stance on indigenous rights could also be considered a necessary compensation for the neglect that the governments have shown in the past.

However, this line of argument has one obvious drawback. Such a reform will have to lead to significant political complications, and it is unclear whether the governments are willing to take such measures. Most people will probably accept that evident wrongs to the Sami should be redressed somehow, but it will be far more difficult to convince people that the Sami should have rights and benefits that are not granted other citizens. Such objections, which here will be referred to as the *equality argument*, may be a major obstacle to the implementation of the convention.

For this reason, an alternative would be to argue along other lines. The equality argument can in fact be invoked also in favour of Sami rights. Instead of emphasizing that they should have special privileges on account of their particular indigenous status it could instead be stressed that they are to be treated according the same standards as the majority population, although with due regard to their particular way of living. The law governing their activities should be compared to the way the legislature would have treated other groups under the same circumstances. By such a comparison, it can be made clear that the Sami can justly claim an amended legal position in several respects, irrespective of their status as an indigenous people. Hence, the reform should aim at avoiding discrimination instead of creating privileges. This aspect has, however, often been disregarded by the opponents of reform.

As will be shown, the proposed convention text can to a considerable extent, though not altogether, be motivated by applying general principles of land law, above all concerning the acquisition of rights. Referring to such principles will be a more convincing and less controversial line of arguing, if the essential intentions of the proposal were to be realized. The status issue should be emphasized only on points where this is necessary to motivate the reform intended.

Choosing between these alternative lines of reasoning should partly depend on which particular rule is being proposed; in some cases, the equality argument will hold, while in others it will be necessary to invoke the minority argument. In the following, a number of possible amendments to the legislation will be discussed with regard to the reasons for the reform in question. The problems are approached from the perspective that a government is considering (or finding itself compelled to consider) some kind of reform. In most cases, the minority argument should be invoked only as a last resort.

The Reindeer Herding Act and the Constitution

Certain shortcomings in the RHA can be amended without accession to the Nordic Sami Convention, as they contain provisions that are difficult to reconcile with the general principles of Swedish land law and, on some points, also with the Swedish Constitution.

A fundamental flaw in the RHA is that the particular traits of the Sami right to land and water – the reindeer herding right – are not defined or analysed. As mentioned above, it is a special type of usufruct right that is protected by the Constitution in the same way as ownership rights. On several points, the legislature has failed to pay due regard to such legal facts. With regard to these cases, there will most likely be no need to invoke the indigenous status of the Sami as it should be enough to refer to the discriminatory character of the present legislation.

Thus, a certain rule in the act (section 30) permits a landowner to make use of the land is a way that negatively impacts reindeer herding rights provided that the impact does not cause considerable detriment; the owner can, for instance, build a tourist centre that will seriously disturb reindeer herding in the area. Compensating the Sami herders for such impacts is not mentioned in the act, although the government Bill states that they may have such a right.[9] This way of dealing with a property right – a kind of private expropriation – is not known in other fields of Swedish property law; it is clearly incompatible with established legislative practice, as well as with the Instrument of Government that prescribes that full compensation should be provided to the owner, and further, that compensation for all kinds of expropriation should be regulated by statute (chapter 2, section 15). Hence, it should be concluded that the present state of the RHA conflicts with Sami minority rights and, at the same time, with the equality argument.

Another example is the particular manner with which the legislature has handled the hunting and fishing right of the Sami in the mountain area.[10] Although part of the reindeer herding right and as such based on immemorial prescription, the Sami are not permitted to dispose over it by granting the use to other people.

---

9   Prop 1971:51, 136. cf Bengtsson, *Samerätt* (n 2) 59–60.

10   cf Bertil Bengtsson, 'Om jakt och fiske i fjällmarken' (2010) *Svensk Juristtidning* 78. See also Chapter 9 by Eivind Torp in this volume.

Instead, the County Administration Board can grant such use on behalf of the Sami and without their permission. The reasons for these regulations were stated in the preparatory works of the first Reindeer Herding Act of 1886. The Sami villages, which at that time were loosely organized, were not considered competent to deal with these questions as they were seen to have difficulties making decisions. The Sami have for a long time protested against this discriminatory rule, which is obviously based on reasons that no longer hold any relevance. The legislature has, nevertheless, refused to change it but, instead, responding to pressure from hunting and fishing organizations and others, has rather encouraged the authorities (by legislation in 1993) to make more use of their competence to grant such use permits.[11]

One reason for this attitude was a government declaration that, according to the Game Act from 1987 and the Fishing Act from 1993, only the state, as owner of the land, had real hunting and fishing rights in these areas. Here, the government ignored the fact that both acts make exception from the owner's rights in case of immemorial prescription. In addition, the state had also over the years and in several ways acknowledged that hunting and fishing were the sole rights of the Sami in the mountain districts.[12]

Here, too, it should be easy to repeal these provisions by referring to the prohibition to discriminate against minorities in the Constitution (chapter 2 section 12 in the Instrument of Government, 1974) as well as to the Constitutional protection of property – provided that a new government dares to address the problem. In addition, certain rules in the draft Nordic Sami Convention, among others article 3 concerning the right of self-determination, will further support reform on these points.

Reforms Proposed in the Nordic Sami Convention

If it enters into force, a reform can be founded on the draft Nordic Sami Convention.[13]

Certain articles that deal with the general reasoning and purposes of the Convention can be mentioned briefly. The aim of the Convention is to affirm and strengthen the rights of the Sami people in such a way that they can maintain and develop their language, culture, livelihood and society notwithstanding the borders of the countries (article 1), and further, that the Sami have a right to self-determination according to international law and the rules of the Convention

---

11   Prop 1992/93:32, 133–51.

12   Thus, for instance, the state acknowledged such a right for the Sami in the Taxed mountain case (see above).

13   For an English translation see <http://www.regjeringen.no/upload/BLD/Nordic%20 Sami%20Convention.pdf> accessed 2 September 2014.

(article 3).[14] The rights laid down in the Convention are minimum rights (article 8). These somewhat abstract provisions will most likely only present minor political difficulties for the government.

However, increasingly difficult challenges arise when provisions proscribe clear advantages to the Sami compared to the majority population. Such provisions must therefore be treated with particular regard to the political complications that may arise.

One such provision may be article 9, which demands that legislators and courts should show 'due respect' (*tillbörlig hänsyn*) to Sami people's conceptions of law, legal traditions and customs in legislative matters and in the application of the law. Certain critics might object that this provision puts the Sami in a privileged position, as customs and traditions among other groups are not explicitly protected by the law. Of course, this provision can be defended with reference to the minority argument, pointing out that the Sami are the only indigenous people in Sweden, but it can also be emphasized that the convention only prescribes 'due respect'. When interpreting the text, the importance of such customs should be weighed against other considerations. The legislature can also point out that customs and traditions are relevant in many legal contexts, not least in land law. For instance, the possibility to acquire rights by immemorial prescription is founded on such considerations. The purpose of the provisions in the convention should therefore be regarded only as a reminder of their importance in cases where reindeer herding is involved.

The rules protecting the Sami culture may be similarly defended. One example is article 33, which protects commercial and economic conditions to maintain and develop Sami culture.[15] Here it can be argued that no other group of Swedish citizens have a particular culture of this kind as it is specific not only from an ethnic and historical point of view but also with regard to Sami occupation and way of living. The reference to culture should serve as a natural acknowledgement of the importance of Sami culture, as often emphasized by the government, without implying any encroachment on the rights of other groups. In this way, the provision can be compatible with the principles of equality.

The most difficult problems from a legislative point of view concerns the rules provided in chapter IV regarding Sami rights to land and water. These rights are defined in a way that might be considered particularly favourable to the Sami. Article 34 prescribes, in paragraph 1, that a protracted use of land or water areas

---

14 'As a people, the Saami have the right of self-determination in accordance with the rules and provisions of international law and of this Convention. In so far as it follows from these rules and provisions, the Saami people have the right to determine their own economic, social and cultural development and to dispose, to their own benefit, over their own natural resources'.

15 'The responsibilities of the states in matters concerning the Saami culture shall include the material cultural basis in such a way that the Saami are provided with the necessary commercial and economic conditions to secure and develop their culture.'

by the Sami should be a basis of their individual and collective ownership of these areas in accordance with national or international rules regulating such protracted usage. Commentators have considered this provision one of the most awkward rules in the convention, probably because it concerns acquisition of ownership. From the Swedish point of view, however, it does not seem so difficult to handle. As mentioned above, it has already been established in the Taxed mountain case (NJA 1981 p 1) that the Sami had a possibility of acquiring ownership on the basis of centuries-long use; the court admitted that, on an historical basis, the Sami might have become the owner of other areas in the northernmost parts of Sweden by their traditional use of the land. Similar statements have been made in the Finnish Parliament on the basis of certain historical research by Kaisa Korpijaakko-Labba[16] and Juhani Wirilander,[17] which also concerned the state of the law in northern Sweden.[18] Thus, it could be argued that the provision in question expresses only the present state of the law. Although it is true that the Swedish government has preferred to disregard this possibility,[19] it is difficult to get away from the pronouncement of the Supreme Court on the subject. It should be pointed out that the statement of the court was not based on the minority argument but on general principles of Swedish land law. In any event, the chance of success of a claim of ownership is uncertain; it would probably demand a long and complicated lawsuit with a doubtful outcome. Still, the possibility does exist.

Similar remarks can be made regarding the provision in article 34, second paragraph, that states that the Sami have a right to continue to occupy and use land and water areas according to what already applies concerning their right of reindeer herding. The rule describes only the present state of the law. Further, the paragraph expresses a duty of mutual regard that is to be shown when the Sami herder and a land owner use the same areas at the same time. Also this agrees with existing principles of law, such as, for instance, that regulating the relations between neighbours. The duty of mutual regard is probably even stricter when the same land is used at the same time by both parties involved.

It is true that some people can feel doubt concerning the statement coming next that particular consideration here should be paid to the interests of the reindeer herding Sami. This may be regarded as providing a particular advantage to the

---

16   Kaisa Korpijaakko-Labba, *Om samernas rättsliga ställning i Sverige-Finland* (Juristförbundets förlag 1994).

17   Juhani Wirilander, *Lausunto maanomistoloista ja niiden kehituksesta saamelaisten kotiseutualueella* (2001).

18   During the relevant time (before 1809), Sweden and Finland comprised one kingdom with the same legislation. Consequently, the state of law in Finland is more interesting from the Swedish point of view than the corresponding Norwegian law (where an acquisition on similar grounds has been accepted by the Supreme Court, see Rt 2001 p 1229, the *Svartskogen* case).

19   Prop 1992/93:32, 90, where the reminder by the Law Council concerning the research of Kaisa Korpijaakko, according to the Government did not motivate any particular statement.

Sami when in conflict with other groups, such as forest owners; will not the Sami interest too often outweigh that of the other party? However, also this provision can be considered to express another general principle applicable for instance in tort cases. If an enterprise involves risks to other activities, one should pay special regard to the fact that some of these are particularly sensitive to interference, and this is undoubtedly true of the reindeer herding practice. Compared to other activities, the effects of disturbances on reindeer herding can be very serious. Also this statement can thus be explained as a well-founded clarification of the present state of the law.

The issue of whether there is traditional use in the sense of the articles is raised in article 34 third paragraph. Such an assessment must take into consideration that the traditional use of land and water by the Sami often leave no permanent traces on the environment. This rule agrees with the general principle that a court should regard the particular difficulties that a party may have in producing evidence of his or her rights; it is a reason for lowering the demand for evidence. The Supreme Court reasoned in this way in the Taxed mountain case concerning the evidence produced by the Sami. Hence, such rule should be regarded only as a confirmation of present law.

According to article 35, the states should take necessary measures to protect the rights described in article 34. Amongst other measures, the Sami should be provided with necessary economic aid to fund court procedures. This economic aspect is a well-known problem when a Sami village is a party to a case. Such a reform will not seem very remarkable from any point of view. The Sami villages are particular subjects of law that are prone, on account of the complicated legal relations to their surroundings, to be involved in particularly costly conflicts. It can therefore be justified that special rules concerning legal aid should apply.

So far, it has been shown that the rules of the convention seem comparatively easy to defend against a critical examination. However, more serious problems will arise concerning article 36, which treats the access to natural resources in areas used by the Sami. The first paragraph will not meet any serious objection; it provides that the rights of the Sami should be particularly protected with regard to their importance for the preservation of their traditional knowledge and culture. This, too, should be regarded as a consequence of the susceptibility of the Sami culture. Similarly, no serious objections can be expected concerning the second paragraph, which prescribes consultations with the Sami concerned and the Sami Parliament before a public authority can provide a permit for prospecting or allowing the extraction of minerals or other resources below ground, or the exploitation of other natural resources in areas where it may adversely affect the Sami. Similar rules concerning the call for consultations with landowners and other concerned parties can be found in several statutes, especially in planning legislation.[20]

The third paragraph is, however, more controversial. It argues that permission to explore or exploit natural resources in the Sami regions must not be granted

---

20   See eg the Planning and Building Act 2010, ch 5, s 11.

if the activity in question will make it impossible or substantially more difficult for the Sami to continue their use of the areas, when this use is essential for the Sami culture, unless the Sami Parliament and the affected Sami have specifically agreed to the activity. Here, the legislation would give a right of veto not only to the representative Sami organization but also to individual Sami. It is true that the rule will be applied only in certain exceptional cases, where mining or similar operations imply a very serious threat against reindeer herding in large areas. Still, it is evident that the Sami would be in a privileged position in relation to other groups to stop a development. The local population can be affected in a comparable way, for instance by the activities just mentioned, but they will have no real possibility to stop the exploitation (unless they can convince the Sami in the same area to act for them). However, also this rule can be defended with reference to the particular sensitivity of reindeer herding and its particular importance for the Sami culture. A Sami village that is prevented from accessing reindeer herding pastures as a result of a mining activity may not be able to find a compatible herding area to use instead.[21] However, this could also be true for the landowner on whose land the expropriation is taking place. In such instances, the Sami would be in a unique position to defend their access to land by halting development. The only argument whereby this could be defended would be in reference to their status as an indigenous population.

Objections based on the equality argument will probably be stronger still if the proposal in the fourth paragraph is realized. Here, the right to be consulted and the veto right of the Sami are extended to other types of encroachment to the regions mentioned in article 34, such as forestry activities, hydroelectric and wind power plants, road constructions, recreational housing, military exercise activities and the establishing of military training grounds. While it is true that some of these activities would, under particular circumstances, cause serious damage to reindeer herding practices, it would be a far-reaching step to allow the Sami, even in unusual cases, to prevent activities of this kind. Should they be allowed to do so, it would provide them with a marked advantage in conflicts, not only in relation to public interests but also with private groups and individuals – such as forest owners or people wanting to build houses on their own land.

The particular rules provided in article 36 can hardly be justified with reference to any existing legal principles. The Environmental Code, 1998 protects the reindeer herding industry against measures that would pose a threat to its continued existence, especially in areas where the industry has national importance, but the Code gives the Sami no right of veto.[22] In conflicts with mining or wind power companies, for instance, the objections of the Sami have often been disregarded, although they have invoked principles of international law.[23] Neither can this rule

---

21   cf Mattias Åhrén's Chapter 13 in this volume.

22   See the Environmental Code, 1998 ch 3, ss 5 and 10.

23   cf Mattias Åhrén's Chapter 13 in this volume on the Rönnbäcken case. His criticism of the present state of the law seems well founded; it remains to be seen if it will

be based on the historical rights of the Sami, as they have never enjoyed privileges of this type. If implemented it would imply that the reindeer herding right would appear stronger than the ownership of land, since an owner does not have the same absolute veto right when he is threatened by expropriation, mining concessions or similar compulsory measures. Also in this case, the only valid argument would be to refer to the special status of the Sami people, but, as pointed out above, it is doubtful that any arguments for such a rule would be accepted by the public.

In this context, attention should also be given to articles 16 and 39. According to article 16, the Sami Parliament has the right to negotiate with the government in matters of major importance for the Sami. It is added, that the state must not take or permit measures that may significantly obstruct the basic conditions for the culture, economic activities or social life of the Sami without the consent of the Sami Parliament. Consequently, the Sami Parliament would have a veto right without any parallel in the Swedish Constitution. Article 39 also provides that the Sami Parliament can exercise this right in the areas mentioned in article 34. On the other hand, these rules can be regarded as a natural consequence of the Sami's status as an indigenous people; since the abstract provisions do not infringe upon the right of other citizens, they can probably be accepted without the same criticism that will meet the more specified veto rules.

Article 37 may cause some discussion as well. Here, the Sami are ensured compensation for all damage caused by activities mentioned in article 36. This, however, agrees with the present state of the law concerning compulsory measures against Swedish citizens. Further, the Sami shall be put on an equal footing with the landowner in so far as he is entitled to part of the yield of the mining operation on his land.[24] It should be pointed out that the right of the landowner, which was reintroduced in Swedish law as late as 2005,[25] is based on the idea that the mineral extracted from his land in effect is his property (although another important aim of the legislation was that the owners should take on a more positive view of mining operations on their land). As for the Sami, the Supreme Court stated in the Taxed mountain case that the Sami had no right to minerals found in the Sami areas. Thus, money paid by a mining company to the Sami cannot be regarded as a kind of compensation for property taken from them. Apart from the difficulty of supporting the rule by a legal construction, it would probably be easier to justify than other advantages prescribed by the convention, as the Sami have the strongest right to the land in question next to the owner.

---

have any effect. If so, the rules in article 36 will be easier to implement.

24 'If national law obliges persons granted a permit to extract natural resources to pay a fee or share of the profit from such activities to the landowner, the permit-holder shall be similarly obliged in relation to the Saami that have traditionally used and continue to use the area concerned.'

25 Prop 2004/05:65.

The last chapter contains certain provisions that protect the economic activities of the Sami. They are formulated in a general way and do not seem very controversial, at least compared to certain articles mentioned before.

Sami outside the Sami Villages

Accession to the convention would not solve one of the most difficult problems of Sami law, that is, the division amongst the Sami themselves, specifically between the members of the Sami villages and other Sami.[26] According to the RHA section 1, the reindeer herding right belong to the Sami people, but reindeer herding can be exercised only by members of a Sami village.[27] The same applies to the particular hunting and fishing rights of the Sami and to other rights accessory to reindeer herding[28] Membership in a Sami village is restricted to reindeer herders and persons closely akin to them (RHA sections 11–14). Of course, other particular minority legislation, for instance concerning the Sami language, protects non-members as well, but the majority of the Sami have no other rights according to the RHA except the possibility of becoming a reindeer herder with the consent of a Sami village. A proposal to open up the villages, and thereby making it possible for other Sami to exercise at least hunting and fishing rights,[29] has not gained any support; the government has consistently refused to extend such rights to all Sami for the political reasons mentioned in the introduction.[30] It is difficult to see why any equality arguments should prevent such an extension. The question concerns land rights that belong solely to the Sami, and it could be argued that the legislature should not intervene in the distribution of such rights.

The draft Nordic Sami Convention deals briefly with these question and provides that the responsibility of the state parties also includes, to a reasonable extent, those Sami who live outside the traditional Sami districts (article 6, paragraph 3). According to the commentary to this rule, it should be guaranteed that their language, culture and trade are developed so that they can take part in Sami social life, though the measures provided to guarantee this may not be the same as for the Sami who reside in the districts. Thus, the proposal can be seen to have the reindeer herding minority as their main focus. Hopefully, the interests of the Sami who fall outside this category will not be neglected should a reform

---

26 cf Chapter 9 by Eivind Torp in this volume.

27 See the RHA s 1, para 3. The particular problems connected with this rule are discussed by Christina Allard, 'Who Holds the Reindeer Herding Right in Sweden? A Key Issue in Legislation' in Nigel Bankes and Timo Koivurova (eds), *The Proposed Nordic Saami Convention: National and International Dimensions of Indigenous Property Rights* (Hart 2013).

28 See the RHA ss 16-18 and 25.

29 SOU 2001:101.

30 cf Bengtsson, 'Om jakt och fiske i fjällmarken' (n 9).

become implemented. Although the different livelihoods will prevent a complete equality in terms of access to rights, the legislature should at least try to eliminate some of the present differences. An opening of the Sami villages according to the proposal just mentioned may be a first step in this direction.

Final Remarks

In this chapter it has been argued that the Swedish government will be confronted with a number of difficult obstacles should the system of the convention be carried out without affording the Sami too conspicuous advantages compared to the citizens in general. Certain reforms can be motivated by referring to general principles of Swedish law, but on other points it is necessary to invoke the minority argument.

One possibility that is worth discussing is to meet possible objections by giving other legal entities the same, or at least similar, influence over the exploitation of nature resources. Even if it is difficult to grant rights of this type to groups of private persons, some parallels can be drawn with municipalities. At times, Sami villages are compared to them in spite of the obvious differences that exist. The municipalities already possess a kind of veto concerning certain types of establishment on their territory. According to chapter 17, section 6 in the Environmental Code, 1998 the government must not permit certain activities (nuclear power stations and several other large scale industrial establishments) unless the municipal council has approved of them specifically.[31] In some cases, when it is very important from a national point of view, the government can disregard the veto, but still there remain situations in which the municipality has the last word.[32]

It may lie near at hand to try to connect the veto of a Sami village and the Sami Parliament to the rule just mentioned about nuclear and similar establishments. It is true that the provision in the convention goes further than the Environmental Code, 1998 in this respect, but if the provision is modified on some points, it might be possible to give a common rule of veto. It will not be too risky to grant a veto right concerning mining operations to the municipalities, as in most cases they will have a positive attitude to such activities as a remedy for unemployment. Such a regulation can meet some of the demands for equality. On the other hand, the modification would probably take away a valuable protection for the Sami, and it would not satisfy all the claims based on their particular status. In any event, it is doubtful that it can silence all critical voices. Even if the idea may be

---

31 The same rule applies concerning certain other activities, if the Government has reserved for itself the right to consider the permissibility.

32 There are also other rules that prescribe a municipal veto, such as wind power constructions; however, they concern only exploitations of a limited scope and cannot be compared to the veto rules in the Convention.

worth a discussion, it does not seem to be an entirely satisfactory solution to the equality problem.

Under these circumstances, the remaining way to gain sufficient support for the convention seems to be to emphasize the international pressure on the government to extend the protection of the Sami as an indigenous people. The mass media have reported on such initiatives from various international organizations, although without any apparent interest. Perhaps the Swedish public has become so accustomed to international reproaches concerning Sami rights that the news value is considered rather small. It will probably be necessary to draw public attention to the international reaction on a much larger scale than before, even if such an expedient might be repugnant to the government concerned. As mentioned before, the attitude to the convention at least in Norway seems to be more positive, and this may be another argument for accession to the convention.

However, it remains to be seen if a Swedish government will take so much trouble for such an end. At least for the time being, the chances of a Sami law reform seem doubtful.

Chapter 7

Sami Reindeer Herders' Herding Rights in Norway from the Nineteenth Century to the Present Day

Kirsti Strøm Bull

Introduction

This chapter describes legal developments in Norway regarding Sami reindeer herders' rights to use traditional Sami reindeer herding areas and spanning the last 150 years.[1] The focus of analysis will be twofold: first I will examine the rights of Sami reindeer herders to use grazing land and other natural resources, and then I will address conflicts between these rights and other economic interests.[2]

A major theme of this chapter will be Sami reindeer herders' historical use of herding lands. An analysis will be conducted regarding the legal significance of this historical use in cases where the use has conflicted with the interests of Norwegian society at large. Traditionally, Norwegian law has viewed the regular and recurring use of land areas known in Norwegian as *utmark*,[3] whether by individuals, extended families or other groups, as an important factor in establishing legal rights of ownership or use. This concept is reflected in Norwegian rules relating to common usage, customary law and ancient use. If we examine the history of Norwegian law in relation to reindeer husbandry we find that attitudes that have varied. Variations in these attitudes have notably occurred concerning the extent to which the historical use of herding lands by Sami reindeer herders may establish

---

1 This account is based on Kirsti Strøm Bull, *Studier i reindriftsrett* (Oslo 1997) 34–55 and Kirsti Strøm Bull 'Yngvar Nielsen med prejudikatvirkninger' in Dag Michalsen (ed), *Rett, historie og metode* (Department of Public and International Law, University of Oslo 2005) 137–49. A historical account of the law as it relates to reindeer husbandry is also provided by Øyvind Ravna in *Rettsutgreiing og bruksordning i reindriftsområder* (Oslo 2008) 320 et seq.

2 The allocation of and rights to pasture land are also key sources of debate within reindeer herding sector. However, this debate between various groups involved in reindeer husbandry, such as cooperative herding partnerships (known in Northern Sami language as *siida*) and 'reindeer pasture districts' (Norwegian: *reinbeitedistrikt*), is beyond the scope of this article. Regarding these issues, see the chapter by Kristina Labba in this volume.

3 The concept of *utmark* denotes natural environments that are not cultivated, such as meadows, mountain pastures, forests, moorland, mountains and coastlines.

rights of land usage. These attitudes have been influenced, in turn, by general Norwegian policy concerning the Sami people.

The Lapp Codicil of 1751

The Sami people inhabit regions of the Nordic countries of Norway, Sweden and Finland, as well as Russia's Kola Peninsula. Northern Sami is the mother-tongue spoken by the majority of Sami living in the northernmost areas of Norway, Sweden and Finland. South of this area the Sami language or dialect is Lule Sami and further south Southern Sami. The Sami are a transnational people; their familial, cultural, linguistic and economic links transcend national borders.

The border established in 1751 between Norway and Sweden/Finland cut directly across Sami territory, also known as Sápmi.[4] Some of the difficulties that the newly established border could potentially cause for the Sami were recognized at the time of its establishment. Securing Sami rights was deemed essential to what a statement of 1750, issued in conjunction with the border negotiations between Sweden and Denmark-Norway, had described as 'the preservation of the Lappish Nation'.[5] Article 3 of the border treaty of 1751 noted that 'Lapps of both sides require the land of both kingdoms for husbandry of their reindeer', and accordingly required the adoption of an appendix to the treaty in order to secure continued rights for the Sami to use land on both sides of the border. The resulting appendix is generally referred to as the Lapp Codicil.

The first sentence of Section 10 of the Lapp Codicil provides that, 'since the Lapps require the land of both kingdoms, as accorded by ancient custom, they shall be permitted to migrate, in autumn and spring, with their reindeer across the border into the other Kingdom'. The wording in the sentence both affirms and recognizes Sami historical use of a region of land, a use that had to be respected despite the fact that a national border was to bisect that region. The Lapp Codicil did not establish a right of land use for the Sami; however it did codify an ancient and unwritten customary law.

---

4 In 1751, Finland formed part of Sweden. The treaty also determined the border between Norway and Finland as far as Utsjok. The border between Sweden and Finland was determined in 1809, when Finland was ceded to Russia as a grand duchy. The borders between Norway and Finland from Utsjok and between Norway and Russia were established in 1826.

5 Declaration of 16 September 1750, quoted in NOU 1984: 18, 187.

The Norwegian Constitution of 1814 and Voting Rights for Sami People

Although not directly covering the main topic of this chapter, this section will briefly address Norwegian attitudes toward the Sami in 1814, which was the year in which Norway gained its own Constitution and parliament (*Storting*).[6] It is helpful to have this attitude in mind when considering different attitudes that later appeared at the end of the same century.

The right to vote in Norway was given to all men over the age of 25 who either (a) held or had held an official office; (b) owned or rented 'matriculated' land in a rural area; or (c) were citizens of, or owned property in excess of a certain size in, a market town. These criteria meant that very few men in county of Finnmark,[7] and certainly no Sami men, were entitled to vote. As early as 1818, a proposal was considered to amend the Norwegian Constitution to secure voting rights for the Sami in Finnmark. In support of the proposed amendment, the Constitutional Committee noted that the voting rules would clearly have been formulated differently if the National Assembly, when it had gathered in Eidsvoll (where the Constitution was drafted) in 1814, had been aware of the situation in Finnmark. Most inhabitants of Finnmark neither owned nor rented land, but were 'itinerant Finns'. Moreover, 'particularly the so-called Mountain Finns' were 'owners of Reindeer and other assets whose value far exceeds the value of the land'.[8]

The committee also emphasized that it was very important for Finnmark to be fully represented in the *Storting*. This inclusion was due to the fact that representatives in the *Storting* were largely ignorant of conditions in Finnmark, which were very different from the rest of Norway. In 1821, the *Storting* unanimously approved the proposed constitutional amendment to secure voting rights for the Sami men of Finnmark.[9]

The Lapp Codicil of 1751 and the Constitutional Amendment of 1821 are evidence of a respect for the Sami people and an understanding of their economy,

---

6   Between 1380 and 1814, Norway was part of a union with Denmark. As a result of the Napoleonic Wars, Denmark was forced to cede Norway to Sweden under the Treaty of Kiel signed in January 1814. According to the terms of the treaty, Norway was to be united with Sweden as a single kingdom. When news of the treaty reached Norway, it fuelled the Norwegian independence movement. Opposition to the treaty led to the signing of Norway's Constitution on 17 May 1814 and to the election of a separate Norwegian king. Shortly thereafter Swedish troops attacked Norway. The result of this attack was that Norway agreed to enter into a union with Sweden, but retained its own new Constitution, subject to such amendments as were necessitated by the union. Norway's union with Sweden lasted until 1905.

7   Finnmark is the northernmost county in Norway.

8   Storthings Forhandlinger (March 1821) 233–41.

9   The proposal put forward in 1818 could not be approved before the next *Storting* met in 1821, because the rules on constitutional amendments set forth in Section 112 of the Constitution specify that proposed amendments may not be approved until after the next general election.

culture and history. However, during the next century, this attitude changed significantly. This change would erode the legal rights of the Sami people.

Sami Reindeer Herders' Use of Herding Land: The Legal Basis

As mentioned above, the regular and recurrent use of *utmark*, whether by individuals, extended families or other groups, is an important factor in establishing the legal rights of ownership or land use in Norway.

In several cases, Norway's Supreme Court has considered the question whether the Sami reindeer herders' long-standing usage of particular areas of grazing land or *utmark* have established rights of use. Usually, the question at hand has been whether Sami reindeer herders' use of a particular area has been sufficiently prolonged and intensive enough to have established rights of use. If the answer is yes, then the deemed-owner of the land in question must respect those rights. Views concerning the effect of Sami reindeer herders' historic use of land have varied over the last 150 years. Such views have been influenced, amongst other things, by prevailing majority Norwegian opinions about Sami history and about the relative importance of agriculture and reindeer husbandry. In particular, conflicting theories about the length of time during which the Sami have been present in certain areas have affected Norwegian courts' findings. These findings include whether or not Sami reindeer herders have established rights to use the areas in question, a situation that has particularly affected reindeer herders in Southern Sami areas.

Until the end of the nineteenth century, the Sami were generally considered to be indigenous inhabitants of Norway, who had been displaced northwards by the arrival of Old Norse-speaking tribes.[10] This view of the Sami as the indigenous population of Norway also formed the basis of Norwegian court judgments. In 1862, for example, the Norwegian Supreme Court reviewed a case[11] in which a Sami reindeer herder had been prosecuted for taking timber and birch bark from privately owned land in Nordland, a county in Northern Norway. The Supreme Court acquitted the reindeer herder on the grounds that he had been exercising an ancient Sami right to use land in the area. According to the court, the Sami were the original inhabitants of the area, and therefore Sami right to use of land had to be respected by Norwegian property owners (who had moved to the area more recently).

Moreover, a report from the so-called Røros Commission, published in 1879, stated that, prior to the establishment of the Røros Copper Works, the rural municipality of Røros was virtually uninhabited; 'only some nomadic Lapps had

---

10　　Peter Andreas Munch, *Det norske Folks Historie* (Christiania 1852–1859).
11　　Rt 1862 p 654.

their temporary residences there'.[12] The Commission referred to several judgments by Norwegian courts of first instance, in which the courts held that the Sami had rights to use land in the area on the basis of having been its original inhabitants.[13]

This view of the Sami as the indigenous inhabitants of southern – as well as northern – areas of Norway abruptly changed in 1889. During the summer of that year, the historian and geographer Yngvar Nielsen hiked through the area of Femunden, east of Røros, and northwards as far as Namskogen. That November 1889 Nielsen gave a lecture at the Norwegian Geographical Society entitled 'The Lapps' advance southwards in the diocese of Trondheim and the county of Hedemark'.[14] Nielsen claimed that ethnic Norwegians had been the first to settle in the Røros area. According to Nielsen, the Sami had arrived from the north at a later stage and had encroached on land already being used by Norwegian farmers. This assertion contradicted the belief by the Sami in the area that they were the original inhabitants of the region. Nielsen put forward two findings in support of his assertion that the Sami had arrived relatively recently: firstly, he had found no Sami place names; secondly, he had found no trace of any Sami burial or sacrificial sites in the area.[15]

According to Nielsen, the Sami arrived in the southern part of the county of Trøndelag only toward the end of the seventeenth century. He claimed that they arrived in the area around Røros even later, during the eighteenth century.[16]

In July of 1889, the same year that Nielsen presented his theory, a commission was established by Royal Resolution to investigate 'The Lapp situation in the counties of Hedemark and Southern and Northern Trondhjem'. This commission, known as the Lapp Commission of 1889, accepted Nielsen's theory without question. Referring to Nielsen's work, the Lapp Commission declared that ethnic Norwegians had started to farm mountain areas in South Trøndelag and

---

12   The Røros Commission was established on 11 January 1875. Its task was to investigate positions of the Røros Copper Works and the Norwegian State with regard to the Works' control of forestry activities. The quotation is taken from page 17 of the Commission's Report.

13   Report of the Røros Commission 1879, 47.

14   The lecture was published in the society's 1891 Yearbook: Yngvar Nielsen, 'Lappernes fremrykning mod syd i Trondhjems stift og Hedemarkens amt' (1891) in Det norske geografiske Selskabs Aarbog 19.

15   ibid 20.

16   The cleric and demographer Thomas R. Malthus travelled within Norway in 1799. One of the places he visited was Røros. In his diaries, Malthus wrote that the director of the Røros Copper Works, Knoph, had informed him that the Sami 'had inhabited these mountains before Roraas was known' (see Patricia James (ed), *The Travel Diaries of Thomas Robert Malthus* (Cambridge 1966) 195). This information contradicts the claims that Yngvar Nielsen made 90 years later. Malthus' diary also contains a lively depiction of his visit to a family of Sami reindeer herders at Tolga, a little south of Røros (ibid 188–95). The information provided to Malthus about the presence of Sami in the area around Røros first became known through the publication of his diaries in 1966.

Hedmark long before the arrival of the Sami to the region. Among other things, the Commission found:

> The claim that the Lapps in bygone times had a presence further south than nowadays, both in Norway and in Sweden, and that they are the true indigenous inhabitants, who have been driven by Scandinavians northwards and away from these areas, where they had been able to lead their nomadic lifestyle without hindrance, can no longer be sustained by anyone, since the incorrectness of such a supposition appears to have been adequately demonstrated by recent academic research.[17]

The Norwegian courts were also quick to accept Nielsen's theory that the Sami had encroached on land that was already being used by Norwegian farmers. This acceptance is demonstrated in two Supreme Court decisions from the 1890s.

The first court case, registered at Rt 1892 p 411, concerned claims by farmers in the area around Røros for damage caused by reindeer to summer grazing land. The reindeer herders denied liability. They argued that they had established land use rights long before the farmers had started to use areas of the *utmark* for mountain pasture and the growing of hay. The reindeer herders lost the case. Referring to Nielsen's theory, the Norwegian Supreme Court found that the Sami, contrary to previous belief, were not the original inhabitants of the area. The court determined that the Sami had started to use the land only after the farmers had established mountain pastures there. As a result, the reindeer herders had to yield to the judgment favouring the perception of the farmers' more long-standing use of the land.

A similar case came before the Supreme Court in 1897, registered at Rt 1897 p 759. Once again, the court found that the Sami reindeer herders had no claim to herding rights, because the farmers' use of the land pre-dated Sami reindeer husbandry in the area.

Even though Sami place names and Sami heritage sites were discovered subsequently in areas where Nielsen claimed that they had not existed, his theory proved very resilient. As discussed below, even a century later, his paper of 1889 continued to exert significant influence in Norwegian court cases concerning reindeer husbandry in Southern Sami areas.

Nation-building and 'Norwegianization'

Starting in the second half of the nineteenth century, general attitudes toward the Sami and Sami culture also began to change. Simultaneously, there was a change in

---

17 *Indberetning fra den ved kongelig Resolution af 12te Juli 1889 til Undersøgelse af Lappeforholdene i Hedemarkens, Søndre- og Nordre Trondhjems Amter anordnede Kommission* [Commission Report] 1892, 4.

attitude toward the rights of the Sami to use land-based resources. These changes coincided with the period of 'Norwegianization', which commenced around 1850. During this period, a growing Norwegian population and an expanding farming sector put pressure on ancient Sami reindeer herding areas. In addition, Norwegian culture focused to a large extent on the process of Norwegian nation-building, in which there was no place for Sami culture, economic activities or society.

The period of Norwegian nation-building that lasted for the remainder of the nineteenth century involved the glorification of everything that was typically Norwegian. In particular, this attitude led to the elevation of farming culture and the adoption of very negative attitudes towards the Sami. In 1900, for example, the deluxe publication *Norway in the nineteenth century* contained descriptions of people from different parts of Norway. While the people of, for example, Østerdalen and Gudbrandsdalen, were eulogized, the description of the Sami people was unflattering to say the least.

A chapter on Western Finnmark in the same book clearly illustrated the efforts being made to Norwegianize the population of Finnmark. In its closing words, the chapter notes that '... Finnmark is a good land, a land for Norwegians, for the Norwegian language and for Norwegian customs.'[18]

Thus, Yngvar Nielsen's theory, discussed in the previous section of this article, that the Sami had arrived in more southern areas of Norway far later than previously believed, was in fact a manifestation of the changing views of the Sami during the period of Norwegianization and Norwegian nation-building. As explained above, one consequence of Nielsen's theory was that in several Norwegian court cases the Sami lost the right to use land that they had previously been accustomed to using for reindeer herding.

In Northern Norway, where the Sami could quite clearly demonstrate their long-standing use of land and natural resources, it was impossible to deny that the Sami had been present since far back in history. Nonetheless, their use of natural resources, however long-standing, was not viewed by the state as protected.

As mentioned earlier in this article, the Norwegian government recognized during the eighteenth century, through the Lapp Codicil, and also throughout the nineteenth century, that long-standing use of land and natural resources by the Sami afforded the Sami rights on the basis of 'use from time immemorial' (*alders tids bruk*). During the twentieth century, however, the use of land and natural resources by Sami reindeer herders was viewed as an example of a 'tolerated use' (*tålt bruk*). The general view was that such 'tolerated uses' had to yield to the 'inexorable law of progress'.

One example of this attitude can be found in a 1955 Norwegian Supreme Court judgment for a case originating from the county of Nordland.[19] The issues in dispute included fishing rights in a privately owned lake. The parties to the case

---

18 Axel Hagemann, 'Vestfinmarken', in Nordahl Rolfsen (ed) *Norge i det nittende Aarhundrede*, vol 2, Christiania (1900) 145.

19 Rt 1955 p 361 (the Marsfjell case).

agreed that the Sami reindeer herders' use of the land and resources, including fishing, went far back in time and pre-dated Norwegian private ownership of the area. Nonetheless, the Supreme Court held that the Sami did not have any rights based on use from time immemorial. In the court's view, pursuant to the Norwegian Reindeer Herding Act of 1933, Sami reindeer herders were entitled to fish only on common land. Even where the Sami could demonstrate historical use, they had no rights other than those established under the Act.

This view of Sami reindeer herders' land rights was developed by, amongst others, Professor Nikolaus Gjelsvik, who was considered to be the foremost expert on Norwegian property law during the early twentieth century. Gjelsvik's textbook *Norwegian Property Law*, stated, for example, 'The right of use that people have to the land in Finnmark has been given to them by the state, and the state may at any time whatsoever withdraw that right'.[20] This view still prevails.

As touched up earlier, in the 1960s, the official view in Norway was that Sami reindeer herders' use of land and natural resources was merely a 'tolerated use'. This view was consequently subordinate to current prevailing legislation. The herders' use of the land was subject to exhaustive statutory regulation, and the rules on use from time immemorial did not entitle the herders to claim rights that extended beyond the statutory rules as described in the following paragraph.

Reindeer herding in Norway thus came to be governed by the Reindeer Herding Act of 1933. However, even though the act mentioned reindeer in its title, its content gave farming priority over reindeer herding. For example, the legal text included extremely harsh rules concerning reindeer owners' liability to pay compensation if their reindeer ventured onto farmland. These rules did not equally address the fact that areas traditionally used for reindeer herding were also subjected to encroachment by, for example, new farming cultivation or road or hydropower construction. In those cases, the general view was that Sami reindeer herders had to make way without any right to compensation.

A Change in Attitudes about Sami Use of Resources: Two Cases in 1968

In 1968, the Supreme Court decided two cases that broke radically with the prevailing orthodoxy that Sami reindeer herders in Norway could not claim rights on the grounds of use from time immemorial.

The first case, the Brekken case, concerned Sami reindeer herders' rights to hunt and fish in a mountainous area of land under co-ownership in Brekken, an area east of Røros.[21] In the Brekken case, the co-landowners claimed that the Sami had no rights to hunt or fish on the land in question. The landowners did not dispute that the Sami had practised reindeer herding in the area for several centuries, including during the period pre-dating the farmers' acquisition of property rights

---

20   Nikolaus Gjelsvik, *Norsk Tingsrett* (Oslo 1926) 133–34.
21   Rt 1968 p 394.

in the area. Nonetheless, citing the Marsfjell judgment[22] and the Reindeer Herding Act of 1933, the landowners argued that the Sami reindeer herders' hunting and fishing rights applied only to common land (*statsallmening*),[23] and not to privately owned land. The Sami reindeer herders argued that they had fishing and hunting rights on the land in question by virtue of the rules on use from time immemorial. The landowners prevailed before the Land Consolidation Court and subsequently at the Court of Appeal.

According to the Court of Appeal, no special legal basis existed for Sami rights to hunt or fish beyond those rights established by the Reindeer Herding Act of 1993. Citing the Marsfjell case, the Court of Appeal found that the Sami reindeer herders' 'centuries-old exercise of rights to use, including in relation to fishing and hunting', did not go beyond the scope of a 'harmless right of enjoyment'(*uskadelige nyttesrett*) that the Sami at all times had been permitted to exercise. The court elaborated, 'This exercise of rights of use cannot, either by virtue of established custom or use from time immemorial, create a particular basis for a right that cannot freely be changed by subsequent legislation'.[24]

On second appeal, however, the Norwegian Supreme Court did not view the Sami reindeer herders' use of the land and resources as a 'harmless right of enjoyment'. With the concurrence of the other judges, the judge first to present his vote held the following:

> It appears to have been the Sami who first took this mountainous area into use, to the extent that it was capable of use, and on the basis of the evidence presented I find that the mountain territory was not used by others until after the Sami's use of the land for reindeer husbandry and other purposes was relatively firmly established. It was certainly the case that each year the Sami moved from place to place, and that their actual use of the land varied, but at least in the area to the east of the subsequently established 'Finn line', their use appears to have been so attached to the place and fundamentally established that it cannot be summarily equated to the exercise of a harmless right of enjoyment or a common right of access.[25]

The judgment in the Brekken case was delivered on 5 April 1968. Just 15 days later, the Norwegian Supreme Court then held in the so-called Altevann case[26] that the Sami reindeer herders' historic use of land and natural resources was an independent legal basis that gave them rights to compensation for state expropriation of their rights. The case addressed whether Swedish Sami reindeer

---

22 Rt 1955 p 361.

23 *Statsallmenning* is *utmark* owned by the state but with extensive usage rights for local people, in particular for local farmers.

24 Rt 1968 p 394, 401.

25 ibid 410.

26 Rt 1968 p 429.

herders, who used summer herding lands in the area around Lake Altevann in the Norwegian county of Troms, had a right to compensation for the expropriation of their rights. A question at hand was if herding rights had been expropriated due to the lake having been dammed for the construction of a hydropower plant. Thus, the case also concerned cross-border reindeer husbandry. The plaintiffs in the case were the Sami villages determined to be a part of the Swedish state who herded their reindeer in Sweden during the wintertime and in Norway during the summers. The existence of cross-border reindeer husbandry was recognized by the Lapp Codicil of 1751, but was more strictly regulated by the Reindeer Grazing Convention of 1919 between Norway and Sweden.

Initially, the Norwegian Waterways authority was prepared to compensate the Swedish Sami for their loss of their herding land. However, the Norwegian Ministry of Foreign Affairs intervened. The Ministry's position was that, under the Reindeer Grazing Convention of 1919 between Sweden and Norway, Sami individuals or groups in one of the states did not have independent rights of the other state when in the other state's territory. In the Ministry's view, the Convention conferred rights on Sami only in the state designated as their state of citizenship. Accordingly, issues relating to compensation for loss of herding land were the concern solely of the two states towards their respective Sami citizens. The Swedish Sami villages disputed this view and claimed that they had herding rights and rights to fish in the waterway on the basis of ancient use, regardless of the convention between the two states.

Due to the intervention of the Norwegian Ministry of Foreign Affairs, the Norwegian Waterways authority in turn claimed that the Swedish Sami had no grounds in private Norwegian law to bring their case forward, due to the reindeer herding rights of the Swedish Sami in the area around Lake Altevann having basis in the conventions and joint acts entered into by Norway and Sweden. According to the Norwegian Waterways authority, the Sami from the Swedish side of the Norway-Sweden border had not used land in the area in such a way as to develop rights prior to the signing of the Lapp Codicil in 1751, and that the Codicil did not imply any recognition of Sami rights. The Norwegian Waterways authority claimed that the Codicil permitted the practice of reindeer husbandry only to the extent that such practice was in accordance with the interests of the two states. According to the Norwegian Waterways authority, this was 'merely a permitted use that the States could at any time whatsoever change, restrict or abolish completely'.[27]

The Norwegian Supreme Court thought otherwise. With the concurrence of the other judges, the first judge to present his vote held the following:

> In relation to the situation in this case, I base my opinion, as did the Court of
> Appeal, on the fact that generation after generation from the district where the
> villages are located, in any event for 100 years before the border was determined
> in 1751, have had dwellings next to Lake Altevann with storehouses, separation

---

27   Rt 1968 p 429, 433.

fences, boats, and other equipment that they needed, and that the Lapps subsequently have used the area annually for grazing and fishing. Accordingly, one must be able to determine, as did the appeal court, that from historic time the Lapps in this particular area have firmly established an essential economic use.[28]

According to this reasoning, Sami reindeer herders from the Swedish side of the Norway-Sweden border had rights in the area around Lake Altevann on the basis of use from time immemorial. This meant that their rights were not based solely on the state conventions or laws that were applicable at any particular time. The Swedish Sami villages received compensation for the effects of lost herding land and for their loss of fishing resources caused by construction of the hydropower plant.

Through these two judgments in 1968 the Norwegian Supreme Court determined, contrary to the basis for its decision in the Marsfjell case in 1955, that Sami reindeer herders' rights were not regulated exclusively by either state legislation or inter-state agreements and conventions. Instead, Sami reindeer herders were to have more extensive rights, and these rights were established on the basis of use from time immemorial. This view has formed the basis of all subsequent judgments by the Supreme Court.

Despite these clear statements by the Norwegian Supreme Court, the Norwegian Ministry of Agriculture, when drafting the new Reindeer Herding Act of 1978, did not wish to recognize that Sami reindeer herders' rights of use were based on use from time immemorial. In the preparatory works to the Act, the Ministry stated that earlier legislation on the subject had been based on the principle that the right to engage in reindeer husbandry in a reindeer herding district was governed exclusively by the relevant legislation. In other words, the scope of the right to engage in reindeer husbandry was determined solely on the basis of the prevailing statutory rules. This was also the Ministry's intended position under its proposed new law. In this context, the Ministry stated the following:

> Such rights as shall at any time be ascribed to the reindeer husbandry sector must be determined by balancing the interests of the sector against those of neighbouring businesses and the interests of society as a whole.[29]

Accordingly, the Ministry ignored the principles upon which the Norwegian Supreme Court had based its decisions in 1968 and subsequently thereafter. It is striking that the Norwegian Ministry of Agriculture, in its preparatory works to the 1978 Act, did not refer to the fact the Norwegian Supreme Court had established in multiple decisions that Sami land rights could exist, regardless of the prevailing law, on the basis of use from time immemorial. Only upon an amendment to the Reindeer Herding Act in 1996 was the court's position addressed. In the 1996

---

28 Rt 1968 p 429, 437–38.
29 Ot prp no 9 (1976-77) 42.

Amendment the Ministry stated that court practice had established that rights relating to reindeer husbandry had a separate legal basis that was independent of the act.[30] In other words, it took nearly 30 years for the Norwegian Supreme Court's position on the land rights of Sami reindeer herders – clearly announced in the two judgments from 1968 – to be adopted officially by the Norwegian Ministry.

In the Altevann case of 1968, the Norwegian Ministry of Foreign Affairs intervened in the matter of paying compensation to Sami villages in Sweden that had lost herding land due to the building of a hydropower dam at Lake Altevann. The background to this intervention was most likely that Norway was preparing to negotiate a new Reindeer Grazing Convention with Sweden, and the Ministry wanted to make it clear that the rights of Swedish Sami in Norway were subject to exhaustive regulation under that convention. The new Reindeer Grazing Convention between Norway and Sweden came into force in 1972, but the Convention made no reference either to customary rights or to the landmark judgment in the Altevann case. The 1972 Convention was intended to remain in force until 2002. This period was extended while negotiations about a new convention continued between Sweden and Norway after 2002, but in 2005 these negotiations broke down, partly due to disagreement between the parties on the significance of customary rights. Simultaneously, the 1972 Convention expired.

Later, following the breakdown in 2005, the negotiations for a new inter-state Reindeer Grazing Convention were revived. These negotiations over the text of the new convention were completed in 2009,[31] and the new convention currently refers explicitly to customary rights.[32] The Convention has not yet been ratified by Norway and Sweden.

The Selbu Case of 2001

Even though the Norwegian Supreme Court recognized, from 1968 onward, that the land rights of Sami reindeer herders were to be based upon on use from time immemorial and not solely on the rules of the Norwegian Reindeer Herding Act, it was difficult for Sami reindeer herders – especially in Southern Sami areas – to

---

30 Ot prp no 28 (1994-95) 28.

31 On this issue, see Else Grete Broderstad, 'Cross-border Reindeer Husbandry: Between Ancient Usage Rights and State Sovereignty' in Timo Koivurova and Nigel Bankes (eds) *The Proposed Nordic Saami Convention: National and International Dimensions of Indigenous Property Rights* (Hart 2013).

32 Article 8 states that the convention does not affect such customary rights to reindeer herding such as those that reindeer herders from one state party possessed within the other state party. Article 8 also provides: 'Judicial determination of questions concerning the scope of customary rights shall accordingly not be restrained by the convention, but shall be determined on the basis of the private law of Norway concerning use form time immemorial and the laws of Sweden concerning use since immemorial prescription.'

prove sufficient use. These reindeer herders struggled to achieve recognition of their rights on the basis of ancient use, see Rt 1981 p 1215,[33] Rt 1988 p 1217[34] and Rt 1997 p 1608.[35]

In all of these cases, the court attached decisive weight to the descriptions of reindeer herders' historical use of the land and natural resources as those descriptions appeared in the Lapp Commission's Report of 1889. Given the nature of the report's description of the reindeer herders' use of the land and natural resources, herders' use was considered in many disputes as neither sufficiently long-standing, nor sufficiently intensive, to establish rights under the prescribed doctrine of ancient use. As mentioned previously above, the Lapp Commission was strongly influenced by Yngvar Nielsen's theories. In accordance with this fact, the Commission formed an opinion that the Sami had encroached on land that was in use by farmers in the area. Even in areas that existed within the boundaries of the land described by the Lapp Commission as Sami reindeer herding areas and that were designated as Sami 'pasture districts' in 1894, Sami reindeer herders lost the right to herd their animals in the *utmark*. This was the outcome of both the Aursunden case in 1997 and the Korssjøfjell case in 1988.

The report from the Lapp Commission stated that the division of land into 'pasture districts' did not establish definitive boundaries with respect to Sami rights. The report also stated that there could be areas within a pasture district in which the Sami did not have a right to practise reindeer herding[36] Even with regard to an area of grazing land that lay within a pasture district, the Norwegian Supreme Court held, in the Korsjøfjell case, that reindeer owners were obliged to establish that their right to herd reindeer through proving historical use.

The Supreme Court's decision in the Korsjøfjell case in 1988 prompted other Norwegian landowners to commence legal actions in an attempt to ban reindeer herding from grazing lands that the landowners owned. In 1995 in Selbu, southeast of Trondheim, a total of 229 Norwegian landowners commenced legal claims that the Sami had no rights to herd reindeer in areas in the possession of the landowners. These claims were made despite the fact that such areas were located within Sami pasture districts. According to the landowners, the right to herd reindeer applied only to common land.[37] The reindeer owners argued that they had been using the areas since ancient times in such a way so as to have grazing rights. The reindeer owners prevailed by slim majorities in both the District Court and the Court of Appeal. When the Selbu case came before the Norwegian Supreme Court, the

---

33 The Trollheimen case.
34 The Korssjøfjell case.
35 The Aursunden case.
36 Commission Report (n 16) 42.
37 *Common Land*, see fn 22.

court considered the issue of such fundamental importance that it decided to hear the case in plenum.[38]

Although the Supreme Court addressed several questions in the Selbu case, only a couple of those questions shall be examined in this article. First, turning to the court's view of the opinions of the Lapp Commission: in relation to questions about the length of time during which the Sami were present in a particular area, the Supreme Court attached weight in both the Korssjøfjell case (1988) and the Aursunden case (1997) for information found in written sources. In these judgments, physical evidence of a historical Sami presence in an area was not capable of overturning the written conclusions of the Lapp Commission. However, the majority in the Supreme Court's judgment in the Selbu case (2001) exhibited a more nuanced view of the historical background. In addition to this, in the Selbu case the court majority had a far more critical view of the Lapp Commission's findings.

The majority in the Selbu case, comprising nine judges, referred to particular methodological difficulties. The difficulties were associated with research into the history of the Southern Sami and owing to the fact that the Sami – in contrast to ethnic Norwegians – did not, historically, have a written language. However, the Sami had an oral tradition. In this regard, on behalf of the majority, the first judge to present his vote declared the following:

> On the other hand, the Sami of course, in common with the permanent residents, possess an oral tradition. Such traditions must be evaluated carefully, but cannot be discounted generally. And if they are supported by other evidence, they may become of increased significance.[39]

In addition, the majority pointed out that consideration should also be given to the fact that misunderstandings could easily occur in communications between the Norwegians and the Sami. Linguistic and cultural differences could lead people to understand each other incorrectly.

According to the court majority in the Selbu case, one should also be cautious in drawing legal conclusions on the basis of a lack of physical evidence of Sami presence in an area. This due to the fact that he Sami were a nomadic people who used mainly organic materials that decomposed and left little to no trace. Accordingly, it was difficult to find physical evidence of reindeer husbandry from past centuries.

A significant factor in the Norwegian Supreme Court's decision in the Selbu case was, in fact, the Lapp Commission's own materials. During its work, the Commission had collated a number of statements from farmers and other people in the region that were recorded in the Commission's minutes. Portions of these statements, which were reproduced in the Commission's report, had been referred to in earlier Supreme Court cases and Appellate Courts cases. However, a new

---

38   Rt 2001 p 769 (the Selbu case). For an English translation of the judgment, see <http://www.galdu.org/govat/doc/selbudommen.pdf> accessed. 22 July 2015.

39   Rt 2001 p 769, 792.

feature of the Selbu case was the producing of the Lapp Commission's minutes as evidence. Anders Løøv, a university research librarian,[40] had undertaken the enormous task of transcribing these minutes. The complete statements, as recorded in the minutes, contained information about what the contemporary informants could relate regarding the ancient Sami use of land areas, for example by referring to ancient Sami camping grounds. This information had been omitted from the partial statements reproduced in the Lapp Commission's Report. The minutes revealed a land use by the Sami herders that was not consistent with Yngvar Nielsen's theory about Sami presence in the area. The Norwegian Supreme Court concluded that reindeer herding took place in Selbu for a longer period than the Lapp Commission had concluded.

In addition, the Supreme Court made some important statements about Norwegian law as it pertains to reindeer husbandry. The court held that the right to herd reindeer was an independent right not based in the Act and that the basis for it was use from time immemorial. Accordingly, the herding of reindeer was and is deemed a right, not simply a tolerated use.

The court decided for a right to be established through use from time immemorial, three factors must be present: the *use* must have been of a particular nature; the use must have taken place over a *long period of time*; the use must have occurred in *good faith*. The court instructed that in the evaluation of the presence of a right, weight should be attached to the 'nature of the right'. The Supreme Court majority hearing the case pointed out that, since the case concerned reindeer grazing rights, account needed to be taken of the nature of reindeer herding. The court deemed that the above criteria should be applied in a way that was relevant to the use of the area both by the Sami and by the reindeer, and that account was to be taken of the fact that the Sami practised a nomadic lifestyle. Accordingly, considerations concerning use that were raised in relation to the grazing of other animals could not automatically be applied to reindeer grazing.

In the Selbu case the Supreme Court majority emphasized that reindeer husbandry required very large areas of land and that the area of land used varied from year to year according to weather conditions, wind, and the quality of the herding area. Accordingly, in the view of the court it was not appropriate to require that the reindeer had to graze in a particular area each year to meet evidence requirements. For this reason, and because the Sami lifestyle was nomadic, an interruption in land use was not to hinder the acquisition of land rights, even if that interruption had been relatively lengthy.

Typically, reindeer roam while grazing. The fact that reindeer may consistently use a primary area, for example when calving, did not mean that the area used by the reindeer was not significantly larger than these primary areas.[41]

---

40 Anders Løøv was a research librarian employed at the Gunnerus Library at the University of Trondheim.

41 Rt 2001 p 769, 789.

After the Sami reindeer herders prevailed in the Selbu case and the Norwegian Supreme Court, landowners to the north of Selbu withdrew their threats of legal action.

Concluding Remarks

Attitudes in Norway about Sami reindeer herders' rights to use traditional Sami grazing lands and herding areas have varied during the last 150 years. Until the late nineteenth century, Sami reindeer herders' use of the herding land (*utmark*) was accepted as a right of use that was of equal status to the rights of use of Norwegian farmers. This right of use was established by many generations' use of the grazing and herding areas. However, this rights-based attitude changed during the period of Norwegianization, which lasted from the mid nineteenth century until around 1960. During this period, Sami reindeer herders' use of the *utmark* came to be considered a 'harmless right of enjoyment' that had to give way to the 'inexorable law of progress'. From the late 1960s, however, this attitude also started to change, due in part to the results of two cases in 1968, the Brekken case and the Altevann case, judged by the Norwegian Supreme Court. Both court judgments were trailblazers for a new attitude towards Sami reindeer herders' rights to use the *utmark*.

Norwegian courts, in the wake of these two Supreme Court cases, began to adopt the view that Sami reindeer herders could establish rights of use in the *utmark* on the basis of use from time immemorial. However, Sami reindeer herders in the southernmost parts of Southern Sami territory within the Norwegian borders still found it difficult to achieve recognition of their long-standing use of land as the basis for an official, legal right of use. The main reason for gap in rights was a theory, advanced in 1889, that Sami reindeer herders had established a presence in that southern region only after farmers had started to use the land as summer pasture for farm animals. This theory was quick to take hold in Norway, both in official reports and in court practices. Despite subsequent research that uncovered a different view of Sami history in the area contested, this same theory continued to influence the Norwegian courts' approach towards the rights of Sami reindeer herders in the area up until recently. However, in the Norwegian Supreme Court Selbu case, decided in 2001, the court held that the Sami had, in fact, been present in the area since further back in time than had been previously established.[42]

---

42   In the years following the Selbu case, archaeologists have discovered evidence of Sami presence in the mountain areas of southern Norway from at least 1,000 years ago. See Jostein Bergstøl and Gaute Reitan, 'Samer på Dovrefjell i vikingtiden - et bidrag til debatten omkring samenes sørgrense i forhistorisk tid' (2008) 1 Historisk Tidsskrift [Norwegian Journal of Historical Studie] 9–27.

Chapter 8

The Swedish State's Legacy of Sami Rights Codified in 1886

Johan Strömgren

Introduction

Sami Rights to Ownership or Use

The current law regulating reindeer herding and Sami land rights in Sweden is the Reindeer Herding Act of 1971 (amended 1993). The main principles of this law were established in the first Reindeer Herding Act of 1886, which was amended in 1898 and then replaced by a new act in 1928. The Reindeer Herding Act of 1928 was in force until the present Reindeer Herding Act of 1971. In 1993, the 1971 Act was adjusted to express clearly that the rights of the Sami People are based upon immemorial prescriptive rights. These rights are deemed as exhaustively regulated by the Act as usufruct rights to reindeer herding lands, hunting, fishing and the use of wood for Sami needs. No other Sami rights to land or natural resources currently exist in Swedish state law, due to the fact that the rights to ownership of land and natural resources belong to someone other than the Sami. The current Reindeer Herding Act also regulates who amongst the Sami People can access and utilize Sami rights.

The 1993 Amendment of the Reindeer Herding Act was a consequence of the famous Taxed Mountains Case of 1981, tried in the Supreme Court of Sweden. The case consisted of Sami plaintiffs in one party and the state defendant in another, and regarded primarily full rights to ownership of non-privatized mountain areas in the county of Jämtland.[1] The ownership of the disputed land was deemed by the Supreme Court to belong to the state. However, the judgment came to verify that the right to reindeer herding is a usufruct right based upon immemorial prescription and belonging to the Sami People, as first codified in the Reindeer Herding Act of 1886. Since its creation in 1886, the Reindeer Herding Act has regulated Sami land

---

1   NJA 1981 p 1. This case seen as the most extensive of all cases in the history of the Swedish courts; it began in the District Court in 1966 and ended with the decision of the Swedish Supreme Court in 1981. The official referendum of the case is a hefty 251 pages and covers the development of the legal rights to the disputed areas from time immemorial to 1981. For an English review of the case see Bertil Bengtsson, in B Jahreskog (ed), *The Sami National Minority in Sweden* (Almqvist & Wiksell International 1982) 143–250.

rights in lieu of any other sources of potentially applicable law, such as customary law. The act refers to and intertwines with Sami customary rights in significant aspects; however, it only does so in ways described by and as an extension of the act itself. Since the Taxed Mountains Case, this legal interpretation, based on ideas of codification and exhaustive regulation through the Reindeer Herding Act, has served as a firm basis for policy regarding Sami land rights in Sweden.[2]

The accuracy of this construction of Sami land rights has been indirectly questioned in research[3] and Public Commission Reports[4] through discussions concerning how to understand the strength, origin and nature of reindeer herding rights and the possible existence of other Sami rights. Such other rights considered include Sami ownership of land and usufruct rights for other groups or persons not entitled to Sami rights in the scope of the Reindeer Herding Act.[5]

The purpose of this chapter is to describe the main components of this legal construction of the state's right to ownership of land in the Sami traditional living areas and the Sami usufruct rights to the same areas, and to discuss some significant problems therein. This is done by looking at the primary lines of reasoning in the Taxed Mountains Case of the Swedish Supreme Court, and its limitations, alongside research on Sami historical land rights to so-called Sami taxed lands, *lappskatteland*[6] and the emphasis on previous legal codification

---

2   See the various commission reports, eg SOU 1989:41 *Samerätt och sameting*; SOU 1999:25 *Samerna – ett ursprungsfolk i Sverige*; SOU 2001:101 *En ny rennäringspolitik*; SOU 2005:17 *Vem får jaga och fiska? Rätt till jakt och fiske i lappmarkerna och på renbetesfjällen*; SOU 2005:79 *Vem får jaga och fiska? Historia, folkrätt och miljö*; SOU 2005:116 *Jakt och fiske i samverkan*, SOU 2006:14 *Samernas sedvanemarker*.

3   Kajsa Korpijaakko-Labba, *Om samernas rättsliga ställning i Sverige-Finland* (Helsingfors 1994); Bertil Bengtsson, *Samerätt – En översikt* (Norstedts Juridik 2004); Christina Allard, 'Two Sides of the Coin: Rights and Duties – The Interface between Environmental Law and Saami Law Based on a Comparison with Aoteoaroa/New Zealand and Canada' (Doctoral dissertation, Luleå University of Technology, 2006) 297–99; Nils Johan Päiviö, 'Från skattemannarätt till nyttjanderätt – En rättshistorisk studie av utvecklingen av samernas rättigheter från slutet av 1500-talet till 1886 års renbeteslag' (Doctoral dissertation, Uppsala University, 2011).

4   SOU 2001:101 (n 2) 172–73 and 264 regarding some aspects within the right to reindeer herding; SOU 2005:17 (n 2) regarding the relationship between reindeer herders' and the landowners' rights to hunt and fish, SOU 2006:14 (n 2) on how to decide far eastward and southward the rights to winter herding lands can be applied.

5   Bengtsson (n 3) 18–24, 40–43; Allard (n 3) 257–64, and for a more thorough discussion on customary rights and immemorial prescription see ibid 264–97.

6   Sami persons and families in Lapland had paid taxes for their lands, *lappskatteland*, which had boundaries and were protected legally in Swedish courts. The lands were also sold, bought and inherited by the Sami. A Sami village, a *sameby*, is a larger entity; in old days a Sami village could encompass several Sami taxed lands. The system Sami taxed lands ceased to exist in the nineteenth century, however in some parts of Lapland the Sami taxed lands existed as late as 1928. cf Korpijaakko-Labba (n 3) and Päiviö (n 3). Sami taxed

within the official Sami policies after the Taxed mountain case. I will then further the discussion by analysing the use of immemorial prescriptive rights and discussions regarding Sami taxed lands in the context of the Reindeer Herding Act of 1886.

Due to the complex nature of the theme, in this chapter I will not go further into other important perspectives regarding the codifying process. Topics such as the development of law and society over time, legal theoretical approaches, problems concerning the legal subjects (the Sami People, Sami villages or *sameby*, groups and individuals) and possible comparisons will remain for a later date.

Some Basic Facts

When discussing Sami land rights, we must bear in mind some basic facts. The north-west part of the Swedish territory occupies a portion of the Sami People's traditional territory. These lands are traditionally used by the Sami for reindeer herding, small farming, hunting, fishing, gathering and other related activities. Reindeer herding is normally carried out in the autumn by moving the herds from summer grazing areas, which are in the Scandinavian mountain range, to winter grazing areas, which are in the forest lands to the east. These winter herding areas often stretch as far as the Gulf of Bothnia. The land in the Scandinavian mountain range of the north-west area is most commonly owned by the state, and the land in the forest area east of the mountain range is usually owned by either the state or by private parties. The forest lands nearer to the coastline of the Gulf of Bothnia are most often privately owned. This land ownership pattern is a result of the land allocation processes, *avvittringarna*, of the state of Sweden that took place in the eighteenth and nineteenth centuries. The colonization pattern went from the coastline of the Gulf of Bothnia westwards, toward the Scandinavian mountain range. The common view on Sami land rights is that they are stronger in the primary living and herding areas, which are considered to be within the mountain range and the adjoining forests (versus nearer to the coastline). Another common view is that Sami rights within some of the primary living and herding areas might, for historical reasons, also be stronger in Lapland (in the north) than in Jämtland (in the South).[7]

---

lands have also existed in the county of Jämtland; however those lands were not organized into Sami villages before 1886 and, according to the Taxed mountain case, seem to have been of a different kind than the Sami taxed lands in Lapland.

7   For more thorough information see for example Bengtsson (n 3) 39–44 and Allard (n 3) 326–40, especially 336–40.

The Taxed Mountains Case and the Understanding of Codified Sami Rights in 1886

The Starting Points of the Legal Discussions

The contemporary understanding of codification of Sami land rights in the 1886 Reindeer Herding Act was formulated when, in the 1960s, the parties to the Taxed Mountains Case elaborated their arguments.[8] The main foundation for the discussions regarding the questions of ownership and the meaning of the Reindeer Herding Act of 1886 can be found in the parties' expert legal witnesses.[9]

In 1966 the expert witness for the Sami parties, Gunnar Prawitz, LLD, made a lengthy descriptive explanation of Sami history. Prawitz's analysis was that the Sami parties' rights were private rights, resulting from long-term land use and not Swedish state law,[10] and that the Sami had always considered themselves to be owners of their lands.[11] The view by the state party was based upon a report from their expert witness, the law professor Svante Bergström. His main arguments were that the starting point of the Reindeer Herding Act of 1886 and the 'common view of that time' were both that the state owned the land and that Sami rights were usufruct rights to those lands. The Swedish government and Swedish Parliament had developed the Reindeer Herding Act of 1886 maintaining the law with the understanding of Sami land use as based upon usufruct rights. After the legislation had come into force, it was solely this legislation and no other source of law that regulated the rights in question.[12]

The Supreme Court of Sweden on the Right of Ownership

In the 1981 Taxed Mountains judgment, the Supreme Court of Sweden determined that it was of fundamental importance to clarify the pre-1886 Sami rights to the disputed areas in the county of Jämtland. The Supreme Court found that pre-1789 the Sami using the land in question had not owned these lands through the rights

---

8   For an English review of the Case see Bengtsson (n 1) 143–250. This was in a time (the 1960s) when Sami rights to use land for reindeer herding were widely seen as a privilege, as something granted by the state, and not necessarily as a right as such. Sami claims for rights to ownership of land were by many regarded as highly controversial.

9   There were many expert witnesses throughout the duration of the trial, however only two of these experts who testified significantly addressed how to interpret the act of 1886, see further Bengtsson (n 1) 144.

10   Gunnar Prawitz, *Om samernas rättigheter* 132, 148–50, in Samisk arkiv (The Sami Archives is a part of the National Archives Serices of Norway), Samisk rettsarkiv, Kautokeino, PA-1037 J-003. See also NJA 1981 p 1, 102–08.

11   NJA 1981 p 1, 152, 157–58.

12   Svante Bergström, *Om rätten till renbetesfjällen* 19–24, 65–72, in Samisk arkiv (See n 10), Samisk rettsarkiv, Kautokeino, PA-1037 J-003. See also NJA 1981 p 1, 88–102, especially at 97, 101.

of a taxed man, *skattemannarätt*, meaning rights equal to those of farmers.[13] The Supreme Court found that Sami rights to the taxed mountains areas pre-1789 had existed as strongly protected usufruct rights of a special kind. Post-1789, the taxed man's rights held by the farmers began to evolve into the rights of ownership that we know today in Sweden.[14] At the same time, after 1789 the rights of the Sami continued to evolve as usufruct rights, which was acknowledged by the Swedish authorities via inter alia official decisions of the Swedish King and County Governors concerning Sami use of the taxed mountain areas.[15]

The Swedish Supreme Court held in the Taxed Mountains Case that the Crown had owned the disputed lands before 1886 up until the present day.[16] This interpretation was based mainly upon a declaration from 1683 regarding the forest land, *1683 års skogsordning*. The court deemed that the starting point for the public administration of the land, as could be seen in official documents, was that all land not demonstrably owned by someone else was thusly owned by the Crown. This was viewed as an established authoritative position and starting point in 1886 according to the Supreme Court. The Sami parties to the Taxed Mountains Case had argued that the opinions of state officials could not be taken as evidence in a claim to Sami land rights. The court agreed that one had to show precaution when using this kind of evidence in a case such as the Taxed Mountains Case, but that the case law referenced had been stable, consistent and based upon reasonable legal arguments and not any abuse of power. Colonialism and racist ideologies existed at the era encompassing 1886; however, according to the Swedish Supreme Court those ideologies had not influenced reindeer herding legislation as such.[17] At the same time, the court clarified that the question of land ownership at hand regarded only the disputed taxed mountains in Jämtland and not the legal position regarding other areas.[18]

---

13 However, the Supreme Court declared that it, at least during the seventeenth century, was possible also for nomads or semi-nomads to acquire rights of a taxed man (an old form of ownership), see Bengtsson (n 1) 249 and Allard (n 3) 261. cf Korpijaakko-Labba (n 3).

14 In 1789, by support of the large peasant class, the Swedish King Gustav III made a radical change in the Swedish Constitution, securing for himself absolutism. In return, the peasants received the possibility to own their earlier taxed lands with a right similar to contemporary ownership rights. cf G Inger, *Svensk rättshistoria*, upplaga 4:1 (Liber Ekonomi 1997) 126–27; M Bäärnhielm, *Sameland och samerätt. Ett aktuellt minoritetsproblem i rättshistorisk belysning*, in KÅ Modéer (ed), *Rättshistoriska studier tillägnade Gösta Hasselberg vid hans avgång från ämbetet 30 juni 1976*, Rättshistoriska studier (femte bandet, Lund 1977) 59; Päiviö (n 3) 197–98.

15 NJA 1981 p 1, 211–14, 227.

16 NJA 1981 p 1, 229–30.

17 NJA 1981 p 1, 227–29.

18 NJA 1981 p 1, 227, 175.

The Understanding of the Codification of Usufruct Rights in 1886

Due to the fact that the Swedish Supreme Court found that the right to land ownership ultimately belonged to the Swedish state, the question regarding the extent of the rights within the Reindeer Herding Act had to be elaborated upon. According to the Supreme Court, the foundation for the Reindeer Herding Act of 1886 was based on the fact that all authorities of the Swedish state had deemed land to be owned by the state, and that Sami land rights were in the form of usufruct rights. The alternative view in 1886 was seen by the court to have been that the Sami did not have any rights at all.[19] In the Reindeer Herding Act of 1886, the Swedish government and the Swedish Parliament actually aimed to protect Sami rights to winter herding lands.[20] According to the Swedish Supreme Court, the main question in formulating the 1886 Reindeer Herding Act was issue of the Sami rights to winter herding lands on private property in forest areas. The court stated that the Swedish government and Swedish Parliament, when formulating the act, had determined that Sami usufruct rights to reindeer herding on these lands were legally justified by customary law and immemorial prescriptive rights. The court further held that this must also have implied that more extensive Sami rights to the mountain area had at least an equal status and protection under Swedish law.[21] However, the Supreme Court made these remarks only briefly and without further elaboration.

It was clear that preparatory works for the formulation of the Reindeer Herding Act of 1886 were built on scanty evidence that did not include thorough investigations of historical land use and Sami rights in the mountain areas. However, this did not mean that the concepts surrounding the question of ownership could be left without regard. That the Swedish government and Swedish Parliament at that time only in brief terms had touched upon the question of the rights to the mountain areas could probably be explained by the fact that the common view at the time concerning ownership of land in the North of Sweden was that it was state-owned.[22] The court could not find evidence that these views had been influenced by ideals of Social Darwinism or market-based capitalist interests, although it was obvious that big economic interests were at stake.[23] The court also discussed the fact that almost all Sami persons who had expressed opinions regarding the Draft Act in 1885 had agreed with the proposed law in the Draft. These facts in turn supported the Supreme Court's judgment that the 1886 Act was a formulation of applicable law.[24]

---

19 NJA 1981 p 1, 225.
20 NJA 1981 p 1, 229.
21 NJA 1981 p 1, 225–26.
22 NJA 1981 p 1, 226.
23 NJA 1981 p 1, 226–27.
24 NJA 1981 p 1, 228.

The Sami rights codified were primarily the right to reindeer herding lands, but also the rights to gather wood, hunt, fish and other land uses typical for Sami needs to live off of the land as reindeer herders. It was determined by the Swedish Supreme Court that the Reindeer Herding Act of 1886 was built upon, and in turn carried forward, the same kinds of rights previously applied and also found in various legal sources. This continuation was interpreted as being due to the fact that such practices were the main methods of land use and rights that the Sami had carried out since before the Reindeer Herding Act of 1886.[25] Thus, the Supreme Court decided that these prior rights had been codified into the Act of 1886.[26] Moreover, after those pre-1886 rights had been codified into the act, they were determined to be exhaustively regulated by the act itself.[27]

Nevertheless, the Swedish Supreme Court held that the 1886 Act was, in one regard, a change from earlier rights. The change pertained to the grouping of taxed lands into larger Sami villages, or *samebyar*. This meant that the taxed lands ceased to exist, and that the rights of the Sami were carried over and to be used within the framework of the new village, the *sameby*.[28] It was also unclear and uncertain if a section of the 1886 Act that prohibited Sami from deeding their own rights to hunting, fishing and gave a corresponding right for the Swedish County Administration was actually legally valid. However, the Supreme Court held that the prohibition did not conflict with the Constitution.[29]

The Geographical Limitations of the Taxed Mountains Case

A key facet of the Taxed Mountains Case is its limitations. The most obvious, often referred to, limitation is the fact that the discussions by the Swedish Supreme Court only regarded the land areas concerned, i.e. the taxed mountain areas in the county of Jämtland. This limitation means at least two things. First, that the arguments presented by the Sami party regarding Sami areas north of Jämtland, i.e. Lapland at the time, were not discussed. This is significant, due to the fact that Jämtland and Lapland have different histories. Jämtland was a part of Norway until 1645 and was, before 1886, subject to different regulations concerning Sami matters. The legal situation in Lapland, however, seems to have been clearer than in Jämtland. Secondly, the Taxed Mountains Case regarded only land presumed to be owned by the state; no private landowner was involved in the trial. This meant, as we will discuss below, that the main regulations in the Reindeer Herding Act of 1886, which addressed the rights of reindeer herders and private landowners, were never thoroughly reviewed in the Taxed Mountains Case.

---

25   NJA 1981 p 1, 233–38.
26   NJA 1981 p 1, 243.
27   NJA 1981 p 1, 244.
28   NJA 1981 p 1, 243.
29   NJA 1981 p 1, 236–37, 243–44.

Official Sami Policy and Emphasis on Previous Legal Codification

The Taxed Mountains Case led to a public inquiry on the legal status of the Sami in Sweden by the Sami Rights Commission, *Samerättsutredningen*, which interpreted its purpose to be to strengthen the position of reindeer herders within current applicable law, not to examine if the Sami People could have had rights historically beyond the law deemed applicable (the Reindeer Herding Act).[30] This work culminated in amendments in 1993 to the present Reindeer Herding Act, which, as mentioned in the introduction of this chapter, says that the rights of the Sami People are based upon ancient prescriptive rights exhaustively regulated by the act as usufruct rights.

This interpretation of the Swedish Supreme Court was later challenged by a thorough legal historical analysis by Kajsa Korpijaakko-Labba in 1989. The subject of Korpijaakko-Labba's Doctoral Thesis was the history of land rights in some parts of Lapland until the 1750s. With convincing evidence and arguments she showed that at that time the Sami taxed lands, *lappskatteland*, in Lapland, which is north of Jämtland and not included in the Taxed Mountains Case, contained Sami rights equal to a right of property ownership. The information she provided included that Sami persons in Lapland had paid taxes for their lands, the lands had boundaries and were protected legally in Swedish courts, and that the lands were also sold, bought and inherited by the Sami.[31] Her studies were based on methodology, evidence and criteria other than what had been used in the Taxed Mountains Case. As a result, she came to a different conclusion than the Swedish Supreme Court regarding one of the key questions in the interpretation of the historical rights to ownership of land in the Sami areas. Following this, law professor and former Judge in the Taxed Mountains Case, Bengtsson, wrote in 1990 that the Sami could be perceived to have a stronger position for their rights in Lapland than in Jämtland. The problem in Lapland was that the 1683 *Skogsordning*, a primary determining factor in the Taxed Mountains Case, was applicable only to land without an owner. Consequently, if Sami groups or individuals could have been seen as land owners until the 1750s, then the Crown would have to show how the right of ownership passed from the Sami to the Crown before 1886.[32]

When making the 1993 amendments to the Reindeer Herding Act, the Swedish government paid no genuine heed to the research of Korpijaakko-Labba. The Swedish government interpreted the grounds of the judgment in the Taxed Mountains Case as valid for the whole of the Sami territory of Sápmi on the Swedish side of the state's borders. However, the Swedish Law Council, which is tasked in the Swedish Constitution to pre-view legislative proposals, said in

---

30   SOU 1989:41 (n 2) 258–60.

31   Korpijaakko-Labba (n 3) 464–68. cf Päiviö (n 3). The old form of Sami taxed lands and the Sami villages in Lapland pre-19th century does not seem to have been created by the Swedish Crown, but existed pre-colonization.

32   B Bengtsson, *Samernas rätt i ny belysning* (SvJT nr 1990) 138–42.

its analysis that already a cautious interpretation of the Taxed Mountains Case contradicted the Swedish government's interpretation. This was due to the fact that the Swedish Supreme Court had left unanswered the question as to whether or not the Reindeer Herding Act of 1886 was actually a codification of Sami land rights in parts of Sweden other than the areas of the taxed mountains.[33]

The Swedish government did not follow up on these remarks of the Swedish Law Council; instead, it determined that adjusting the wording in some sections of the law, based on what was deemed official available knowledge at that time, was most appropriate. This knowledge was based on the Taxed Mountains Case: if the view regarding the justification of Sami land rights was to change in the future, then the law itself could also be changed.[34] This seems to have been the official position of the Swedish government and the Swedish Parliament ever since. From 1993 onward the Swedish government has made several Commission Reports on various themes concerning reindeer herding and Sami land rights. All of these Commissions have been more or less explicitly instructed to look upon questions regarding Sami rights within the current Reindeer Herding Act of 1971, with amendments from 1993.[35]

Some Aspects of the Legal Codification in 1886

Introduction

I aim in this section of the chapter to explain the use of immemorial prescriptive rights and the discussions regarding Sami taxed lands, *lappskatteland*, in the context of the Reindeer Herding Act of 1886. This analysis was not performed in the Taxed Mountains Case, and, as a result, there is no direct insight available into discussions on customary rights and immemorial prescriptive rights when the 1886 Act was made. I will first discuss the application of immemorial prescription and how it was used to explain why Sami rights to reindeer herding during the winter time still existed on land that had been recently allocated to settled farmers. Following that I will examine an important discussion on the nature of 'original' Sami land-use and the Sami-taxed lands in the mountain areas and adjoining forests. Then an analysis will be made as to how and why the sustainability of such a discussion can be questioned, in light of the research of Korpijaakko-Labba.

---

33 Lagrådets utlåtande (Statement of the Law Council) 1990-06-18, in Prop 1992/92:32, 299–304.

34 Regeringens protokoll (Protocol from the government) in Prop 1992/93/32, 90, cf the statement of the Law Council at 300.

35 SOU 1999:25 (n 2) 271–75; SOU 2001:101 (n 2) 555–62; SOU 2005:17 (n 2) 11–12, 179–81; SOU 2006:14 (n 2) 543–50 (cf also at 15–16).

The Main Legislative Process and its Starting Points

The main legislative process was, essentially, that the Swedish government appointed a Royal Committee to perform the related work in 1882. A year later, in August 1883, the Committee produced a report along with a draft law, entitled *On the regulation of the relationship between the Sami and the settled farmers*. This title also reflected the Committee's commission and starting points.³⁶ The draft law was subjected to strong opposition and intense discussions in the hearings prior to the government Bill,³⁷ and in the Parliament's Special Committee Report,³⁸ as well as in debates within the Swedish Parliament's two chambers.³⁹ Nevertheless, the draft law, its structure and its arguments remained relatively unchanged throughout the process of creating the government Bill and the passing of the Bill in the Swedish Parliament in 1886. The name of the law would, however, be changed by the Swedish government from the above-mentioned title proposed by the 1882 Committee to the Reindeer Herding Act.⁴⁰

In the context of the Reindeer Herding Act, creating a new law regulating land-based relations between settled farmers and Sami reindeer herding also caused a need to codify Sami customary rights and previously dispersed regulations of regional rights applications.⁴¹

---

36   Förslag till förordning angående de svenska lapparne och de bofaste i Sverige samt till förordning angående renmärken, afgifna af den dertill utaf Kongl. Maj:t förordnade komité, Stockholm 1883 (hereafter cited as RCR 1883, ie Royal Commission Report 1883) 1, 3–5, 21, 80–81 and 64–66 regarding the Counties of Norrbotten and Västerbotten, and at 66–71 regarding the county of Jämtland (cf the references in n 42). Starting points for the Reindeer Herding Act 1886 are also briefly discussed, but not further elaborated, by Päiviö NJ (n 3) chapter 10, and by Eivind Torp, 'Renskötselrätten och rätten till naturresurserna. Om rättslig reglering av mark- och resursanvändingen på renbetesmarken i Sverige' (Doctoral dissertation, Tromso University, 2008) 47 et seq.

37   Kongl. Maj:ts nådiga proposition 1886:2 till Riksdagen, med förslag till lag angående de svenska Lapparnes rätt till renbete i Sverige och till lag angående renmärken (herafter cited as Prop. 1886:2).

38   Särskilda utskottets utlåtande 1886:1 (hereafter Special Committee Report, SCR 1886:1).

39   Riksdagens protokoll 1886, första kammaren, nr 17, 17 April (hereafter Parliament Protocol 1886, first chamber 17 April). Riksdagens protokoll 1886, andra kammaren, nr 41, 17 April (hereafter Parliament Protocol 1886, second chamber). Between 1866 and 1971, the Swedish Parliament had two chambers, hence the two Parliament protocols from the same day.

40   Prop 1886:2 (n 37) 1. There was also a need to harmonize the Swedish state law with the recently adopted 1883 Act between Sweden and Norway, *den gemensamma lapplagen*, relating to herding reindeer across the mutually held state border, see RCR 1883 (n 36), 78–79. This will not, however, be further elaborated upon in this article.

41   Prop 1886:2 (n 37) 33–34. See also Parliament Protocol 1886, first chamber (n 39) 9–10. These regulations were Royal Letters concerning liability when herding reindeer, allocation of land, an old administrative regulation (*lappfogdeinstruktionen*) from 1760,

Immemorial Prescription as Justification of Sami Reindeer Herding Rights on Privatized Land

It is, of course, important to understand the circumstances surrounding the use of a certain legal rule or discussion to understand its comprehensive meaning. When crafting the 1886 Reindeer Herding Act, the primary need to regulate the relationship between settled farmers and reindeer herders was a result of deep conflicts between private landowners and reindeer herders in the specific parish, or Swedish administrative division, of Härjedalen in Jämtland.[42] The severe conflict in Härjedalen had its roots in the Crown's allocation and privatization of large areas of land to farmers and other predominantly Swedish businesses through land allocation processes – the *avvittringarna* in Jämtland from the 1820s through the 1840s. Out of the Jämtland area of 4,924,000 acres, only 80,000 acres in the mountain area remained non-privatized after the Crown's land allocations were completed. This meant that all of the winter grazing lands in Jämtland necessary for reindeer herding had been privatized and belonged to predominantly Swedish homesteads, and that the remaining areas in the mountain range, the summer herding lands, were allocated by the Crown as lands for the Sami herders.[43]

The privatized lands had been used by Sami families as reindeer herding lands during the wintertime when Sami families, due to harsh weather conditions, moved with their herds from the mountains to the forests in the lowland. However, the land allocations had taken place without first acknowledging and reserving the rights of the Sami who were to be affected. The private landowners received their land allotments without any statutory obligation to accept reindeer herding on their lands, despite the reindeer herders needing their access to these lands to survive. Therefore, the main legal question regarding the Reindeer Herding Act of 1886 became whether the Sami rights to reindeer herding during the winter on private land areas had continued to exist post-privatization.[44]

---

and the 1873 law on allocation of land in Lapland (1873 års avvittringsstadga). None of the Letters contained deeper discussions of the justification of Sami land rights as there were determined.

42   RCR 1883 (n 36) 66–71, Prop 1886:2 (n 37) 33–36. Prop 1886:2 the Supreme Court Opinion (an appendix in the proposition 1886:2) 2–11. The task of the Swedish Supreme Court was, according to the Swedish Constitution, to provide interpretation of new legislation. In 1909 this task was replaced by the Law Council's role of previewing new legislation. SCR 1886:1 (n 38) 23, (cf the opposition against the Reindeer Herding Act of 1886 led by the County Governor in Jämtland); Parliament Protocol 1886, first chamber (n 39) 6–8.

43   Lars Rumar, in L Lundmark and L Rumar, *Mark och rätt i Sameland* (Rättshistoriska skrifter 10, 2008) 169 et seq. In the northern part of Jämtland and in Lapland, the relations were seen as relatively positive.

44   RCR 1883 (n 36) 64–71. Parliament Protocol 1886, first chamber (n 39) 6–8, Parliament Protocol 1886, second chamber (n 39) 3–7.

This question regarding private lands and herding rights started a complex debate. The Swedish Minister of Justice, Nils Vult von Steyern, and the Governor of the County of Norrbotten, Henrik A Widmark, argued in favour of existing winter-herding-area Sami land rights, while the newly appointed County Governor of Jämtland, John Ericsson, and the Justice of the Supreme Court of Sweden, Knut Olivecrona, argued against such rights. The main argument of the Minister of Justice and others in agreement with him, consistent with the opinion of the Sami concerned, was that the Sami, through customary land use and immemorial prescriptive rights, had obtained a real property right to use these lands. In this view, the existence of these rights was to be acknowledged in the act and given the same legal protection as a right of ownership. This did not mean that the landowners' rights to ownership ceased to exist. Rather, it meant that the rights of the Sami and of the landowners existed simultaneously on the same land and with the same legal protection.[45] The main argument against Sami land rights to winter herding areas was that there was no statutory obligation of the landowners to accept these rights since these lands had been privatized without mention of reindeer herding rights. Hence, the customary land use of winter herding areas could not be held as a right as such, despite the fact that it had been carried out for many years without meeting objections from other land users.[46]

The resulting Swedish government Bill, along with the opinion of the Swedish Minister of Justice and the positions of the Justices of the Swedish Supreme Court, went to the Swedish Parliament for decision. A Special Committee prepared the Bill before it was debated and decided upon by the Swedish Parliament. The majority within the Special Committee expressed in the Committee Report that the Sami by long-standing, customary land use, and immemorial prescriptive rights, had obtained a real property right to winter herding lands. This property right was deemed comparable to the nature of an easement; it was expressed that the Crown could not have given through the colonial processes more exclusive rights to land to farmers than those rights that the Crown had owned itself. Hence, the Sami rights to reindeer herding on private lands still existed, despite the private land allocations.[47] These rights, written into the 1886 Reindeer Herding Act, were debated and approved by the Swedish Parliament.

In the Taxed Mountains Case, the Supreme Court of Sweden applied the very same legal justification to the mountain areas that had not been privatized and were at stake in the case. As the court determined in the Taxed Mountains Case, since the right to reindeer herding was legally justified in the winter grazing lands before, the more extensive Sami rights to the mountain areas in question must have had at least the same value and protection by law (as discussed earlier in this

---

45   Prop 1886:2 (n 37) 34–35.
46   Prop 1886:2, the Supreme Court Opinion, (n 42) 2–3.
47   SCR 1886:1 (n 38) 16–18, cf the Minister of Justice in Parliament Protocol 1886, first chamber (n 39) 15–16. See also Päiviö NJ (n 3) 224–227.

chapter).[48] This logic is reasonable, given immemorial prescription and customary rights are the only outright legal justifications of historical Sami land rights within the preparatory works to the Reindeer Herding Act of 1886. The question is, however, if this is the best way to explain and legally justify Sami rights in parts of Lapland also.

On the Rights to the Mountain Range and Adjoining Woods

Sami land rights to primary Sami living areas in the mountain range and adjoining forests, where there were only few settlements and hence few to almost no conflicts between farmers and reindeer herders, were not seen as a direct part of the assignment for the 1882 Royal Committee. Rather, these areas were treated as an exception to its commission on the Sami People and their relation to settled farmers.[49] However, Sami land use in these areas and the relationship between the Crown and the Sami People, as well as Sami internal affairs and the Sami taxed lands, were discussed by the 1882 Committee. This was done within the scope of certain sections of the draft law text concerning the public administration of Sami affairs.[50] The Committee was motivated to create this exception due to its position that stable Sami internal affairs would presumably have a positive effect on the reindeer herders' relations with the farmers.[51] The Committee seems also to have been motivated by a desire to maximize the economic utility of the land used for reindeer herding.[52]

A key component of the Committee discussion regarding administrative themes concerned the taxed lands the Sami used and lived on that existed both in Jämtland and within the Sami villages in Lapland (as far north as the three northernmost Swedish administrative parishes of Gällivare, Jukkasjärvi and Enontekis). The land use in the northernmost Sami villages was not interpreted as grouped into taxed lands used by certain persons and families, but as land collectively used within the community of the Sami villages based upon old Sami custom. The 1882 Royal Committee interpreted the taxed lands to be a new legal construction based both on written permission given by the County Governors and on Sami collective land use. Sami collective land use was deemed to be the older, original Sami land use, natural for a nomadic way of living and suitable for maximization of the utility of the lands. As a result, a return to the old order was preferable in the eyes of the Swedish authorities at the time, and they needed the power bestowed upon them by Swedish law to make decisions of governance accordingly. This

---

48 See also NJA 1981 p 1, 225–26.

49 RCR 1883 (n 36) 80.

50 RCR 1883 (n 36) 7–8, 71–74, 87–89. The discussions concerned the themes of how to arrange Sami living areas into Sami villages, to deed rights to inter alia hunting and fishing and the displacement of reindeer herders.

51 RCR 1883 (n 36) 80.

52 RCR 1883 (n 36) 73.

interpretation of land use and history was only discussed in short terms, with few and somewhat unclear references, however it motivated new articles of law on administrative authority in the Reindeer Herding Act 1886.[53]

The common land use and nomad descriptions were also a part of the legitimating of regulations concerning the reindeer herders' common liability for damages on farmers' hay.[54] Regulations concerning liability can be seen as central to the main purpose of the 1886 Act.

Interestingly, the foundation for this part of the discussion in the 1883 Royal Committee Report was contradicted by the research of Korpijaakko-Labba in 1989. Korpijaakko-Labba did not argue against the Committee's preparatory works, but she did show that the taxed lands that the Sami used and lived on in Enontekis and adjoining parts of Lapland, which were the very same areas that the Committee referred to as the older, original collective land use areas, had until 1750 been individualized and possessed by Sami persons with the rights of a taxed man contributing to the Sami village payment of taxes to the Crown. Hence, this discussion within the 1883 Committee Report seems insufficiently supported.

Later in the Special Committee Report, Sami rights to taxed lands were mentioned as strong, but only to the degree that was necessary for Sami to continue living as nomads, and not as equal to rights of land ownership; the right of land ownership was deemed to ultimately belong to the Crown.[55] This was mentioned only very briefly and so as to justify the Crown, not the Sami, as having the right to sell permits to use the land that was allocated to Sami land use.

Reflections on the Understanding of Codification

In this last part of this chapter we will discuss various problematic aspects of the above-mentioned components of the legal construction of the states right to ownership and the Sami usufruct rights, to the same areas. We will first briefly emphasize some significant contingencies regarding the right to ownership, and then reflect on various aspects of the meaning of the Reindeer Herding Act of 1886 and the understanding of codification and exhaustive regulation of Sami land rights.

The Taxed Mountains Case defines arguments as to why the state has the ownership rights, and the Sami usufruct rights therein, to the land areas at stake in the case. Through the amendments of Reindeer Herding Act in 1993 these arguments have been given a determining effect also on Sami land areas in Lapland. Two important arguments regarding the question of ownership were that the starting point of public administration of land was that the state owned the land, and that the forest regulation of 1683 was applicable to the case. However, it

---

53   RCR 1883 (n 36) 71–74, 87–89, see also 25–35.

54   RCR 1883 (n 36) 76, 90–97.

55   SCR 1886:1 (n 38) 31.

seems inadequate to assume without further investigation that the Swedish public administration of land in Lapland was as strict and consistent as in Jämtland. Meaning, while the differences between Jämtland and Lapland were perhaps not that significant, the extent of the differences cannot be taken for granted. Furthermore, and as discussed first and foremost by Bengtsson (see above), the research of Korpijaakko-Labba raises the important question as to whether the forest regulations of 1683 are applicable in the northernmost region of Sweden. This key question has yet to be answered.

The work by Korpijaakko-Labba also gives new perspectives on important aspects of the preparatory works of the Reindeer Herding Act of 1886, especially in regards to the 1882 Committee's brief discussions concerning the Sami taxed lands. As the Supreme Court stated in the Taxed Mountains Case, the preparatory works of the 1886 Act did not include thorough investigation of historical land use and Sami rights in the mountain areas. The research of Korpijaakko-Labba gives reason to take the Swedish Supreme Court's indirect criticism one step further, by also questioning how sufficient the foundation for the 1882 Committee's discussions in this aspect really was. Furthermore, the primary reason for the 1882 Committee to have been discussing the Sami taxed lands does not necessarily seem to have been to codify legal standards at that time; rather, motivation seems to have been that of the granting of powers to sectors of Swedish administration within the scope of the Reindeer Herding Act.

When interpreting the Reindeer Herding Act of 1886, one must bear in mind that its aim was primarily the relationship between reindeer herders and settled farmers, not the legal position of the Sami in their primary living areas. The act of 1886 can be seen as having been a tool created by the state to regulate and balance the interests between the already-existing Sami reindeer herding and the expanding Swedish farming society in the north – a legal solution to a new legal question that had arisen in a society during change.

The problem at hand today is that the discussions regarding the nature of Sami land rights, customary rights and immemorial prescription in 1886 had taken place to answer a very specific legal question that by nature presumed one land owner and one land user. Problematic then is the fact that in 1981 the Swedish Supreme Court applied the legal justification of the 1886 Act when analysing the situation of the taxed mountain areas in Jämtland. Additionally problematic is that the same legal justification was again maintained in 1993 as applicable to all Sami areas throughout the Swedish state, even within northernmost Lapland, through the 1993 amended Reindeer Herding Act. This means that historical land rights in Lapland are still rather unclear, and that Sami rights in these areas can be regarded as currently being held at a minimum standard.

The main problem when understanding the Reindeer Herding Act of 1886 is perhaps not that it can be seen as a codification of Sami rights, because it did codify Sami rights to reindeer herding in the winter grazing areas. The main problem seems to be that interpretations of the 1886 Act also created an understanding that this codification *exhaustively* regulated Sami rights, while the rights to the primary

Sami living areas can be interpreted as likely stronger than the Sami rights to winter herding lands. The emphasis on an exhaustive consideration implies that there cannot be any rights other than these that are either stronger or applicable to other types of land use. The understanding of an exhaustive consideration does not seem to have been discussed in the preparatory works of the 1886 Act. Furthermore, the preparatory works for the 1886 Act do not specify what was meant by the word 'codification' the few times that it was mentioned. Neither Professor Bergström nor the Swedish Supreme Court discussed the possible meanings of the word in the 1886 context other than as a codification of land rights into the 1886 Act. Can the word 'codify' have meant that the drafters truly codified every possible right? Or, could it have meant that the drafters were simply putting together various existing regulations along with winter herding rights into one legislative act, leaving other, undisputed rights and possible questions for examination at a later date?

There are many questions concerning the thought process surrounding legal codification in 1886, and, until such questions are clarified, it is perhaps best to not draw further conclusions. Placing too much emphasis on and belief in the concept that all rights were, in fact, codified and exhaustively regulated in 1886 poses a risk. This risk resides in thus being blinded to other possible explanations as to why the rights of the Sami have evolved in the ways that they have, as well as to why the Sami People at times have perspectives differing from those of the state regarding the strength and nature of those rights. Additional research will further clarify these questions.

Chapter 9

Sami Hunting and Fishing Rights in Swedish Law

Eivind Torp

Introduction

This chapter aims to clarify the position on Sami hunting and freshwater fishing rights in Swedish law. An examination will be made with regard to how these rights have been regulated in Swedish law and how the Swedish courts have subsequently applied relevant legislation. By examining how Sami hunting and fishing rights have been treated in Swedish law, I will demonstrate how the Swedish state views the matter of Sami land and water rights.

Sami hunting and fishing rights have long been a bone of contention in the relationship between the Sami people and the Swedish state for several reasons. In recent decades, hunting and fishing have become recreational activities that appeal to a growing segment of the Swedish population. For this reason, the Swedish legislature has had an interest in accommodating rising demand by increasing general state population access to hunting and fishing. A resulting conflict that garnered much media attention had followed the related statutory amendments implemented by the government in the early 1990s. According to the amendments, the Sami no longer had exclusive hunting rights on state land. The change sparked widespread protest in the Sami society,[1] and the situation ultimately prompted a decision by the National Association of Swedish Sami (SSR)[2] to sue the Swedish state for better Sami hunting rights within a limited territory of northern Sweden.[3] Moreover, there is significant lack of clarity in the Swedish state legal regulation of Sami hunting and fishing rights, which has given rise to increased tension between the Swedish state and the Sami people.[4]

However, many people contend that the real injustice in the matter of Sami hunting and fishing rights is that the rights accrue only to Sami who are members of

---

1 Sametinget, *Beslutet om småviltsjakten – En studie i myndighetsutövning* (Kiruna 1994).

2 A special interest organization for the reindeer herding industry in Sweden.

3 Gällivare district court, case T 323-309, Office of the Chancellor of Justice, ref no 3360-09-05. The complaint was filed through the Girjas Sami village; the trial is in progress.

4 cf Swedish government report SOU 2005:17.

a so-called Sami village (*sameby* in Swedish).[5] Of the approximately 20,000 Sami people in Sweden, only about 2,000 are members of one of the 51 Sami villages in Sweden.[6] Hunting and fishing rights are thus exclusive rights for only about 10 per cent of the Sami population in Sweden. In the vernacular in Sweden, Sami hunting and fishing rights refer to the rights of only a minority of Sami. The present focus is the legal foundation of this condition; that is, how Sami hunting and fishing rights have been regulated in Swedish law, and how the Swedish legislature has expressed the extent to which, if at all, these rights should be regarded as accruing to the entire Sami population.

The matter is interesting beyond the perspective of legal history. Sweden has recognized the Sami as a distinct people[7] and the Swedish government has, on several occasions, expressed a desire to ratify the ILO Convention No 169 concerning indigenous and tribal peoples in independent countries. For these reasons, it is pertinent to examine the extent to which the regulation of Sami hunting and fishing rights is consistent with the principles of international law. A secondary aim of this chapter is thus to direct attention toward the question of what hunting and fishing rights the Sami may be considered to possess, regardless of their chosen livelihood. In the following, I will begin with the legislation through which Sami hunting and fishing rights were first regulated and thereafter follow subsequent developments chronologically.

Earlier Regulation of Hunting and Fishing Rights

The Swedish Parliament passed a reindeer herding act in 1886 that comprehensively regulated Sami reindeer-herding rights in the part of northern Scandinavia that had, since the end of the middle ages, gradually become a part of the Kingdom of Sweden.[8] This act defined who had the right to herd reindeer and when, where, and how this could be pursued. The main aim of the act was to regulate legally the relationship between the livelihoods of the Swedish population of fixed abode and the (at the time) nomadic Sami population – between farmers and reindeer herders. According to Swedish lawmakers, the act entailed codifying rights that certain Sami possessed, based on the principles of occupation of lands and immemorial prescription. In the drafting history of the legislation, it was acknowledged that

---

5   Swedish government report SOU 2005:116, 316–17. A Sami village is an association of reindeer herders for the organizing of reindeer herding over a geographically defined area.

6   Swedish government report SOU 2005:116, 88. There are no official statistics on the number of Sami village members in Sweden.

7   Instrument of government (1974:152) ch 1, s 2, para 6.

8   At this time, Sami land and water rights had already been recognized in certain Swedish legal documents, but there was no comprehensive understanding of the consequences on Sami reindeer herding.

the Sami were the indigenous population of the northern territory of Sweden and that hunting and fishing were their original livelihoods, but that reindeer herding had gradually become their primary livelihood. Against this background, Sami hunting and fishing rights were appended as auxiliary rights to the reindeer-herding right.[9] Hunting and fishing rights were thus included in the 1886 Act as an element of Sami rights to use the land, and the rights were regulated in relation to the territories that Sami reindeer herders occupied at various times of the year.

Clearly, not all Sami were engaged in reindeer herding when the act of 1886 was enacted. A commentary on the act pointed out that there were various categories of Sami within the Sami community structures (for example, paupers, fisher-folk and herders), who did not own reindeer and were not involved in reindeer herding.[10] The Swedish legislature did not, however, address this fact. The restriction of hunting and fishing rights to reindeer-herding Sami may have been made with the best interests of the Sami people in mind, but perhaps it occurred without further examination of the legal basis of the rights. This may seem understandable, considering the legislature's primary aim with the law, namely, to regulate legally the relationship between two livelihoods (Sami nomadic reindeer herding and settled Swedish farming). However, such reasoning seems ill-founded in light of the legislature's determination that Sami hunting and fishing rights were based on immemorial prescription.

The act was eventually rewritten, initially so in 1898, although no significant amendments were made at that time.[11] However, a need arose in the early 1900s for a more detailed specification of Sami rights. The next legislative reform in 1928 thus entailed several changes. Several committees of inquiry in the early twentieth century had noted that a large segment of the Sami population was not engaged in reindeer herding. The Lapp Committee of 1919, for instance, had reported statistics on the Sami population that indicated that two-thirds of the Sami population within Sweden was not involved in reindeer herding. On that basis, it was considered important that the so-called 'Lapp privilege' – the Sami reindeer-herding right – not apply to anyone other than those who needed it. The primary aim of the act was thus to introduce restrictions regarding Sami reindeer-herding rights.[12] Several provisions of a private legal nature were included in the act with respect to reindeer-herding Sami. These provisions included where herders had the right to build *goahti* (Sami tents) or 'permanent *goahti* and huts', the conditions under which buildings had to be transferred to another reindeer-herding Sami or be dismantled, and how many goats (five) could be grazed

---

9   Swedish Parliament 1886, The Special Committee, statement No 10; see also The Supreme Court NJA 1981 p 1, 240.

10   Christian L Tenow, *Lappfrågan* (Looström 1893) 82.

11   Reindeer Herding Act (1898:66).

12   Eivind Torp, 'The Legal Basis of Sami Reindeer Herding Rights in Sweden' (2013), *Arctic Review on Law and Politics* 43–61.

on state land.[13] The new law sharply curtailed the opportunities of the Sami to combine several livelihoods, which increasing numbers of Sami needed to do. The biggest change, however, was that reindeer-herding rights were confined to Sami who were members of a Sami village.[14] The Sami people were thus divided into two categories: Sami who were members of a Sami village and held reindeer-herding rights, and the Sami who were not members of a Sami village and had no such rights according to the Swedish state.[15] At a stroke of the legal pen, hunting and fishing rights were restricted to Sami who were members of a Sami village.

The prevailing view at the time seems to have been that the Swedish state had the right to impose restrictions on reindeer-herding rights as the state itself saw fit. However, many of the parliamentary bills that preceded the 1928 legislative process had stressed a need to reform the act, which was based on the oppressed position of non-reindeer-herding Sami.[16] Some pointed out that non-reindeer-herding Sami were left with no rights to their own land and that the legislation did not pay sufficient regard to ancient custom.[17] As already evident, views of this type were given no credence in the Reindeer Herding Act of 1928.

Sami Understanding of Justice

As the 1928 Act came to be drafted, it was obvious that the law was out of step with Sami traditions. It later became apparent that several provisions of the act conflicted with how the Sami themselves understood their rights to land and water. The strict requirements of the legislation concerning who should be considered a member of a Sami village, above all, caused problems for the Sami.[18] Certain provisions of the act came to be applied more rigorously, and it became obvious that certain parts of the legislation conflicted with the Sami understanding of justice.[19] This conflict manifested primarily in the context of the issue of hunting and fishing rights. Some of the problems that the Sami faced were discussed at the Sami National Assembly in Arvidsjaur in 1943. The following challenge directed at 'those whose business it is to decide' was presented at the meeting:

---

13   The Reindeer Herding Act (1928:309) s 42.

14   Reindeer Herding Act of 1928, s 1(2), 7, 8.

15   I have chosen to overlook the right to 'have reindeer in the care of another' according to s 14(2).

16   See Swedish government bill 1928:43, 35.

17   Swedish Parliament private member's bill no 163 (1908).

18   As early as the Sami National Assembly (organized optional meetings among the Sami in Sweden) in 1918, the Sami had made it clear that someone could not be considered as having abandoned reindeer herding because he had *exclusively* devoted himself to another occupation; Swedish government bill 1928:43, 59.

19   *Samefolkets Egen Tidning* (1944) No 4, 1 and 40–41.

In recent years, quite a few nomads have been forced by poverty to abandon reindeer herding as their sole livelihood and devote themselves to fishing, hunting, or other temporary work. They have increased the numbers of homeless people in the Lapp population. This is especially true near the Stora Lulevatten Lake, where the homeless must live in peat huts or board with other families, a situation detrimental to both parties. New settlements or dwellings are therefore needed. Our plea now is that the authorities must allow new construction above the cultivation boundary as well, preferably on the shores of Stora Lulevatten. This lake has long been the highway of their forefathers. Many of their relatives live there, and that is where they feel at home ... Regarding fishing and hunting above the cultivation boundary, we must emphasize in this respect the desirability of allotting the same rights to the aforementioned Lapps as those thus far enjoyed by both the nomads and older Lapps of fixed abode. At the least, they should be allowed to retain the right to fish in the mountain lakes along the waterways of the Great Lule River.[20]

Most Sami who spoke during the meeting considered the motion reasonable and worth supporting.[21] It must, as declared at the meeting, be considered 'a general public interest' that this group of Sami people be permitted 'at least to retain their right to fish'.[22] As evident in the motion, the act was designed in such a way that those who were forced by various circumstances to combine reindeer herding with other occupations risked losing their status as reindeer-herding Sami. Thus, they also risked losing their hunting and fishing rights.

That the Sami maintained a different position on the matter of hunting and fishing rights was obvious in connection with various court proceedings. In the mid 1940s, the Swedish Supreme Court reviewed the provision on hunting and fishing rights in two separate cases. A Sami man had been prosecuted in 1944 for having fished in a lake within a Sami village's grazing lands. It was uncontested in the case that members of the Sami village had fishing rights in the area. However, the prosecutor argued that the accused should be considered as having forfeited his membership in the Sami village. It was further uncontested that the accused owned about 90 head of reindeer and that he participated in reindeer herding every year to a certain extent. This meant that the accused had a right to pursue reindeer herding. The legal question, however, was whether the accused had 'persistently engaged in another occupation';[23] if so, he could be regarded as having lost his right to membership in the Sami village. During the trial, the accused testified that he had devoted himself exclusively to reindeer herding from age 15 to 23 and had thereafter taken on temporary jobs in addition to reindeer herding. He testified that he owned a partial interest in a small farm, but that there were no buildings or

20   *Samefolkets Egen Tidning* (1944) No 1, 5.
21   ibid 6.
22   ibid 6.
23   Reindeer Herding Act of 1928, s 8(b).

animals on the farm, and it was otherwise uncultivated. He also stated that he still participated in the work with his own and others' reindeer and should therefore be regarded as a member of the Sami village. In the Court of First Instance, the accused was acquitted on the grounds that he participated in reindeer herding every year to a certain extent and should therefore be regarded as a member of the Sami village. In his response to the prosecutor's appeal of the judgment, the accused argued that the fact that he could not survive on the income from his reindeer herd, and that he was therefore forced to earn supplementary income, should not mean that he had lost the rights included within the scope of the reindeer-herding right, as long as he still pursued reindeer herding. The accused lost in the Swedish Court of Appeal. The Supreme Court affirmed the ruling of the Court of Appeal, upheld that the accused had persistently engaged in an occupation other than reindeer herding, and therefore imposed a sentence for unlawful fishing.[24]

Two years later, the Supreme Court reviewed the same legal issue in a similar case. Three Sami men in the Sirka Sami village were prosecuted for having participated in a moose hunt. The men were regarded as not having hunting rights, according to the same provision in the Reindeer Herding Act of 1928 as in the abovementioned case. They were prosecuted for having assisted in a hunt – none of the accused had taken any game. It was uncontested in the case that all of the accused owned reindeer (one accused owned more than 100 head), that they were recorded as nomadic Sami in church records, and that all of the accused had participated in reindeer herding to various extents. During the preliminary investigation, all three stated that their main income was derived from lake fishing. The prosecutor argued that not one of the accused was a nomadic Sami and that the men participated in reindeer herding only as a side interest. One of the accused conceded that he was of fixed abode but argued that he still engaged in reindeer herding and fishing and therefore could not be regarded as having switched to another occupation. The other two accused considered themselves nomads, who worked to varying degrees in reindeer herding. Their statements were supported by an affidavit signed by 28 Sami in the Sirka Sami village. The affidavit stated that, in the 'firm opinion' of the signers, the two had pursued reindeer herding and therefore must be considered as belonging to the category of Sami who possessed hunting and fishing rights. The accused held that the temporary and short-lived periods of employment in road construction and logging could under no circumstances be considered equivalent to the phrase 'other permanent occupation'. The accused particularly objected to the prosecutor's contention that their fishing activities should be considered an occupation other than reindeer herding and argued the following:

> Every nomad had the right to fish as much as he pleased. This was part of his legal rights ... That a nomad exercised this right to such an extent that he could sell fish and thereby gain a much-needed addition to his financial support did not mean that he was pursuing another occupation. Fishing could hardly be regarded

---

24   The Supreme Court NJA 1944 p 117.

as another occupation for a reindeer-herding Lapp, who always pursued this sideline alongside his reindeer herding, that is, a livelihood that was entirely legitimate by virtue of both old customary law – which predated reindeer herding – and section 55.[25]

The accused further argued that it would violate the sense of justice if a reindeer-herding Sami were to lose his reindeer-herding privileges by virtue of his industriousness. The argument was expanded upon, stating that it was actually beneficial to the reindeer husbandry industry that some reindeer owners be able to pursue other occupations during certain periods. The extent to which the accused had engaged in occupations other than reindeer herding and fishing was not examined in the case. The charge was dismissed by the Court of First Instance, on the ground that the accused were considered members of a Sami village. The prosecutor appealed the ruling. The Court of Appeal and the Supreme Court found that the accused should have been regarded as having permanently pursued another occupation and imposed a sentence for unlawful hunting.

Of particular interest in this context is that the Supreme Court ignored the issue of whether the accused might have had hunting and fishing rights based on customary law.[26] Customary law was an unquestioned principle of Swedish law when these cases were heard, and it is still a fundamental principle in legislation concerning Sami land and water rights.[27] This neglect is even more remarkable when one considers that the accused had explicitly referred during the trial to the fact that their hunting and fishing rights – in addition to the relevant statutes of the law – were based on custom. A troubling consequence of the legal system's strict application of the relevant statutes must be noted. Individual Sami who do not pursue other temporary work, but who have the same connection to reindeer herding as the accused, would be considered members of the Sami village and would therefore retain their hunting and fishing rights.[28] Otherwise, the zeal of the authorities responsible for administering justice, so as to take legal action against the accused in the aforementioned cases, should be recognized. That the courts demonstrate a clear allegiance to the aims expressed by the Swedish legislature in the justification of the legislation must be regarded as a tradition in Swedish law.[29]

The relevant statute and especially how it was applied within the state reindeer herding administration was criticized amongst the Sami, for example in an article in *Samernas Egen Tidning* (the Sami People's own magazine). Under the heading

---

25 The Supreme Court NJA 1946 p 94.

26 The Supreme Court NJA 1944 p 117, NJA 1946 p 94. See also The Supreme Court NJA 1942 p 336.

27 Eivind Torp, 'The Legal Basis of Sami Reindeer Herding Rights in Sweden' (2013), *Arctic Review on Law and Politics*, 43–61.

28 Reindeer Herding Act (1928:309) s 8(b).

29 Richard Nordquist, 'Förarbetenas rättskällestatus – ett historiskt perspektiv' (2011) *Juridisk Publikation*, 141. See also Christina Allard's Chapter 5 in this volume.

'How reindeer herding statutes could be detrimental to reindeer herding' scathing criticism was expressed, addressing the fact that the legislation did not consider 'the primeval rights of the Sami people to their ancient lands'. Arguments voiced in the context included the following:

> To attach, in a statute as recently enacted as 1928 and with no further ado, the right to hunt and fish, the most primordial livelihoods of the Sami, to membership in a Sami village, by which a great many Sami are instantly deprived of an historically determined right, is quite simply an expression of pure arbitrariness and thus cannot be just.[30]

However, no changes of the statutes considered especially problematic were made in subsequent revisions of the act.[31] However, the Swedish legislature later devoted some attention to the matter of fishing rights for Sami people who were not members of a Sami village. I will return to that subject shortly.

Current Regulation of Sami Hunting and Fishing Rights

As Sweden gradually evolved in the twentieth century into a modern industrial nation, in which various primary industries, including agriculture and forestry, underwent drastic efficiency improvements, it became obvious to the government that this evolution was bypassing one industry: Sami reindeer herding. In response, the government initiated a new Reindeer Herding Act in the 1960s. The principal aim of this legislative reform was to enable new forms of operation and make various efficiency improvements in what was now called reindeer 'husbandry'.[32] The livelihood of the Sami would now also undergo necessary structural transformation. The legal arrangements would mainly be the same as before; that is, the new act was expected to be based on the same principles as was the 1928 Act.[33]

From this point of departure, it was a logical consequence that the relevant committee of inquiry for the work of formulating the new act should submit a proposed bill that retained the connection between membership in a Sami village and hunting and fishing rights that had prevailed since 1928. The arguments for this were, first, that extending uncontrolled rights to other Sami could cause difficulties for reindeer-herding Sami attempting to engage in subsistence hunting and fishing and, second, that the value of hunting and fishing rights for license

---

30   *Samefolkets Egen Tidning* 1944 No 4, 40.
31   cf Swedish Code of Statutes 1944:76; 1947:225; 1960:145.
32   Swedish government report SOU 1968:16, 36.
33   Swedish government report SOU 1968:16, 36. I am overlooking the Minister's specification that the new act should not contain provisions regarding differences in rights for men and women, which was the case in the Reindeer Herding Act (1928:309).

to outsiders would decline. At the time, licences were a significant source of income for the State Sami Foundation, and demand for fishing opportunities was expected to increase sharply in the future. This financial interest, in particular, was considered crucial in restricting the number of Sami with hunting and fishing rights. According to the committee of inquiry, however, it was justifiable to make an exception to one principle: members of any Sami village who had abandoned reindeer herding and switched to another occupation should be able to retain the right to hunt and fish within their own Sami village for a period of 10 years. This exception was embraced out of a desire to encourage more Sami to leave reindeer herding as an occupation, so that the herding industry would become more viable and profitable. The proposal was part of the package of efficiency measures the Swedish government had called for.[34]

The government, however, rejected the proposal to allow Sami village members who had left reindeer herding for another occupation to retain hunting and fishing rights. Under current legislation, hunting and fishing rights are still conditioned upon membership in a Sami village.[35] A Sami village may, however, grant the right to engage in subsistence hunting and fishing to a former member of the Sami village.[36]

The matter of alternative forms of membership in a Sami village was subsequently examined by several committees of inquiry, starting in the early 1970s. This occurred when the Swedish government inquired into the particular problems that the Sami were encountering in Swedish society. The rationale was that declining numbers of Sami were able to support themselves through reindeer herding, leading to a significant employment problem in the Sami population. Among other matters, the Swedish government's directive tasked the committee with investigating the matter of alternative forms of membership in a Sami village.[37] Against that background, the committee proposed that a Sami village should be given the option of accepting people who held reindeer-herding rights (but did not pursue reindeer herding) as auxiliary members of the Sami village in which the prospective members originated.[38] The aim was to tighten the bonds between the majority of the Sami people who had left reindeer herding and the minority still involved in the industry. According to the proposal, an auxiliary member of a Sami village could be allotted the right to fish with hand-held equipment and to hunt small game within certain periods of time and in certain areas determined by the Sami village. However, the proposal did not lead to any initiative from

---

34   Swedish government report SOU 1968:16, 191. The proposal was not included in the final bill, cf Swedish government bill Prop 1971:51 and JoU 1971:37.

35   Reindeer Herding Act (1971:437) s 25.

36   ibid s 31, para 2.

37   Swedish government report SOU 1975:99, 37–38.

38   Ibid 163–71; cf in particular the opinion of the Sami members of the committee of inquiry, who proposed that the option to accept auxiliary members should be expressed in the text of the act, 241–42.

the Swedish government or Parliament. Another committee of inquiry presented a similar proposal[39] in the early 2000s, but the Swedish government still did not choose to present a bill to the Parliament on the matter.[40]

In summary, first, the requirement that hunting and fishing rights be conditioned upon membership in a Sami village introduced in the 1928 Act still applies. Second, current legal regulation of Sami hunting and fishing rights is inconsistent with Sami traditions in this area, and third, the legislature has taken no initiative to change the legal order in force since 1928.

Sami Fisher-folk

Not all Sami complied with the regulations established by public authorities. It became known during the first half of the 1900s that there were permanent settlements of Sami people near several lakes in northern Sweden who supported themselves through hunting and fishing combined with small-scale farming, but for whom the sale of fish was the most important source of cash. This group of Sami, designated 'Sami fisher-folk' by the Swedish authorities, created certain problems for the legislature, because they diverged from the pattern of Sami livelihood and thus the legal basis for their activities was unclear.

In connection with the committee of inquiry appointed ahead of the 1971 Act, the Sami fisher-folk were mentioned explicitly for the first time in a legislative context. Without any preceding investigation, the committee held the following position:

> In the matter of the Sami who have never belonged to a Sami village, such as the so-called Sami fisher-folk, we do not believe we can recommend any amendment to the law by which they are accorded Sami hunting and fishing rights.[41]

The committee presumed that any amendment to the act would lead to the expansion of the collective to whom the rights were accorded and would include a group that was very difficult to define. The committee held the view that this 'would, among other matters, significantly curtail already limited opportunities to intervene against the poaching of fish and game'.[42] The Sami fisher-folk were considered dependent upon fishing within the reindeer-herding territory. Consequently, it was believed that they should not be deprived of the opportunity to hunt and fish, but that their permission to hunt and fish should be arranged through individual no-fee

---

39   Swedish government report SOU 2001:101, 193–94.

40   See, however, Ministry Communication Ds 2009:40. For a more detailed analysis of how the government has acted in the matter, see Bertil Bengtsson, 'Om jakt och fiske i fjällmarken' (2010) *Svensk Juristtidning,* 84.

41   Swedish government report SOU 1968:16, 191.

42   ibid 191.

licences and not through legislation.[43] In the committee's opinion, the Sami fisher-folk did not have hunting and fishing rights, although there was talk of giving them 'some precedence over other applicants'.[44]

The Swedish government agreed with the committee of inquiry's opinion that the possibility of Sami fisher-folk pursuing fishing was not a matter that needed to be regulated in any particular provision of the law. According to the 1971 Act, the licensing of hunting and fishing rights to Sami should incur a fee, unless special reason exists to allow an exemption.[45] In agreement with the committee, the government found that it could 'be justifiable' to make exceptions to the fee provision for 'certain Sami people who do not belong to the reindeer-herding population group, but who are dependent upon fishing within the reindeer-herding territory to support themselves'.[46]

The Sami fisher-folk were thus granted no rights in currently applicable legislation. The government's phrase 'may be justifiable' can be considered as a signal to relevant public authorities that no-fee arrangements may be applied. It would be a matter of possible benefit in relation to the general public, as the benefit is not reserved only for Sami fisher-folk. The permanently settled farming population in the interior parts of the two northernmost counties was provided the same benefit. For that group, however, the language used was somewhat more peremptory, stating that that group of people should be 'ensured no-fee fishing rights'.[47] From the legislature's point of view, the idea of a fee exemption was a gesture of compensation to citizens who reside in an area in which business opportunities are limited. The proposal was not based on deliberations concerning what fishing rights the favoured groups may have.

The legal situation of the Sami fisher-folk was paid further attention following that. Only a year or two after the new act had gone into effect, a committee of inquiry investigated the employment problems of the Sami population. The circumstances of Sami fisher-folk and what needed to be done to secure their possibilities to earn an income were examined.[48] The committee determined that the Sami fisher-folk earned their principal income from the sidelines associated with reindeer herding but that the matter of their fishing rights was unresolved.[49] With regard to Sami who had previously pursued reindeer herding, the committee argued the following:

---

43   Swedish government report SOU 1968:16, 212.

44   ibid 192.

45   An important reason for this was that licences were thought to create conditions for higher incomes for Sami who pursued reindeer herding; cf Prop 1971:51, 59.

46   ibid 170.

47   ibid 135.

48   Swedish government report SOU 1975:99, 39.

49   With regard to fishing, the committee of inquiry focused on the significance of fishing to Sami people in general – that is, apart from the question of by what right the fishing occurred; Swedish government report SOU 1975:99, 223.

According to applicable statutes, persons who cease to pursue reindeer husbandry and switch to another occupation to support themselves lose their membership in the Sami village and thus also their hunting and fishing rights. In practice, however, Sami who give up actual reindeer herding and switch to only hunting and fishing for their livelihood are allowed to retain their membership in the Sami village. In the opinion of the Sami Committee, this practice is justified, because hunting and fishing rights are auxiliary rights included in reindeer-herding rights.[50]

In the 1970s, internal Sami community practices still meant that Sami who gave up herding reindeer could remain part of the Sami collective and retain their rights to hunt and fish. According to the committee of inquiry, the Sami had adapted their practices in relation to the legal rules in such a way that Sami traditions concerning hunting and fishing rights could be maintained even though the provisions of the act said otherwise.[51] The committee's report did not, however, lead to any changes in the legal circumstances of Sami fisher-folk.

The legislature's adoption of a stance in the 1960s and 1970s that Sami fisher-folk had no hunting and fishing rights may seem surprising considering that the issue of the rights of non-reindeer-herding Sami had long been a familiar problem to the legislature. Very early on, before the 1928 Act was enacted, a committee of inquiry had pointed out that, in all likelihood, non-reindeer-herding Sami also had the right to hunt and fish:

> The Reindeer Herding Act of 1898 – like its predecessor of 1886 – lacks rules concerning the legal circumstances of Lapps other than reindeer herders. The Lapps who instead of pursuing reindeer herding occupy themselves with fishing and hunting could not, however, based on the aforementioned restriction of the rules of reindeer-herding legislation, be considered devoid of rights; in order to determine their legal position, one must apply older law and, primarily, analogies from the reindeer-herding laws ... In principle, the rights of non-reindeer-herding Lapps should not be as far-reaching as those of the reindeer herders; like them, they should have the right to use the forest and to hunt and fish ...[52]

Although such a view has not been expressed in legislation, the Supreme Court and Supreme Administrative Court on several occasions in the late twentieth century articulated the question of the land and water rights of non-reindeer-herding

---

50   ibid 229.

51   Practices of this kind can, however, entail certain problems in connection with conflicts of interest between a Sami village and an individual member in relation to hunting and fishing, because both the Sami village and individual members have legal standing in such matters; cf Prop 1971:51, 161.

52   Swedish government report SOU 1922:10, 74.

Sami through observing the principle that reindeer-herding rights accrue to all Sami people and not only members of a Sami village. This has mainly applied in disputes over compensation after limitations on fishing, when the courts have noted that the auxiliary rights included in the reindeer-herding right are also a collective right of all Sami people.[53]

Conclusions

As the percentage of the Sami population not involved in reindeer herding became significantly larger than the percentage of reindeer-herding Sami, the matter of the rights of non-reindeer-herding Sami became an increasingly important political issue. This development occurred partially against the backdrop of the court opinion in the Taxed mountain case.[54] Even though the Sami village lost the case, the opinion would prove germane to the legal assessment of Sami rights. As a point of departure for Sami rights, the Swedish Supreme Court found as follows:

> One certain point of departure, however, appears to be that the core of the rights was constituted of that which is still the foundation of Sami livelihood in the mountains: reindeer herding, hunting, fishing, and certain uses of the forest. This was a matter of rights that relied on immemorial prescription from the beginning and which over the ages have taken on other significance as the practice of Sami livelihood developed and took on partially new forms. The emphasis had originally been on hunting and fishing but had later shifted, especially after the Sami transition to full nomadism, to reindeer herding.[55]

The court then assessed how Sami rights based on immemorial prescription have been transformed in legislation and found that the act exhaustively regulates the rights and duties that reindeer-herding rights entail.[56] At the same time, the Supreme Court noted that Sami rights are of such a nature that they are protected under the Swedish Constitution against expropriation without compensation and continued:

---

53   The Supreme Court NJA 1979 p 1; NJA 1981 p 610; and The Supreme Administrative Court RÅ 1993, ref 24.

54   Eivind Torp, *Renskötselrätten och rätten till naturresurserna* (University of Tromsø 2008) 63–70.

55   The Supreme Court NJA 1981 p 1, 233.

56   ibid 244.

> The circumstance that the right is in this case regulated by legislation does not
> mean that it lacks such protection. While the right[57] can certainly be abolished
> through legislation, as long as it is asserted it cannot be taken from the possessors,
> either in law or otherwise ...[58]

This must be understood to mean that it cannot be precluded that the Sami may
have certain rights based on custom that are not expressed in legislation.[59] This
has since been confirmed in a court ruling, in a case in which a reindeer-herding
Sami man was being prosecuted for having gathered reindeer lichen within a
nature preserve in violation of the Environmental Code of 1998. The Court of
Appeal found that gathering lichen in connection with herding reindeer was a
Sami custom and therefore part of the reindeer-herding right, and the charges were
dismissed on those grounds.[60] In the Taxed mountain case, the Supreme Court's
comprehensive review of the grounds for Sami land and water rights led to both
stronger acceptance of Sami demands for greater influence in society and more
flexibility in interpreting Sami rights.[61]

The relatively comprehensive committee of inquiry examining Sami rights
following the Taxed mountain case Supreme Court ruling, and whose remit was
'to clarify the special needs that may be attributed to the position of the Sami as
indigenous people',[62] proceeded from the Supreme Court's opinion regarding the
nature of Sami rights. The inquiry found in that line that Sami people who were
not members of a Sami village might have special rights based on immemorial
prescription.[63] This applied primarily to Sami fisher-folk, who were still engaged in
commercial fishing. Consequently, the committee proposed that Sami people who
were not members of a Sami village, but who were permanently residing within
a Sami village's hunting and fishing territory, should be allowed to hunt and fish
on state land within the designated territory. The committee elaborated that this
should be so when reasonable, in consideration of the individual's opportunities to
earn an income and other circumstances.[64] The arrangement was intended to cover
only those Sami people who were occupied with fishing and were dependent upon
it for their livelihoods.

The Swedish government, however, did not accept the committee's proposal
on this matter, because it found the group of Sami fisher-folk to be too small. In

---

57   In the context, the Swedish Supreme Court is addressing usufruct rights, that
is, the right to use land and water with consideration given to all the rights included in
reindeer-herding rights, such as the right to hunt and fish.

58   ibid 248.

59   ibid 84 and 245.

60   The Court of Appeal Northern Norrland, case B 69-04, 21 December 2005.

61   G Svensson, *The Sami and Their Land* (Oslo 1997) 171.

62   Swedish Government Directive DIR 1983:10.

63   Swedish government report SOU 1990:91, 187.

64   ibid 193.

the bill, the government expresses it thus: '... opportunities to earn a living for the small group of Sami fisher-folk[65] [are] a matter that can be resolved without special legislation'.[66] In the eyes of the government, how the matter should be resolved was determined by the numeric strength of the group and not the legal basis of the right. When few individuals were affected, practical resolution of the issue was considered more appropriate than resolution based on legal considerations.

In so doing, the Swedish government adopted a position suggesting that it understood the issue of the land and water rights of Sami fisher-folk to be a matter of regulation of a benefit given to the Sami fisher-folk by the government itself. This position, however, is not in line with the Supreme Court's findings that Sami land and water rights are based on occupation and immemorial prescription.[67] If the legislature had accepted the Swedish Supreme Court's conclusions in this respect, the hunting and fishing rights of Sami fisher-folk would have been regulated in observation of the same principles of private law upon which the established rights rely.[68] As the Supreme Court expressed in the ruling, state officials have long had difficulty translating Sami legal relations into the conceptual language of private law.[69] Even though one might wish otherwise, this situation remains.[70]

In summary, the Swedish legislature's position and legal point of departure in assessing the land and water rights of non-reindeer-herding Sami people are still unresolved.[71] That non-reindeer-herding Sami people currently have no land and water rights is clear. However, the legal arguments that led to the statutes that regulate these rights are characterized more by a desire to find politically acceptable solutions to a rights problem, rather than by a respect for the legal principles upon which the rights are based.[72] By referring to undetermined future measures, the government has ignored that the problem was considered in the

---

65   In the former report the number was estimated to fewer than one hundred persons; Swedish government report SOU 1990:91, 189.

66   Swedish Government Bill Prop 1992/93:32, 180. In the preceding inquiry, the number had been estimated at fewer than one hundred people; Swedish government report SOU 1990:91, 189.

67   cf Reindeer Herding Act (1971:437) s 1. Regarding the application of the doctrine of immemorial prescription, see The Supreme Court NJA 1956 p 161 and NJA 1984 p 148.

68   The Supreme Court NJA 1981 p 1, 175 and 248.

69   ibid 181.

70   Bertil Bengtsson and Eivind Torp, 'Svensk samerätt: Något om den senaste utvecklingen' in Øyvind Ravna and Tore Henriksen (eds), *Juss i Nord: Hav, fisk og urfolk* (Tromsø 2012).

71   Another committee of inquiry has proposed that non-reindeer-herding Sami should be able to be members of a Sami village; cf Swedish government report SOU 2001:101. However, no Swedish government has been able to present any bill on the matter to the Swedish Parliament. The present Swedish government's negative stance on the issue is illustrated by the handling of Ministry of Communication 2009:40.

72   cf The Supreme Court NJA 1981 p 1, 140.

legislative process. Even though hunting and fishing constitute traditional Sami livelihoods, and even though Sami land and water rights in Sweden are based on occupation and immemorial prescription, most Sami in Sweden today have no hunting and fishing rights. This circumstance also constitutes an important basis of political mobilization in the modern Swedish Sami community: The Hunting and Fishing Sami, whose platform demands hunting and fishing rights for all Sami, is now the largest party in the Swedish Sami Parliament.

Chapter 10

Local Community Right to Fish: A Sami Perspective

Susann Funderud Skogvang

Introduction

Presentation and the Objective

The question of fishing rights for the coastal Sami population in Norway has been vigorously debated.[1] Norway has been criticized for not securing or respecting Sami fishing rights by the UN Special Rapporteur on the rights of indigenous peoples,[2] the UN Permanent Forum on Indigenous issues,[3] the UN Committee on the Elimination of Racial Discrimination (CERD)[4] and in the scholarly literature.[5]

After examining and discussing Sami fishing rights in Norway for decades, Norway passed new legislation on Sami fishing rights in 2012.[6] The new legislation was a direct response to proposals from the Coastal Fisheries Committee [Kystfiskeutvalget]. In 2008, this Committee unanimously proposed stronger

---

1   For further reading about the Coastal Sami people in Norway, see Steinar Pedersen, 'The Coastal Sámi of Norway and their Rights to Traditional Marine Livelihood' (2012) *Arctic Review on Law and Politics* 51–80.

2   Report of the Special Rapporteur on the situation of human rights and fundamental freedoms of indigenous peoples to the UN Human Rights Council, Eighteenth Session, Agenda item 3. 'The situation of the Sami people in the Sápmi region of Norway, Sweden and Finland', June 2011.

3   Permanent Forum on Indigenous Issues. Report on indigenous fishing rights in the seas with case studies from Australia and Norway, E/C.19/2010/2.

4   CERD/c/nor/co/19-20, 5.

5   See also Valmaine Toki, 'Indigenous Peoples' Fisheries Rights – A Comparative Perspective between Maori and Sami' (2010) *Arctic Review on Law and Politics* 54; Svein Jentoft, 'Governing Tenure in Norwegian and Sami Small-scale Fisheries. From Common Pool to Common Property?'(2013) 1 *Land Tenure Journal* 9.

6   For more about this process, see Ministry of Fisheries: Prop 70 L (2011–12) Endringar i deltakerloven, havressurslova og finnmarksloven (kystfiskeutvalet), hereinafter Prop 70 L; Carsten Smith, 'Fisheries in Coastal Sami Areas: Geopolitical Concerns?'(2014) *Arctic Review on Law and Politics* 4–10; Jørn Øyrehagen Sunde, 'A Geographical, Historical and Legal Perspective on the Right to Fishery' (2010) *Arctic Review on Law and Politics* 108–30.

protection for the fishing rights of the coastal Sami population in Finnmark (the northernmost county of Norway).[7] International law and fishing from time immemorial was the legal basis for the proposal.[8] The Norwegian Parliament declined to accept this proposal and therefore several of Committee's proposals to promote coastal Sami fishing rights were not followed up by either the Norwegian government or the Norwegian Parliament.[9]

However, some important changes were made to the prevailing fisheries regulations. One change was a stronger implementation of international law in Norwegian fisheries legislation. Section 6 of the Marine Resources Act already provided that the 'Act applies subject to any restrictions deriving from international agreements and international law otherwise'. The same rule was even more clearly expressed in clause 1(a) dealing with participation: 'The act must be applied in accordance with international law on indigenous peoples and minorities'. This means that applicable international law restricts the interpretation of Norwegian law, and, in case of a conflict, international law will prevail. Another amendment was a new clause 7 (g), which states that it is important that the Norwegian fisheries management help to maintain the material basis for Sami culture.

The most significant change was an amendment to the Finnmark Act clause 29[10] which requires the Finnmark Commission[11] to investigate collective or individual rights to fish in marine and coastal areas in Finnmark if required by someone with a legal interest in such a clarification. This statutory rule presupposes the existence of property rights to fish. Such property rights may be established through fishing from time immemorial, according to clause 5 of the Finnmark Act clause 5 which states:

> Through prolonged use of land and water areas, the Sami have collectively and individually acquired rights to land in Finnmark.
>
> This Act does not interfere with collective and individual rights acquired by Sami and other people through prescription or immemorial usage ...

---

7   NOU 2008:5 *Retten til fiske i havet utenfor Finnmark* [The right to fish in coastal areas outside Finnmark], hereinafter NOU 2008:5. The author was a member of this committee.

8   NOU 2008:5 p 14.

9   Prop 70 L.

10   Act 17 June 2005 No 85 relating to legal relations and management of land and natural resources in the county of Finnmark (Finnmark Act).

11   The Finnmark Commission was established pursuant to The Finnmark Act clause 29 in March 2008 to investigate rights to land and water in Finnmark. The commission is obliged to establish the scope and content of the rights held by Sami and other people on the basis of prescription or use from time immemorial or on some other basis.

With this provision the Norwegian government has recognized claims for collective or individual home-fishing rights in certain areas in Finnmark. This is an exception to the main rule of free fishing for all Norwegian citizens but still in line with the existing legal framework for fishing rights in Norway as we will see later in this chapter.

I will elaborate on this amendment to the Finnmark Act and the criteria for the recognition of fishing rights in tidal waters acquired through immemorial usage. I consider whether fishing, including fishing by the coastal Sami population, qualifies for establishing local community rights to fish according to Norwegian law.[12] I also consider whether the Sami as an indigenous people enjoy certain rights or protection for these activities. I will examine the extent of the protection the Sami have for their fishing according to Norwegian and international law. Does international law provide any protection for indigenous peoples' traditional hunting and fishing in coastal waters? The topic is not discussed in detail by the Finnmark Fishing Commission or in the literature.

Background and Topicality

Many indigenous peoples around the world depend upon marine resources for their livelihood and have been hunting and fishing in coastal areas from time immemorial. This is not surprising, as 71 per cent of the globe is covered with water, most of it saltwater. The coastal Sami population in Norway is among those who depend upon marine resources for their livelihood. Indigenous peoples' rights, including the right to natural resources, have improved substantially during the last several years, particularly through the UN system. During that same period, however, overexploitation of marine resources has been an increasing challenge. Currently, 80 per cent of the global fish stocks are 'fully exploited',[13] over-exploited, or depleted primarily because of intensive commercial fishing.[14] Decreased fish stocks have necessitated strict regulations, and special measures have been introduced to improve fisheries management and to obtain sustainable fisheries.

To save the fish stocks, fisheries management around the globe has had a privatizing character during the last centuries, as fishing rights are often allocated through different private quotas.[15] In Norway the management of the most

---

12 Local community rights are held by a community of people not by individuals, corporations or entities, see Anthony Charles, 'Community Fishery Rights: Issues, Approaches and Atlantic Canadian Case Studies' (2006) IIFET 2006 Portsmouth Proceedings 2. I will also use the term 'home-fishing rights', as the rights are based on fishing in the fjords and coastal waters near the residence.

13 This means that they are being fished at or near sustainable limits.

14 FAO, *The State of World Fisheries and Aquaculture* 2012, <http://www.fao.org/docrep/016/i2727e/i2727e00.htm.> last accessed December 2014.

15 For more see Richard Barnes, *Property Rights and Natural Resources* (Portland 2009), with a thorough list of list of literature regarding this privatization, 313.

important commercial fisheries is arranged through an individual transferrable vessel quota system.[16]

Indigenous marine resources are also under constant pressure from other commercial industries. In Norway, Sami fishing consistently lose to modern activities. A recent example is the mining project called Repparfjord/Ulveryggen by Nussir ASA, in which the company plans to use traditional Sami fishing grounds as a waste disposal with the consent of the Norwegian government.[17] Experience from other fjords in Norway demonstrates that waste from mining and other polluting industries is devastating for marine life.[18] In addition, the fish farming industry in coastal areas sometimes conflicts with traditional Sami fishing rights, as these farms are located in spawning areas for cod or important traditional fish sites. During the last decades, the tourist recreational fisheries have increased and might also conflict with small-scale, local community fishing.

Privatization of fishing rights and area conflicts in tidal waters, together with an increased emphasis on indigenous rights, are among the most important factors that have put discussions about fishing rights on the agenda.[19] The privatization of the fisheries has raised substantial questions about who is and should be entitled to fishing rights. These are important questions in global fisheries management discourses, and Barnes, among others, has discussed different elements of property rights in fisheries thoroughly.[20]

The Right to Marine Natural Resources in General

Marine resources as such are usually considered common property.[21] In Norway, as in many other countries, fish stocks are considered to be common pool resources. Fluctuating fish stocks are considered ownerless as long as they are wild. Whoever captures these fish becomes the owner through so-called 'original acquisition'.[22] Fish and other fluctuating marine natural resources are therefore not subject to private ownership. The fish are regarded as a national resource, and the state is responsible for administering that resource for the benefit of the citizens of the country. This principle that fish are a national resource is currently

---

16   <http://www.fisheries.no/resource_management/Resource-management/#. UvTlRxBc_40.> last accessed December 2014.

17   For more information about their ongoing projects, see NUSSIR ASA, www. nussir.no.

18   See, for instance, the decision from the Frostating Appeals Court regarding compensation for local fishermen for lost fishing caused by dumping, published in RG 1967 p 351.

19   Siri Ulfsdatter Søreng, 'Fishing Rights Discourses in Norway: Indigenous Versus Non-indigenous Voices' (2008) 6 (2) *MAST* 77–99.

20   Barnes, *Property Rights and Natural Resources* (n 15).

21   ibid 318.

22   Thor Falkanger and Aage Thor Falkanger, *Tingsrett* [Property Law] (Oslo 2013) 58.

set out in section 2 of the Marine Resources Act which states: 'Wild living marine resources belong to the Norwegian society as a whole'.[23] Nevertheless, the actual management of these resources through the transferrable vessel quota system has resulted in privatizing this resource.

One may also, to a limited extent, acquire certain use rights or other property rights to fish, for instance through immemorial usage. In Norwegian legislation, there is a tradition of dividing rights between property rights (private rights) on the one side and public law privileges on the other. The allocation of fishing quotas, withdrawal regulations and participation in the management of fisheries are examples of the latter, and a particular right to fish in a certain area is an example of the former. It is important to consider both types of rights in order to make the fishing rights regime effective and relevant, especially for indigenous peoples.

Property Rights in Coastal Areas in Norway

Introduction

Property rights to fish in freshwater, lakes and rivers are well-established in Norwegian property law.[24] The basic rule is that freshwater is fully subject to property rights, including private ownership, and that the owners have exclusive fishing rights on the same basis as with any other property. These rights have an uncontested legal basis and legal protection in Norwegian law.

In contrast, property rights in tidal waters, such as fishing rights in fjords and coastal waters, do not have any clear or investigated legal basis. The main rule in Norway is that saltwater areas are common property and that fishing is free for all Norwegian citizens. This goes back in time and might be because it is physically impossible to limit the oceans.[25] Concepts of property in the coastal area are much less advanced and more difficult to conceive because of the three-dimensional nature of the sea and the fluidity of the object and its resources.[26] The rule that fishing is free for all has not been explicitly expressed in any legislation, but it is provided in other sources of law. The Supreme Court has in several cases applied the rule of free fishing. In a decision from 1985, the Supreme Court concluded that: 'Basically this is a kind of fishing that is free for all'.[27]

---

23   Act relating to the management of wild living marine resources (Marine Resources Act) 6 June 2008 no 37.

24   See Thor Falkanger and Aage Thor Falkanger, *Tingsrett* [Property Law] (Oslo 2013) 107; Skogvang, *Retten til fiske i fjorder og kystnære farvann*, 17.

25   Barnes, *Property Rights and Natural Resources* (n 15) 314.

26   Francis T Christy, Jr, 'Territorial Use Rights in Marine Fisheries: Definitions and Conditions', FAO Fisheries Technical Paper 227, Food and Agriculture Organization of the United Nations (Rome 1992) 5–6.

27   ibid.

There are several exceptions to this general rule that saltwater fishing is free and open for all. Various private property rights exist in saltwater fishing in Norway according to formal legislation, local customary law and case law.[28] Various private property fishing rights have always existed in Norway, particularly in the fjords and the closest coastal waters. Norwegian legal doctrine has in recent years discussed these rights in historical and modern views.[29]

In this section, I will discuss the legal basis for collective property rights to fish, such as home-fishing rights in Norway. One of the most progressive proposals from the Coastal Fishery Commission was a priority right or preference right to fish in the fjords for the population living alongside that specific fjord. This was a home-fishing right that gave preference to the local communities based on a property principle of adjacency.[30] Other fishers would not have the right to fish in that fjord without special permission. This proposed rule was in line with customary fishing in coastal Sami areas. This concrete proposal was largely set aside by the Norwegian Parliament.[31] However, such fjord fishing rights may still exist, and claims can be made before the Finnmark Commission according to the new section 29 of the Finnmark Act. Such rights must be identified separately with a concrete view to the conditions for acquiring rights obtained through immemorial usage.

Conditions for Local Community Fishing Rights/Home-fishing Rights

Local community rights to fish can be acquired through use from time immemorial. The point of departure for immemorial usage was expressed by the Supreme Court in the Selbu-case:

> The acquisition of a right through *use* from time immemorial rests on three elements: There must be a certain amount of use, which must have taken place for *a long time* and been exercised in *good faith*. However, there are no fixed criteria for the determination of whether the individual conditions have been satisfied.[32] (Emphasis added)

---

28   Act relating to Salmonids and Fresh-Water Fish section 16, Act relating to legal relations and management of land and natural resources in the county of Finnmark [Finnmark Act] section 29.

29   Sunde, 'A Geographical, Historical and Legal Perspective' (n 6)108–30; Kirsti Strøm Bull, *Kystfisket i Finnmark* [Coastal fishing in Finnmark] (Universitetsforlaget 2012).

30   NOU 2008:5 Retten til fiske i havet utenfor Finnmark (The right to fish in coastal areas outside Finnmark) 414.

31   Prop 70 L.

32   Rt 2001 p 769, 788–89.

These criteria hold a relative relationship and are neither static nor cumulative. The criteria must be flexibly interpreted and adjusted to the relevant field and territory.[33]

The requirements for local community rights are based on premises found in a series of Norwegian Supreme Court decisions regarding questions of rights acquired by use from time immemorial, for instance fishing for a group of people in a defined geographical area. Such rights are held by a community or a group of people as collective rights. Individuals cannot dispose of or enforce these rights alone. Collective rights are allocated to a larger or smaller group of persons.[34] Collective rights and common rights have previously been seen as equal types of rights. However, collective rights may also include property rights for smaller groups. Eriksen, a Norwegian property law expert, states that collective rights can provide 'individual economic benefit' to the participants even if the right is not individually owned.[35]

The case study (Norwegian Supreme Court cases) includes cases regarding rights in saltwater, but also consider general questions regarding area-based rights, including questions about redress and compensation for loss of rights. Other sources of law are also examined, such as the legal doctrine and the extensive work done by the Norwegian government in the Fisheries case before The International Court of Justice against the United Kingdom from 1951.[36] In the Fisheries case, Norway recognized and documented the existence of private property fishing rights.[37]

The criteria in brief are extensive fishing in a defined area for a long period of time (from time immemorial).[38] One has to make a detailed evaluation of the actual fishing (intensity, exclusivity, continuity, the fishers' needs, the time aspect and more). Further, the group of claimants and the geographical area that is subject to home-fishing rights must not be too large and must be located close to the fishers' residence.[39] A firm interpretation of the law, good faith regarding the right to fish, and dependence on the marine resource are also elements considered by the Norwegian Supreme Court when recognizing local community rights.[40]

---

33   ibid.
34   See Gunnar Eriksen, *Alders tids bruk* (Immemorial usage) (Fagbokforlaget 2008) 108.
35   ibid.
36   The Anglo-Norwegian Fisheries case, *ICJ Reports* 1951, 116–44.
37   *ICJ Reports* 1951, 116–44; Susann Funderud Skogvang, 'Fiskerigrensesaken mellom Norge og Storbritannia og sakens betydning for norsk rett 60 år senere' (The Anglo-Norwegian Fisheries case of 1951) (2012) *Arctic Review on Law and Politics* 81–107.
38   See more Susann F Skogvang, *Retten til fiske i fjorder og kystnære farvann*, [The right to fish in the fjords and in coastal waters] (Oslo 2012) 197–251.
39   ibid 239.
40   ibid 250.

The Character of Local Community Fishing Rights

If a local community fulfils the abovementioned requirements, the community will have an area-based right to fish. The concrete character of the right must be determined individually, but it is not a type of property right that is subject to transfer.[41] A territorial use right in marine fisheries (TURF) is a well-known concept in theories of property in fisheries.[42] This concept fits well with the community right to fish acquired through immemorial usage in Norway. Actual fishing practices will determine the concrete character of the right, but some elements are common. First, there is some kind of right to exclude others from fishing in the same area; second, there is a right to participate in the management of the fishing in the area; third, there is a right to extract benefits from the use of the resources within the territory, and, fourth, there will be predictable future returns from the use.

One of the most important proposals from the Coastal Fishery Commission was for a priority right or a preference right to fish in the fjords for the population living alongside the specific fjord [fjordretten]. This was a home-fishing right that gave preference to the local communities based on a property principle of subsidiarity.[43] Other fishers would not have the right to fish in that fjord without special permission. This proposed rule was in line with customary fishing in coastal Sami areas.

How Does this Apply to the Coastal Sami People?

Norwegian law does of course apply to the Sami population as it does to the Norwegian population at large. Fishing of a character that meets the conditions mentioned earlier has lasted to this day in coastal Sami areas. This means that Sami local communities along the Norwegian coast may establish local community rights to fish according to use from time immemorial. The most important Supreme Court decision regarding protected local community fishing rights is from a traditional coastal Sami fjord.[44] In that case, local fishermen received compensation after loss of fjord fishing due to river-damming.

The Sami as indigenous people further enjoy protection of their lifestyle and culture. The Norwegian constitution in particular protects the Sami in clause 108: 'It is the responsibility of the authorities of the state to create conditions enabling the Sami people to preserve and develop its language, culture and way of life'. Special measures might be required to achieve equality between the Norwegian

---

41 Susann F Skogvang, *Retten til fiske i fjorder og kystnære farvann* (n 38) 252–74.

42 Barnes, *Property Rights and Natural Resources* (n 15) 319; Francis T Christy Jr, 'Territorial Use Rights in Marine Fisheries: Definitions and Conditions' (n 26).

43 NOU 2008:5 *Retten til fiske i havet utenfor Finnmark* [The right to fish in coastal areas outside Finnmark] 414.

44 Rt 1985 p 247 (Fjordfiske i Kåfjord/ Fjordfishing in Kåfjord).

and the Sami people. That Sami use of natural resources qualifies for the acquisition of rights is undoubted and expressed in two important Supreme Court decisions from 2001.[45] This is also clearly expressed in clause 5 of the Finnmark Act as shown above.

International Legal Framework for Indigenous Peoples' Fishing Rights

General

In addition to the national legal protection, the Sami people enjoy protection for their culture and for their rights as indigenous peoples according to relevant international law. National protections must be interpreted in accordance with international legal obligations. In the next section, I will discuss the most important international law rules applicable to coastal fishing activities in indigenous areas. The questions here are whether international law adds something to the Norwegian property rights regime and whether international protection for an indigenous culture is stronger or more far-reaching than Norwegian domestic regulations.

Even though international law provides indigenous peoples extensive substantial and procedural rights to their natural resources, there is no specific provision in international law that states that indigenous peoples have a certain right to fish in coastal areas. Such a right must be based on more general rules and general principles of law. However, indigenous peoples have a solid foundation for their fundamental rights and the right to their natural resources.

Fishing Right as a Right to Culture

Drawing on Article 27 of the UN Covenant on Civil and Political Rights (ICCPR) Indigenous peoples have the right to their culture, including a strong legal protection for the material basis for their culture. Article 27 states:

> In those States in which ethnic, religious or linguistic minorities exist, persons belonging to such minorities shall not be denied the right, in community with the other members of their group, to enjoy their own culture, to profess and practice their own religion, or to use their own language.

The article protects the material basis for the culture of indigenous peoples, including protecting their natural resources. The provision sets up an absolute barrier to preventing indigenous peoples from exercising their culture. In its practice and general comments, the Human Rights Committee that monitors implementation of the Convention (see ICCPR Part IV Articles 28–45) has interpreted the provision

---

45   Rt 2001 p 769 (Selbu); Rt 2001 p 1229 (Svartskogen).

in a dynamic and expansive fashion.[46] The Committee has interpreted the phrase 'culture' to include land rights, especially when it applies to indigenous peoples. In *Ominayak v. Canada*, the Committee concluded that the exploitation of oil and gas on the territory of the indigenous Lubicon Lake Band amounted to a violation of Article 27, because such activities destroyed traditional hunting and fishing grounds.[47] Although Article 27 is described in passive terms the Committee has also expressed that the Article obliges state parties to take positive measures to secure this right.[48] Therefore, all ratifying states are required to ensure that the practice of this right is protected. The Human Rights Committee in the Mahuika case emphasized that the cultural practices protected by Article 27 may evolve over time:

> The right to enjoy one's culture cannot be determined *in abstracto* but has to be placed in context. In particular, article 27 does not only protect traditional means of livelihood of minorities, but allows also for adaptation of those means to the modern way of life and ensuing technology.[49]

In addition, ILO Convention No. 169 Concerning Indigenous and Tribal Peoples in Independent Countries (ILO-169) Article 23 (1) states that indigenous peoples' right to fish is vital for their culture and protects their traditional livelihood such as local community fishing:

> Handicrafts, rural and community-based industries, and subsistence economy and traditional activities of the peoples concerned, such as hunting, fishing, trapping and gathering, shall be *recognised as important factors in the maintenance of their cultures* and in their economic self-reliance and development. governments shall, with the participation of these people and whenever appropriate, ensure that these activities are strengthened and promoted. (Emphasis added)

The main objective of ILO-169 is to provide indigenous peoples the right to preserve their identities and to uphold, maintain and develop their livelihood and culture on their own terms, and to require the authorities to support this work actively. This understanding of the protection of indigenous peoples' culture is also

---

46   See UN Human Rights Committee, General Comment No 23: The Rights of Minorities, UN Doc CCPR/C/21/Rev.1/Add.5 (8 April 1994). See also Donald K Anton and Dinah L Shelton, *Environmental Protection and Human Rights*, 550 (CUP 2011), 550.

47   UN Human Rights Comm, Views of the Human Rights Committee under Article 5, Paragraph 4, of the Optional Protocol to the International Covenant on Civil and Political Rights, Communication No 167/1984, UN Do. CCPR/C/38/D/167/1984 (10 May 1990).

48   UN Human Rights Comm, General Comment No 23: The Rights of Minorities, UN Doc CCPR/C/21/Rev.1/Add.5 (8 April 1994).

49   Communication No 547/1993, *Apirana Mahuika et al v New Zealand*, views adopted on 27 October 2000, para 9.4.

expressed in several articles of the UN Declaration on the Rights of Indigenous Peoples (UNDRIP),[50] such as Article 11, 25 and 31.

These international legal obligations are of great importance to indigenous people, but they do not strongly protect indigenous fishing rights.

Fishing Right as a Right to Property

Another important right for indigenous peoples is the right to and protection of property. Property rights are a fundamental human right, which does not exclude indigenous peoples.[51] This right is expressed in the Universal Declaration of Human Rights Article 17.[52] A general protection of property rights is also expressed in Article 1 of Protocol 1 of the European Convention on Human Rights (ECHR)[53] and in The American Convention on Human Rights (ACHR)[54] Article 21. According to the International Convention on the Elimination of All Forms of Racial Discrimination[55] (CERD) Article 5 (d)(v), state parties undertake to prohibit 'discrimination in all its forms and to guarantee the right of everyone, without distinction as to race, colour, or national or ethnic origin, to equality before the law, notably in the enjoyment of the right to own property alone as well as in association with others'. According to the subsequent practice of the CERD Committee, and in particular the CERD Committee General Recommendation No. 23,[56] states shall pay special attention to indigenous peoples' property rights:

> 5. The Committee especially calls upon States parties to recognize and protect the rights of indigenous peoples to own, develop, control and use their communal lands, territories and resources ... [57]

This means that indigenous property rights shall be acknowledged to the same extent as other citizens' property rights. If a state allows the establishment of property rights to fish for its citizens, these rights must also apply for indigenous peoples. The principle of non-discrimination asserts that, if domestic law acknowledges property rights to natural resources for the non-indigenous peoples in non-indigenous areas, then the indigenous peoples' property rights on their

---

50   Declaration on the Rights of Indigenous Peoples, GA Res 61/295, Art 2, UN Doc A/RES/61/295 (13 September 2007).

51   S James Anaya, *Indigenous Peoples in International Law* (2nd edn, 2004) 141.

52   Universal Declaration on Human Rights.

53   ECHR, Protocol 1, Art 1.

54   American Convention on Human Rights, Art 21, *opened for signature* 22 November 1969, OEA/Ser.LV/11.50, doc 6 (1980) (entered into force 19 July 1978).

55   Committee on the Elimination of Racial Discrimination.

56   Committee on the Elimination of Racial Discrimination, *General Recommendation XXIII: Indigenous Peoples*, UN Doc CERD/C/51.Misc 13/Rev 4 (18 August 1997).

57   CERD Committee General Recommendation No 23 section V.

traditional territories must be recognized as well.[58] That this also includes the coastal Sami communities' fishing right finds support in a CERD questionnaire addressed to Norway in 2011.[59]

> In addition, ILO-169 protects indigenous property fishing rights. Article 15(1) states:

>> The rights of the peoples concerned to the natural resources pertaining to their lands shall be specially safeguarded. These rights include the right of these peoples to participate in the use, management and conservation of these resources.

Indigenous fishing rights must be specially safeguarded including the right of these peoples to the natural resources and the right to participate in the management of fisheries resources. The character of the right takes into account both the right to access and the right to withdrawal and management. Article 15 must be read together with Article 14 concerning the right to ownership and possession and the right to use.

Protection for indigenous property rights to lands and natural resources is also expressed clearly in UNDRIP Article 26. The UN Declaration on the rights of indigenous peoples prescribes in Article 26:

> 1. Indigenous peoples have the right to the lands, territories and resources which they have traditionally owned, occupied or otherwise used or acquired.

> 2. Indigenous peoples have the right to own, use, develop and control the lands, territories and resources that they possess by reason of traditional ownership or other traditional occupation or use, as well as those which they have otherwise acquired.

> 3. States shall give legal recognition and protection to these lands, territories and resources. Such recognition shall be conducted with due respect to the customs, traditions and land tenure systems of the indigenous peoples concerned.

The recognition of the right to natural resources including fishing rights is the most fundamental element in a sustainable future for indigenous peoples.

Procedural Rights

Indigenous peoples also have certain procedural rights according to international law. These rights are important in making substantive rights effective and applicable. These rights are the right to participate in the management of natural

---

58   Mattias Åhrén, *The Saami Traditional Dress & Beauty Pageants: Indigenous Peoples' Rights of Ownership and Self-Determination over their Cultures* (Tromsø 2010) 122.
59   CERD/c/nor/co/19-20, 5.

resources and the right to be consulted regarding issues of importance to them. This is partly reflected in ILO-169, Article 6, 7 and 15, and in UNDRIP, Articles 5, 11, 18, 19, 20 and 32.

Indigenous peoples must be consulted and participate in the management to achieve the goal of sustainable fish stocks. Policies to achieve this goal must be established in collaboration with the relevant indigenous people, whose traditional knowledge must be included in the decision-making. Additionally, the Convention on Biological Diversity (CBD) Article 8 (j) calls for state parties to pay adequate attention to indigenous peoples' traditional knowledge and practices relevant to the sustainable use of biological diversity in the management of natural resources.

Norwegian Implementation

All general fundamental human rights also apply to the Sami people in Norway. These rights must be interpreted and implemented taking into account the specific historical, cultural, social and economic circumstances of the Sami.[60] In addition, as an indigenous people, the Sami people are entitled to a separate set of rights as discussed above. It is undisputed that international law on indigenous peoples applies to fisheries legislation and restricts governmental fisheries management. That the Sami have the right to their property and their culture is solidly rooted in Norwegian law.[61] Norway has also ratified and, at least formally, implemented amongst others the ICCPR, the CERD and the ILO 169.[62] The Norwegian government has also stated that Norwegian Sami policy complies with the UNDRIP.[63]

Norway also recognizes local community property fishing rights. Geographically demarcated area-based fishing rights may be the subject of property rights in Norway. According to Norwegian law, one may to a limited extent establish local community rights to fish in coastal waters. The criteria is that, alone or as a part of a group, one has been fishing in the same area continuously, intensively and more or less exclusively for a long time, often referred to as from time immemorial.

---

60 UN Doc A/HRC/9/9, 11 August 2008; Promotion and protection of all human rights, civil, political, economic, social and cultural rights, including the right to development, 7.

61 See Susann F. Skogvang, *Samerett* (Sami Law) (Oslo 2009); Malgosia Fitzmaurice, 'The New Developments Regarding the Saami Peoples of the North' (2009)16 *International Journal on Minority and Group Rights*, 67–156.

62 Act of 21 May 1999 No 30 relating to the strengthening of the status of human rights in Norwegian law (Human Rights Act) Section 2; Act of 3 June 2005 No 33 on prohibition of discrimination based on ethnicity, religion, etc (Anti-Discrimination Act) Section 2; Act of 17 June 2005 No 85 relating to legal relations and management of land and natural resources in the county of Finnmark (Finnmark Act) Section 3.

63 Proposition No 1 to the Storting (2007–08).

This must also apply to Sami fishing. Any other outcome would be discrimination based on ethnic origin.

In addition, the Sami people in Norway enjoy rights to the material basis for their culture. An important guiding principle for Norwegian fisheries management is further expressed in the new section 7(g) of the Marine Resource Act which states that it is important to ensure 'that management measures help to maintain the material basis for Sami culture'. Therefore, the coastal Sami population in Norway enjoys strong legal protection for their substantive and procedural fishing rights in Norway.

Concluding Remarks

The coastal Sami population has the right to coastal fishing based on property rights and their right to culture and the material basis for their culture, within ecologically sustainable conditions. They are also entitled to participate in the management of the marine resources and to determine the content and the nature of sustainable development. States are obliged to ensure that the right of indigenous peoples to coastal fishing can continue under sustainable conditions and that this fishery is managed in a sustainable manner in line with their traditional knowledge and their participation in resource management. A state may comply with these obligations in different ways.

For marine-oriented indigenous peoples, land and seascapes are integrated within systems of customary tenure, traditions, local knowledge and resource use and management.[64] Therefore, to a larger extent than urban people, they are dependent on access to and the management of marine natural resources for their subsistence. The right to fish is of little value if it is not accompanied by the right to participate in the management of the fisheries and the right to withdrawal. Norway therefore needs to adopt new legal standards that will ensure the compliance of fisheries management and rights allocation with international law on indigenous peoples' rights. A protected and valuable fishing right must include both the right to access and the right to withdrawal and management. This is in line with Jeremy Waldron's definition of the concept of property: 'The concept of property is the concept of a system of rules governing access to and control of material resources'.[65]

Clause 29 of the Norwegian Finnmark Act, together with the implementation of relevant international law, may better safeguard local community fishing rights for the coastal Sami.

---

64 Monica E Mulrennan and Colin H Scott, 'Mare Nullius: Indigenous Rights in Saltwater Environments' (2000) 31 *Development and* Change 681–708, 702.

65 Jeremy Waldron, *The Right to Private Property* (New York 1988) 31.

Chapter 11

The Legal Organization of Sami Reindeer Herding and the Role of the *Siida*

Kristina Labba

Introduction

Reindeer herding is a long-standing Sami livelihood that has been pursued since time immemorial in *Sapmi*, the territory in which the Sami people traditionally live and which today constitutes northern Sweden, Norway, Finland and the Kola Peninsula in the Russian Federation. It is an essential part of the Sami way of life, as it holds, among other things, traditional knowledge about reindeer, nature and social relationships, some of which is embedded in the Sami *siida* custom that is related to the livelihood.[1] My aim in this chapter is to address the role of the Sami *siida* custom in reindeer herding and the need to recognize and strengthen the custom through legislation. The discussion is based on a brief comparison of the relevant parts of the Swedish and Norwegian reindeer herding acts. Literature describing Sami reindeer herding in the northernmost areas of Norway and Sweden is particularly informative with respect to the norms associated with the reindeer herding custom and the role of the *siida*.

Although Swedish and Norwegian Sami share the same reindeer herding traditions, there are significant differences in the national reindeer herding laws especially after Norway enacted a new Reindeer Herding Act in 2007. This Act gave legal recognition to the Sami *siida* custom, which has led to an individualization of rights to land areas within reindeer herding.[2] In contrast to the Swedish law, the developments in Norwegian law better protect Sami reindeer herding traditions. During the last 10 years, Norwegian courts have recognized the role of the *siida* in land use conflicts.[3]

According to traditional societal structures, reindeer herding was pursued by individuals primarily of the same family who lived in specific land areas.[4] Due to

1   Ot prp nr 25 (2006–07) 11–13; SOU 2006:14, 71.
2   Norwegian Reindeer Herding Act 2007 pt 6, s 51; Ot prp nr 25 (2006–07) 36–38; NOU 2001:35, 92–97. See also Gunnar Eriksen, *Alders tids bruk* (Fagbokforlaget 2008) 108.
3   Rt 2000 p 1578; LH2012-106514; LH-2013-162742.
4   Erik Solem, *Lappiske rettsstudier* (Universitetsforlaget 1970) 184, 190–91; Nils Oskal and Mikkel Nils Sara, *Reindriften i Finnmark: Rettshistorie 1852–1960* (Cappelen 2001) 299–307; Nils-Johan Päiviö, *Från Skattemannarätt till nyttjanderätt: En*

conflicts between settlers and farmers on the one hand and Sami on the other during the colonization of *Sapmi*, land area rights for reindeer herding in Sweden and Norway in the late 1800s were collectivized and the right-holders administratively divided into Lap villages[5] and reindeer herding districts,[6] respectively.[7] These specific administrative organizations, although named differently, were tasked in both countries to manage reindeer herding over a geographically defined area. The present-day 51 Sami villages and approximately 80 reindeer herding districts, which consist of unique associations regulated by national reindeer herding acts,[8] have defined borders and together cover a large area from the high north to the southern mountain ranges of Sweden and Norway. Each village and district with its members (reindeer owners and herders), has, since collectivization, been recognized as the primary holder of the land area rights within its defined borders.[9]

Many Sami customs play a significant role in Sami society,[10] but as long as customs do not receive legal recognition they are vulnerable; either they risk disappearing completely, or they cause internal conflicts where they contradict national legislation. In reindeer herding, this creates problems locally if one group of reindeer herders applies the provisions in the Reindeer Herding Act, and another group relies on contradictory *siida* custom and norms.

Sami Reindeer Herding in Practice

Sami reindeer herding is characterized by a close connection with nature; the herding represents a complex coupled system of interchange among animals,

---

rättshistorisk studie av utvecklingen av samernas rättigheter från slutet av 1500-talet till 1886 års renbeteslag (Uppsala universitet 2011) 128.

5   *Lappbyar*. When the current Swedish Reindeer Herding Act was enacted in 1971, the term 'Lap village' was replaced with the term 'Sami village' (*sameby*).

6   *Reinbeitedistrikt*.

7   Förslag till Förordning angående de svenska Lapperne och de bofaste i Sverige (1883); NOU 2001:34, 92. See also Tomas Cramér and Gunnar Prawitz, *Studier i renbeteslagstiftning* (PA Norstedt & Söners förlag 1970) 40; Kirsti Strøm Bull, *Reindriften i Finnmark: Rettshistorie 1852–1960* (Cappelen 2001) 100–103; <www.sametinget.se/samebyar>; <http://www.reindrift.no/?id=300&subid=0> both accessed 1 June 2014.

8   Swedish Reindeer Herding Act 1971; Norwegian Reindeer Herding Act 2007.

9   Swedish Reindeer Herding Act 1971 ss 1, 6 and 8; *Taxed mountain case* NJA 1981 p 1; Nordmaling case NJA 2011 p 109; Norwegian Reindeer Herding Act 2007 pt 1 s 6, pt 6 ss 42 and 51. See also Christina Allard, 'Who Holds the Reindeer-herding Right in Sweden? A Key Issue in Legislation' in Nigel Bankes and Timo Koivurova (eds) *The Proposed Nordic Saami Convention* (Hart Publishing 2013) 207.

10   Susann Funderud Skogvang, *Samerett* (2nd edn, Universitetsforlaget 2009) 26; Mattias Åhrén, 'Indigenous Peoples' Culture, Customs, and Traditions and Customary Law: The Saami People's Perspective' (2004) 1 Arizona Journal of International and Comparative Law 63, 105–107.

ecology and reindeer herders. By and large, seasons and ecological conditions decide reindeer migrations and activities, and herders follow the reindeer. Reindeer require large areas to accommodate their biological needs, and they usually migrate between different subdivided seasonally based pasture areas throughout the year.[11] For example, female reindeer migrate to the same specific calving grounds every spring to calve and to other specific areas for summer grazing, rutting and winter grazing.

Reindeer constitute individual property identified by complex reindeer earmarks that are officially registered.[12] Within the associations, each reindeer herder usually runs his or her own reindeer herding business from which the sale of reindeer meat represents taxable income. Reindeer are herd animals. A herd usually consists of reindeer belonging to different owners. To keep each owner's reindeer separated in a Sami village or a reindeer herding district the entire year would demand unreasonably large land areas and would be very burdensome practically and economically.[13] Especially during the winter-time, reindeer in the villages and districts are separated into *siida* herds, which usually consist of reindeer owned and herded by individuals belonging to the same (large) family.[14]

The Sami *Siida* Custom

For a long time, the Sami have had their own system of managing reindeer, land use and the distribution of natural resources.[15] The *siida* custom represents a part of the system and consists of a reindeer herding entity, which is associated with norms developed in a Sami reindeer-herding context. These norms provide instructions, for example, about competence, actions and consideration. The members of the *siida*, involving individuals often in the same family, pursue reindeer herding together on specific land areas.[16]

---

11   Nikolaus Kuhmunen, *Renskötseln i Sverige förr och nu* (Sámi Girjjit 2000) 19–60; Mikkel Nils Sara, *Reinen: et gode fra vinden* (Davvi Girji 1991) 15. <http://www. sametinget.se/underlag>; <http://www.reindrift.no/?id=974&subid=0> both accessed 1 June 2014.

12   Regulations on the design and registration of reindeer earmarks, ss 3 and 4; Norwegian Reindeer Herding Act 2007 pt 5 s 38. See also <http://www.sametinget.se/ renmärkesregister>; http://www.merker.reindrift.no/sok.aspx accessed 1 June 2014.

13   Sara, *Reinen: Et gode fra vinden* (n 11) 81; Kuhmunen (n 11) 53–55.

14   Kuhmunen (n 11) 53. See also <http://www.sapmi.se/nar_1_0.html> accessed 1 October 2014.

15   Kaisa Korpijaakko-Labba, *Om samernas rättsliga ställning i Sverige-Finland: en rättshistorisk utredning av markanvändningsförhållanden och -rättigheter i Västerbottens lappmark före 1700-talet* (Juristförbundets förlag 1994) 61; Lennart Lundmark, *Så länge vi har marker: Samerna och staten under sexhundra år* (Rabén Prisma 1998) 33; NOU 2001: 34, 425; Päiviö (n 4) 35, 119.

16   Solem (n 4) 184–85; Oskal and Sara (n 4) 302–305; NOU 201:34, 449.

In comparison to the present-day Sami villages and reindeer herding districts, the *siida* is usually a smaller entity in terms of the number of members and the size of land areas. A *siida* usually consists of members of a family or relatives,[17] while villages and districts can consist of several family groups and therefore several *siidas*. In some villages and districts the structure in terms such as the number of individuals and their social relationship is reminiscent of one *siida*. The land area that a *siida* customarily used may cross an administratively defined border of a village. In that event, the boundary was probably administratively created without regard to Sami reindeer herding customs in the area.

There are two distinct uses of the term *siida* in relation to land use. The term is also often used for the historic Sami societal organization (hereafter the historic *siida*), which mainly consists of a cohesive land area on which hunting and fishing were the main livelihoods for the families in the area.[18] Most scholars agree that reindeer herding evolved originally from a livelihood based on reindeer hunting collectively in the historic *siidas*, which later became increasingly intensive based on the herding of reindeer within the *siidas* referred to in this chapter.[19] This dual use of the term *siida*, referring to both the historic *siida* in which hunted reindeer constituted a collective property, and the reindeer herding entity that probably originated in the historic *siida*, may have contributed to confusion in Sweden about the rights connected to reindeer. The legislative processes which led to the adoption of Swedish reindeer herding acts have failed to acknowledge and recognize rights based on Sami reindeer herding traditions. Instead, as will be discussed further below, individual reindeer herding rights have been collectivized. In short, the understanding that rights connected to reindeer had a collective character in the historic *siida* may have been transferred to apply also to herding reindeer within the former Lap villages and the present-day Sami villages.

Siida *Flexibility and Stability Values*

There are two main values in the structure of a *siida*, flexibility and stability. Flexibility responds to the need to adapt the number of members and reindeer, for example, to varied climate situations and access to vital natural resources.[20] New short-term *siida* constellations can arise to cope in the best possible way with unexpected conditions, such as climate. Herders express that winters have become increasingly problematic because of climate change. Rainfall during the winter creates a hard ice layer on the ground through which reindeer cannot dig to get food.[21] Larger herds require

---

17   Robert N Pehrson, *The Bilateral Network of Social Relations in Könkämä Lapp District* (Universitetsforlaget 1964) 81–98, 107–108.

18   Solem (n 4) 81–83.

19   Lars Ivar Hansen, Bjørnar Olsen, *Samenes historie: fram til 1750* (Cappelen Akademisk Forlag 2004) 203; Lundmark (n 15) 34; Päiviö (n 4) 252–57.

20   Oskal and Sara (n 4) 302–303.

21   See for example <http://samer.se/GetDoc?meta_id=4369> accessed 4 February 2014.

larger pastures. Dividing a *siida* in response to problematic weather events related to climate change which adversely affects pastures, may allow herders to cope better by affording them the opportunity to spread herds on different pasture areas.[22] New long-term constellations can be motivated by marriage, for example. A *siida* is also dependent on stability. By nature, reindeer instinctively oppose unnecessary migration to new land areas. In addition, the best possible use of land areas is usually based on traditional knowledge of the areas, which in turn is based on repeated use of them by families through the generations.[23]

Norms about Decision-Making and Relations with Neighbouring Siidas

To herd reindeer effectively, cooperation is required among reindeer herders at the local level. This has likely stimulated the development of norms associated with the *siida* custom, such as how to make decisions and how to relate to neighbouring *siidas*.

Decisions in a *siida* are made at four levels: the individual, the household, the *siida* and the *siida*-leader.[24] The household is a smaller group of reindeer owners, typically the husband, wife and their children; the *siida* is a collection of independent households.[25] The individual is sovereign in all matters concerning his or her individual property, i.e., their own reindeer.[26] Usually, however, decisions of individual character affect and involve the household. Matters affecting all individuals and households in the *siida* are matters for the *siida*, such as matters regarding strategies about land area use and relations with neighbouring *siidas*.[27] A common understanding on these matters is sought at the *siida* level. Individual and household level decisions can also sometimes be issues for the *siida* level, if, for example, they are contrary to standing *siida* policies or prior decisions.[28] Given the need for rapid decision-making and the difficulties with communication in field conditions, individuals on an ad hoc basis can make decisions affecting an entire *siida* during herding. On such occasions, the individual may make important and sometimes complex snap decisions based on rapidly changing conditions, using his or her own knowledge, prior experience and best judgment.[29]

To gain flexibility, membership in a *siida* does not have to be based on a prior connection to the specific land areas; it can also be based on other factors, such

---

22 Sara, *Reinen: et gode fra vinden* (n 11) 104.
23 Solem (n 4) 190–91; Oskal and Sara (n 4) 300–301.
24 Oskal and Sara (n 4) 299; Geir Hågvar, *Den samiske rettsdannelse i indre Finnmark: Om nordsamenes rettsorden, grunnlovsvernet og selvbestemmelsen* (Diedut no 2, 2006) 145–51.
25 NOU 2001:34, 249.
26 Sara, *Reinen: Et gode fra vinden* (n 11) 99; Hågvar (n 24) 145.
27 Hågvar (n 24) 143–45.
28 Oskal and Sara (n 4) 303.
29 Sara, *Reinen: Et gode fra vinden* (n 11) 100–101.

as the spirit of cooperation among individuals. However, for stability reasons the consent of the individual members of a *siida* is preferable when new individuals or families seek to be admitted. An increase in the number of reindeer in a *siida* can have unfortunate ecological consequences and can lead to an overcrowding of reindeer, sometimes at the expense of neighbouring *siidas*. Land use without agreement from *siida*-individuals holding customary land area rights can create conflicts.[30]

A well-working relationship based on mutual respect between neighbouring *siidas* is important. In such a relationship, the *siidas* exchange information when necessary and consult on activities that affect them both. Sometimes reindeer belonging to individuals in one *siida* (A) cross the border and mix with reindeer belonging to another *siida* (B), especially if they are geographically close to each other. Norms associated with the *siida* custom instruct how the situation can be dealt with. The instructions depend, however, on various practical circumstances, such as, for example, the cause of the mix, the pasture situation for the affected *siidas*, and the condition of the reindeer. Very briefly, if an accident causes the mix, *siida* (A) can usually require a separation of the reindeer in order to recover their reindeer. If the mix is desired and caused by *siida* (A), it is mainly up to *siida* (B) to consider whether it is appropriate to separate the reindeer belonging to *siida* (A) from the herd. Often it is possible to find out the reason for the mix. There are no explicit sanctions for violation of norms, but selfish behavior can adversely affect the relationship.[31]

Exercise of the Siida *Custom*

The *siida* custom has a long-standing tradition within Sami reindeer herding, but for a long time national authorities, especially in Sweden, have undermined the role of the *siida*. Gaps in lawmakers' knowledge and understanding of Sami reindeer herding and customs may have led to this approach. For example, the preparatory works to the Swedish Reindeer Herding Act recognized that reindeer herders regularly cooperate within *siidas*, but also that this cooperation was unstructured.[32] The Sami language has a well-developed terminology concerning reindeer herding and the exercise of the *siida* custom. Because the terminology incorporates a huge part of the traditional knowledge about the field,[33] the lawmaker's lack of knowledge in the Sami language may have led to an undermining of the role of the *siida*.

---

30   Kirsti Strøm Bull, *Studier i reindriftsrett* (Tano Aschehoug 1997) 92; Oskal and, Sara (n 4) 318–20.

31   Solem (n 4) 192.

32   Prop 1971:51, 35, 37.

33   Mikkel Nils Sara, 'Land Usage and Siida Autonomy' (2011) 2 Arctic Review on Land and Politics, 140.

Sami historical land area use has not been properly investigated in Sweden. Consequently, it is somewhat uncertain who holds the land area rights within reindeer herding at the local level.[34] In some Sami villages, there may be a common understanding among the members that rights to all land areas within the village are collective; in other villages, the understanding might be different. Some Swedish scholars have pointed out that the uncertainty is problematic especially in terms of property rights related to land areas within reindeer herding.[35] More recent materials indicate that previous connection to land area has traditionally been essential for individuals within reindeer herding.[36] Some have expressed the view that former individual land area rights were collectivized when the Reindeer Herding Act 1886 was enacted.[37] However, individuals still exercise the custom, more so in some regions than others.[38] There are no recent surveys or research to confirm this situation,[39] but the manner in which reindeer herding is pursued indicates this to be the case. Particularly during the winter season, when access to the appropriate food plants is greatly restricted by snow cover, reindeer are dispersed across different land areas in the form of *siida* herds.[40]

National Legislation on Reindeer Herding

Both Sweden and Norway have their own reindeer herding acts.[41]

Swedish Legislation

The first strictly national Swedish Reindeer Herding Act was enacted in 1886, three years after the bilateral Swedish-Norwegian Common Lap Treaty,

---

34 Bertil Bengtsson, *Samerätt: En* översikt (Norstedts Juridik 2004) 32.

35 Bertil Bengtsson, 'Några samerättsliga frågor' (2000) SvJT 36, 45; Bertil Bengtsson, *Samerätt* (n 34) 32, 39–40; Allard, 'Who Holds the Reindeer-herding Right in Sweden?' (n 9) 219.

36 Korpijaakko-Labba (n 15); SOU 2006:14, 115; Päiviö (n 4) 128; Oskal and Sara (n 4) 304–305.

37 Cramér and Prawitz (n 7) 40.

38 *Fastsetting av rammebetingelser i reindriftsnæringen: Delprosjekt Siidaindeling i Vest Finnmark* (Reindriftsforvaltningen 2006) 7–9; Øyvind Ravna, *Rettsutgreiing og bruksordning i reindriftsområder: En undersøkelse med henblikk på bruk av jordskiftelovgivningens virkemidler* (Gyldendal Norsk Forlag AS 2008) 390, 403–407.

39 Prop 1971:51, 174; Kuhmunen (n 11) 61.

40 Kuhmunen (n 11) 61, 156; <http://www.sapmi.se/nar_1_0.html> accessed 1 October 2014.

41 Oskal and Sara (n 4) 302–305; Swedish Reindeer Herding Act 1971 ss 1, 6; Norwegian Reindeer Herding Act 2007 pt 1 s 6, pt 2 ss 9 and 10, pt 5 s 32. See also NOU 2001:34, 265–77; NOU 2001:35, 163.

Felleslappeloven entered into force.[42] Like the treaty, the Swedish Act was supposed to function on a national level to reduce the increasing conflicts between Sami reindeer herders and other types of land users (e.g., for farming and logging). To more readily assign blame for damages caused by reindeer, the land area on which reindeer herding had been pursued since time immemorial was divided into Lap villages. In every village, all reindeer herding individuals became jointly and severally liable.[43] Areas that in varying degrees had been used by specific *siidas* thus became collectivized regardless of the extent of prior use. Thereafter, all members of a Lapp village formally gained uniform rights to the land areas within it.[44] Under the reformed Reindeer Herding Act (1928), orders of the County Administrative Board regulated the internal organization of the village.[45] Every Lap village had its own specific order that stated, among other things, if and how the land areas were divided internally.[46] By means of these orders state authorities and their officials strongly controlled and decided on the usage of land areas and the internal organization of reindeer herding in Sweden until the current Reindeer Herding Act was enacted in 1971.[47]

The current Act is based on an old Swedish cooperative association model. The model was considered to benefit the internal organization of reindeer herding.[48] The older term 'Lap village' was replaced with the term 'Sami village', but the presumption introduced in the first Act to the effect that all members of the village have the right to use all land areas within it has been maintained.[49] According to the current act, the Sami villages hold annual general meetings during which the majority rules, a principle that means that the greatest number of votes exercises power over such issues as membership in the Sami village, land area use and the joint economy.[50]

Norwegian Legislation

In Norway, reindeer herding in *Troms* County and counties to the south experienced a similar scenario to that of Sweden in 1886. The land area on which reindeer herding has been pursued since time immemorial was divided into reindeer herding districts by Norwegian authorities according to authority granted in the

---

42   Swedish Reindeer Herding Act 1886.
43   Appendix to the Parliamentary Protocol: Protocol on Legal Matters, Meeting held at the Supreme Court 1884 1886 10.
44   Swedish Reindeer Herding Act 1886 s 5. See also Cramér and Prawitz (n 7) 40–41.
45   Swedish Reindeer Herding Act 1928 s 11; SOU 1968:16, 46.
46   SOU 1968:16, 46.
47   Prop 1971:51, 30.
48   Prop 1971:51, 37.
49   Swedish Reindeer Herding Act 1971 s 15.
50   Swedish Reindeer Herding Act 1971 s 59.

Common Lap Treaty.[51] Every reindeer owner was thereafter obliged to report district affiliation to make it easier to assign blame for damage that reindeer caused others.[52] When the first strictly Norwegian Reindeer Herding Act was enacted in 1933, reindeer herding in *Finnmark* County was also divided into reindeer herding districts.[53] The County Administrative Board had to ensure that the regulations were carried out.[54]

In the second national Reindeer Herding Act, enacted in 1978, the reindeer herding district was emphasized in a way that caused Sami reindeer herding customs (e.g., the *siida*) to lose prominence.[55] For example, the term 'shared pastures',[56] which was introduced in the legislation, emphasized that land area rights were uniform and collective. Many reindeer herders disagreed with this emphasis which often led to conflicts between herders about borders.[57] A change in the Act in 1996 authorized administrative officials to allocate land areas with regard to Sami customs.[58]

The committee that drafted the updated Reindeer Herding Act of 2007 (the current version) concluded that the Act needed to acknowledge legally the *siida* and to reflect variability in the rights of individual reindeer owners in relation to each other.[59] This is in contrast with the previous presumption that the herding right in a district is a uniform and collective right for its members. Thus, the *siida*, defined as an entity of reindeer herders who conduct reindeer herding together on specific reindeer grazing land areas, was incorporated into the Act of 2007 as a legal subject, with certain legal capacities; the Act also recognized the concept of the *siida*-share.[60] According to the Act of 2007, a *siida* consists of one, several or many *siida*-shares, and the creation of a new *siida*-share requires, among other things, that leaders of the existing *siida*-shares in the relevant *siida* agree to the new share. The creation of a new *siida*-share is associated with various conditions, for example, that the new share cannot threaten the *siida*'s economic, ecological and cultural sustainability. Each *siida*-share must have at least one leader; the leader(s) can be an individual, spouse or cohabitant. The decision about who shall lead the share must be based on the individual's efforts in the *siida* and his or her living conditions, meaning, for example, that a person who actively works in the *siida* should be prioritized. The role of the leader(s) involves determining who

---

51   Common Lap Treaty 1883 s 6.
52   Strøm Bull, *Reindriften i Finnmark* (n 7) 101–102.
53   ibid 235.
54   NOU 2001:35, 51–52.
55   Hågvar (n 24) 177–81.
56   *Fellesbeiter*.
57   Stortingsmelding nr. 28 (1991–92) 7.
58   Strøm Bull, *Studier i reindriftsrett* (n 30) 91.
59   NOU 2001:35, 29.
60   Norwegian Reindeer Herding Act 2007 pt 6, s 51; Ot Prp no 25 (2006–07) 36.

is allowed to own reindeer in the share and how many reindeer each may own.[61] Each *siida*-share controls five votes at the annual *siida* meeting, during which members elect a board for the *siida*. The *siida*-board in turn has the responsibility to organize and manage activities in the *siida*.[62] To be able to own reindeer in Norway, both a reindeer earmark and ownership of a *siida*-share are required. A *siida*-share consists of a reindeer herding family or an individual.[63]

Decision-Making According to Statutory Law and the Sami Siida *Custom*

Cooperation between individuals such as reindeer herders at the local level depends upon an appropriate decision-making mechanism. According to the Swedish Reindeer Herding Act, decisions in a Sami village must be based on majority rule, by which reindeer herding members jointly decide issues that have economic significance, such as issues about leadership, land area use and membership in the village.[64] Membership does not require previous connection to a land area, but the person must be a Sami who is or has permanently been involved in or pursued reindeer herding within the boundaries of the Sami village. Such a person can qualify as a reindeer herding member.[65] There are no definitions of what involvement in and pursuit of reindeer herding actually consist of. The preparatory works state that these are determined by custom (*praxis*). According to the same source, the village has the primary right to decide these matters.[66] According to the Norwegian Act, establishment of a *siida*-share, the entity that best corresponds with a reindeer herding member in a Sami village, requires consensus among the existing *siida*-shares. The *siida*-share leader(s) in turn controls reindeer-owning and reindeer herding membership in the share. These Norwegian regulations are based on Sami traditions, and the intention is to preserve stability. The preparatory works mention that not all who want to herd reindeer may do so; ecological conditions in combination with land area connection decide who can own and herd reindeer in a *siida*.[67]

The Swedish Act does not require consensus among existing reindeer herding members about letting in new members to the Sami village, nor does it require a connection to the land area. Consequently, there is a potential risk for misuse of the majority rule to strengthen the majority's position of power. A village can consist of groups of individuals that more or less coincide with the structure of possible *siidas* in the village. In practice, the misuse can occur by giving Sami village membership and reindeer herder status to Sami who support the majority.

---

61 Norwegian Reindeer Herding Act 2007 pt 2, ss 10–11 and pt 6, s 51.
62 Norwegian Reindeer Herding Act 2007 pt 6 ss 51–55.
63 Norwegian Reindeer Herding Act 2007 pt 2 ss 9, 10.
64 Swedish Reindeer Herding Act 1971 s 59; Prop 1971:51, 179–81.
65 Swedish Reindeer Herding Act 1971 ss 11–12.
66 Prop 1971:51, 161–63.
67 NOU 2001:35, 99.

Over the long run those in the minority in a *siida* may lose out. The situation can be especially difficult if a dominating part of a Sami village relies on the collectivization presumption of the Act, while another part relies on contradictory and unrecognized Sami customs and norms.

Land areas constitute essential resources for traditional reindeer herding. Allowing entry for new members and indirectly allowing an increased number of reindeer also increases competition among the *siidas*, especially if land areas are understood as collective for all members. Literature produced in Norway indicates that competition between individual reindeer herders or *siidas* for access to land areas is one of the causes of internal reindeer herding conflicts.[68] From a *siida*-perspective, the Swedish Act may seem flexible in this respect. However, somewhat simplified, if constellations are based mainly on flexibility, over-exploitation of, or unfortunate internal competition over, natural resources can arise. Identifying land area right-holding individuals could promote stability and better clarify where flexibility is appropriate. The possibility of excluding usage is, however, a basic element in the property rights regime.[69]

Discussion and Closing Remarks

Failing to recognize Sami customs in legislation can cause different consequences and ultimately violate Sami individuals' and group's human rights, such as protected property and cultural rights.[70] An apt example arises when commercial, or other entities, formally deal with the Sami village in agreements for such things as industrial projects and mineral extraction activities. These agreements may involve land traditionally used by a specific *siida* as opposed to the village as a whole. This could create a situation in which the most directly affected *siida* has little or no say in what can and will be done with what is traditionally their land. Opinions about the extraction may differ between the directly affected *siida* and the Sami village; the *siida* may oppose it because it is entirely dependent on the area in question, while the Sami village, although not being entirely dependent upon the specific portion of land, may want to reap the benefit. Further, this could lead to a questionable, and possibly disturbing, distribution of any proceeds and benefits from the use of the land.

According to the provisions in the Reindeer Herding Act, all members of a Sami village have the access and use of all land areas within that Sami village. This creates a situation in which a *siida* that loses proper use of its traditional land

---

68   Strøm Bull, *Studier i reindriftsrett* (n 30) 92; Sara, *Reinen: Et gode fra vinden* (n 11) 102–103.

69   Erling Eide, Endre Stavang, *Rettsøkonomi* (Cappelen akademisk 2008) 162–63.

70   European Convention on Human Rights art. 1 Protocol 1; International Convention on Elimination of All Forms of Racial Discrimination, art 5; International Covenant on Civil and Political Rights, art. 27. See also A/HRC/24/41.

area may be forced to find another suitable area in which to pursue their reindeer herding. With the right of access to all other land within the Sami village, the suitable area may be no farther than the land of the *siida* next door. This opens the opportunity for an environment ripe for internal and unsustainable competition, and conflict. In the end, this can result in the affected *siida* feeling that the only option is to leave the reindeer herding society completely, thereby leaving behind their culture, heritage, and not least their land without compensation.

A progressive and effectively irreversible loss of lands is one of the greatest threats to reindeer herding in Sweden and Norway.[71] The loss of land exerts great pressures on reindeer herders, because, ecologically, it implies a reduction in reindeer carrying capacity. Economically, it means that fewer herders can maintain viable incomes from reindeer herding, and many whose incomes become insufficient have to quit reindeer herding. In cultural terms, it can mean that individuals lose their culture and identity. In Sweden, almost no attention has been given to the legal (and rights) consequences of the loss of land areas for individuals involved in reindeer herding.

However, legal recognition of the *siida* is not unproblematic. In times of declining land areas due to, for example, the extraction of natural resources, the individualization of land area rights can make individuals and *siidas* more vulnerable, especially if their cultural and property rights are not respected, e.g. in terms of being able to oppose planned activities. If the land area is lost, the individuals or *siida* may be forced to quit reindeer herding. With individualization, the collective also can become vulnerable, because the flexibility around land use is reduced.

The collectivization of the land area rights, with all that it implies, may have extinguished a large part of possible customary rights in Sweden. By comparison, the situation in Norway for the legal recognition of the *siida* differs somewhat primarily due to the manner in which reindeer herding during the 1900s was regulated and managed by national authorities. The *siida* custom was largely exercised within reindeer herding in *Finnmark* County in Norway until the 1970s without any major negative impact from the Act.[72] Thereafter, it lost prominence for some 10 years. The situation in *Finnmark* probably facilitated the legal recognition of the role of the *siida* in Norway as a whole.

Even if customary subdivisions of land areas in all present-day Sami villages may no longer exist, at least certain norms associated with the *siida* custom deserve further examination in future legislative processes. The custom is associated with norms that, in different ways, could create predictability in decision-making for individuals within reindeer herding. To a large degree, I think this applies also to Norway, where the legal framework for the organization of reindeer herding

---

71   NOU 2001:35, 29. See also Kristina Labba, 'Mineral Activities on Reindeer Grazing Land in Sweden' (2014) 1 Nordic Environmental Law Journal 93.

72   Sara, *Reinen: Et gode fra vinden* (n 11) 44–45.

should better reflect knowledge, customs and practices related to the *siida*.[73] In conjunction with writing this chapter, I have experienced that it is difficult to refer to the norms of the *siida* because they are far from being systematized or even available in written form; indeed, they are mainly transmitted orally in conjunction with reindeer herding activities. However, my study indicates that the *siida* custom still has a central role in Sami reindeer herding. Consequently, it deserves to be recognized in legislation in an insightful and respectful manner. This requires that efforts be made to study and document the custom thereby facilitating the lawmaking processes.

---

73   Sara, 'Land Usage and Siida Autonomy' (n 33) 154.

Chapter 12

The Definition of a Sami Person in Finland and its Application

Tanja Joona

Introduction

This chapter draws attention to the contemporary discussion on Sami identity and legal recognition of Sami identity in Finland. The government of Finland has taken steps to strengthen the rights of its indigenous people, the Sami. The ratification of the international ILO Convention No 169[1] and the renewal of the Sami Act prepared by the Ministry of Justice of Finland during 2013–14 were on the agenda of the Finnish government 2012–15. One of the main issues in this regard was the evaluation of the definition of a Sami person in the act. This chapter deals with the application of the current act and the proposed changes in the law.

The current discussion on Sami identity and subjectivity are related to the survival of the entire Sami culture, due to the fact that the majority of the Sami population is living in cities far away from their traditional lands. In Finland, 70 per cent of the Sami children are born outside their home region. Those traditional lands are, however, often described in public rhetoric as the basic element of their 'indigenousness' and culture. However, the Finnish Sami subjectivity is strongly connected with the right to vote in the elections of the Sami Parliament and is, therefore, the basis of Sami rights as indigenous people. A broader viewpoint of the chapter introduces the model of indigenous membership-based governance, which, in Finland, has roots in the 1960s. These decisions have had far-reaching consequences for the official status of many Sami people, and this fact will continue to affect the lives and identities of Sami in Finland for future generations.

In the modern Nordic welfare states, the Sami are acknowledged as an indigenous people within the nation states and as a people with their own culture, customs, beliefs and identity. Some of the Sami still practise unique traditional livelihoods, although the modern and globalized world has also affected the Sami society in ways that have developed quickly. In many cases, the situation of indigenous peoples has been obscured by issues of broader concern, including land rights and political representation. These concerns are, of course, fundamental

---

1   C169 – Indigenous and Tribal Peoples Convention, 1989 (No. 169) Convention concerning Indigenous and Tribal Peoples in Independent Countries (Entry into force: 5 September 1991) Geneva, 76th ILC session (27 June 1989).

to indigenous communities, but it is nonetheless crucial that these issues and situations are considered together with targeted action to safeguard the distinct identity of indigenous peoples and to promote the realization of indigenous rights.

This chapter examines the official status of a Sami person in Finland and how that status is connected with the right to vote in the elections of the Finnish Sami Parliament. The electoral roll of the Sami Parliament in Finland consists of 5,483 persons, and, when counting their descendants, the official number of the Sami is about 9,200 persons.[2] Approximately 60 per cent of the Sami in Finland are living outside their traditional territories in big cities like Rovaniemi, Oulu and Helsinki. The trend is similar in Sweden and Norway. The situation of the Sami languages is not good; only 1,930 persons identify one of the Sami languages as their mother tongue in Finland.[3]

The Finnish Sami Parliament is deemed the representative and political body of the Sami with origins from within what is now Finland.[4] A Sami person in Finland is defined under the Sami Act[5] as a person who has the right to vote in the elections of the Finnish Sami Parliament. Section 3 of the current act provides:

> For the purpose of this Act, a Sami means a person who considers himself a Sami, provided:
>
> 1. That he himself or at least one of his parents or grandparents has learnt Sami as his first language; or
>
> 2. That he is a descendent of a person who has been entered in a land, taxation or population register as a mountain, forest or fishing Lapp; or
>
> 3. That at least one of his parents has or could have been registered as an elector for an election to the Sami Delegation or the Sami Parliament.

Finland's Ministry of Justice requested statements from and negotiated with the Finnish Sami Parliament from 2012 to 2014 concerning the new act, both in regards to the Finnish Sami Parliament and especially concerning the new definition of 'Sami' in Finland. Resulting drafts of the related subsection 2 of the act have been introduced to the public from time to time. The latest version was accepted into the Finnish government Bill[6] and was also approved by the majority

---

2 The Sami Parliament <http://www.samediggi.fi> accessed 20 October 2014.

3 The Official Statistical Office of Finland, *Suomen virallinen tilasto* (SVT): Väestörakenne [verkkojulkaisu]. ISSN=1797–5379 (Tilastokeskus 2013) <http://tilastokeskus.fi/til/vaerak/2013/vaerak_2013_2014-03-21_tie_001_fi.html> accessed 20 October 2014.

4 Act of Sami Parliament 17.7.1995/974.

5 ibid s 3.

6 Hallituksen esitys eduskunnalle laeiksi saamelaiskäräjistä annetun lain ja rikoslain 40 luvun ja 11§:n muuttamisesta. Government Bill (HE) 167/2014 vp.

of the Finnish Sami Parliament on 27 June 2014, which formulates subsection 2 in the following way:

> 2) so that he/she has in his/her family relations acquired the Sami culture and maintained his/her contact with it and is a descendant of a person who has been entered in a land, taxation or population register as Lapp ...

An electoral board consisting of five persons at the Finnish Sami Parliament makes a decision on membership to the electoral roll, which at the same time, constitutes the formal status and membership of a person in the Sami society in Finland. The possibility to appeal is first to the governmental body of the Finnish Sami Parliament and then, if rejected, to the Finnish Supreme Administrative Court.[7] The electoral roll has its foundation in interviews made in the 1960s by young students in a limited area in Northernmost Lapland.[8] The purpose of the interviews was to interview every inhabitant of the Sami region whose parents or grandparents spoke Sami as their first language.[9] Later, the language criteria also became the criteria for Sami identity in Finnish law.[10] Current problems relate both to those interviews and to the 'self-governing' power of the electoral board to decide membership. This is further elaborated upon below. The Finnish approach to the situation has two sides to the same coin: identity/formal status and the right to vote. In Finland, it is difficult to call yourself a Sami if you are not on the voting roll. Hence, I draw attention to the Finnish situation, in which governance of membership, or *membership governance*, plays a significant role in the identity formation and the formal status of an indigenous person. The recent debate in Finland concerns the membership selection and how the definition of a Sami is applied in practice. The majority in the Finnish Sami Parliament have demanded changes in the legislation, seeking to adopt an even more restrictive approach and a stronger position for the group's, i.e. Finnish Sami Parliament's, own right to decide on the members.[11] The minority relies more on how

---

7   See more on the electoral board of the Sami Parliament in Finland <http://www.samediggi.fi> accessed 20 October 2014.

8   Erkki Nickul, *Suomen saamelaiset vuonna 1962. Selostus Pohjoismaiden saamelaisneuvoston suorittamasta väestötutkimuksesta* (Tilastotieteen pro gradu-tutkielma.Helsinki 1968); Asetus saamelaisvaltuuskunnasta 824/73 1 s 2 mom; See also Saamelaisasiain neuvottelukunnan mietintö I. Ehdotus saamelaislaiksi ja erinäisten lakien muuttamiseksi. KM 1990:32, 30.

9   Erkki Nickul, *Suomen saamelaiset vuonna 1962. Selostus Pohjoismaisen saamelaisneuvoston suorittamasta väestötutkimuksesta* (Tilastotieteen pro gradu-tutkielma, Helsinki1968).

10   Act on Sami Delegation 1973 s 1 para 2.

11   Saamelaiskäräjälakityöryhmä, puheenjohtaja Riitta-Leena Paunio, sihteeri Camilla Busck-Nielsen. *Oikeusministeriö, Mietintöjä ja lausuntoja* 55/2013, 30.10.2013<http://urn.fi/URN:ISBN:978-952-259-340-5> accessed 20 October 2014.

the act has been arbitrarily interpreted in practice.[12] This means that some persons and families have been left unfairly outside the roll. The problem may be in the law itself, but certainly there are difficult approaches in the application. The background for the act and examples of its application are introduced later in this chapter.

Membership governance is an interesting approach theoretically, because it combines both law and policy aspects of membership selection.[13] Rules and principles governing indigenous membership have a dual aspect. First, a group's capacity to decide its own membership is an essential element of indigenous self-governance. The Sami leaders in Finland practise their own indigenous membership selection, fearing that too liberal an approach to membership selection would allow non-Sami to enter into the roll and thereby destroy the existing Sami culture.[14] Self-constitution is both an expression of self-governance and its precondition. Second, a person's claim to membership is sometimes supported by human rights, especially the right to enjoy one's culture in community with other members of a minority. Because of this duality, in some instances, the interests of a self-constituting group and the interests of a self-identifying individual are directly opposed,[15] which is the case for the Sami in Finland.

Membership disputes involving indigenous communities often involve the most conceptually difficult claims to address using human right methodologies and related institutions. It is argued that exclusions are necessary if indigenous communities are to be communities, but not all exclusions can be justified in a liberal democracy.[16] In whatever forum they are heard, be

---

12 *Inarinsaamelainen: Pahinta on kun oma kansa syrjii.* An interview of Anu Avaskari, an Inari-Sami and member of the Sami Parliament, who expresses her view on discrimination by the Sami themselves. Finnish Braodcasting Company (YLE) <http://yle.fi/uutiset/inarinsaamelainen_pahinta_on_kun_oma_kansa_syrjii/6586220> accessed 2 October 2014.

13 Kirsty Gover, *Tribal Constitutionalism: States, tribes and the Governance of Membership* (OUP 2010); Austin Badger, 'Collective v. Individual Human Rights in Membership Governance for Indigenous Peoples' (2011) 26 (2) American University International Law Review 485–514; Kirsty Gover, 'Genealogy as Continuity; Explaining the Growing Tribal Preference for Descent Rules in Membership Governance in the United States' (2008–09) American Indian Law Review 243.

14   KHO:n uusi tulkinta saamelaisuudesta kuohuttaa. 8.10.2011 <http://yle.fi/uutiset/khon_uusi_tulkinta_saamelaisuudesta_kuohuttaa/5436701> accessed August 27 2014.

15 Kirsty Gover, 'Indigenous Membership and Human Rights: When Self-identification Meets Self-Constitution' in Corinne Lennox and Damien Short (eds), *Routledge Handbook of Indigenous Peoples' Rights, Abingdon* (Routledge 2013) <http://papers.ssrn.com/sol3/papers.cfm?abstract_id=2262558> accessed 28 August 2014.

16 ibid 1. See also Kristian Myntti, *Suomen saamelaisten yhteiskunnallinen osallistuminen ja kulttuuri-itsehallinto.* Raportti Oikeusministeriölle Osa 1. Lainvalmisteluosaston julkaisu (Helsinki 1997); Kristian Myntti, 'Saamelaismääritelmä oikeudelliselta kannalta' in Irja Seurujärvi-Kari (ed), *Beaivvi Mánát, Saamelaisten juuret ja nykyaika* (Tietolipas 164, Suomalaisen kirjallisuuden seura 2000) 216–26.

it tribal, national or international, indigenous membership disputes raise two fundamental questions:

1. What is the optimal inclusivity of an indigenous community?
2. Under what circumstances may a person reasonably be excluded from an indigenous community?[17]

The recent Finnish discussion is related to inclusions in and exclusions from group membership. Since the other side of the coin refers to identity, the exclusion and inclusion become problematic. In addition to identity and the right to vote, the extra value of the entry into the Finnish Sami Parliament electoral roll is also often questioned.

In such a situation, a Sami person is a citizen of Finland in addition to his status as an indigenous person. Furthermore, due to the fact that, in Finland, a Sami is defined as a person who has the right to vote in the elections of the Finnish Sami Parliament, the electoral register also gives the person formal Sami status. Status as member of a state government-recognized indigenous group can determine legally whether one is entitled to certain benefits provided by the state.[18] These benefits may range from the basic right to live in a certain area to usufruct rights for practising a livelihood, such as reindeer herding. As these financial benefits grow, so does the importance of determining that status as an indigenous person in a just manner.[19] In Finland, Sami persons, when registered into the roll, have the right to participate in the political decision-making and the use and governance of the financial resources granted to the Finnish Sami Parliament.[20] The operation of the Finnish Sami Parliament is funded by the state.[21]

In addition to cultural autonomy, the Finnish Sami Parliament has political influence through the demand for consultation on all matters concerning the

---

17   Gover (n 13) 1.

18   Austin Badger, 'Collective v. Individual Human Rights in Membership Governance for Indigenous Peoples' (2011) 26 (2) American University International Law Review 493.

19   ibid.

20   The Finnish Sami Parliament (*Samediggi*) is the self-governing body of the Sami from within what is now Finland, as legislated at the beginning of 1996. The Parliament consists of 21 members and 4 deputies, and its main purpose is to plan and implement the cultural self-governance guaranteed to the Sami as an indigenous people. The Sami Delegation (Sami Parliament), founded under a decree, was a predecessor to the Sami Parliament and operated from 1973 to 1995. The Finnish Sami Parliament is the supreme political body of the Sami in Finland. It is an independent legal entity of public law, which, due to its self-governance nature, is not a state authority or part of the state public administration. The Finnish Sami Parliament functions under the administrative sector of the Ministry of Justice. The Sami Parliament in Finland represents the Finnish Sami in national and international connections, and it tends to the issues concerning Sami language and culture and Sami position as an indigenous people. The Sami Parliament can make initiatives, proposals and statements to the state authorities. <http://www.samediggi.fi> accessed 27 August 2014.

21   ibid.

Sami in Finland, including, for example, land use, environmental issues, natural resources, traditional livelihoods, and social and health services.[22] Even academic research is subject to consultations enforced by the local Lappish authorities.[23] Most importantly, the formal identity recognition places, in the view of the Finnish state, a Sami in the position of rights holder via international human rights conventions concerning the rights of indigenous peoples.[24] Without the registration in the voting roll, a person lacks all of these rights in Finland in the eyes of Finnish law.

Identity preservation and connection with culture are challenged when membership to a certain group is not based on objective criteria or the law, but is instead subjected to random selection based on similar political interests between the selector and the candidate. This can also be described as a 'democratic paradox',[25] a situation in which the legitimacy of the people is questioned – how should the legitimate constitution of the Sami 'people' be determined? The constitution of a people is typically brought up as a question of identity – whether the feeling of a (Sami) identity needs to be thick or thin for democracy to be able to work – whereas its legitimacy remains unexplored.[26] In the Finnish Sami context, by selecting the members for the electoral roll, from the Sami point of view, the selector is actually approving voters for the next elections.[27]

In comparison to Sweden and Norway, Finnish Sami membership selection is more restrictive. In Norway, 15,005 persons were marked into the electoral roll of the Norwegian Sami Parliament in 2013.[28] According to research by Torunn Pettersen, 'we are unable to know how large this population could have been if all persons with known or unknown Sami background considered themselves to be Sami and decided to join the electoral register'.[29] Pettersen continues that this remains unknown primarily because Sami affiliation had

---

22   Act on Sami Parliament s 9.

23   For example, the Regional Council of Lapland and The Centre for Economic Development, Transport and the Environment (ELY Centre in Lapland) interpret the Sami Act s 9 concerning the consultations, so that they must hear the opinion of the Sami Parliament when issues or applications concerning the Sami are received.

24   Draft Government Bill 19.5.2014 on the ratification of the C 169 <http://oikeusministerio.fi/fi/index/valmisteilla/lakihankkeet/kielellisetjakulttuurisetoikeudet/saamelaistenoikeudetalkuperaiskansanaosallistuasaamelaistenkotiseutualueellaerityisestimaankayttoakoskevaanpaatoksentekoon.html> assessed 21 November 2014.

25   See more Chantal Mouffe, *The Democratic Paradox* (Verso 2000); Sofia Näsström, 'What Globalization Overshadows' (2003) 31 (6) Political Theory 808–34.

26   Sofia Näsström, 'The Legitimacy of the People' (2007) 35 Political Theory 624.

27   Juha Joona, 'Kuka kuuluu alkuperäiskansaan – historian vastauksia tämän päivän kysymyksiin' Lakimies (2013) 47 747.

28   Elections of 2013 <http://www.samediggi.no> accessed 20 October 2014.

29   Torunn Pettersen, 'The electoral register of the Sámediggi in Norway 1989-2009: Basis, growth and geographical shifts' (Paper prepared for presentation at European

not been registered in the Norwegian censuses since 1930. Combined with previously prevailing negative attitudes toward being Sami, this could have caused many persons to be unaware of their Sami heritage, or to make those who were aware their heritage reluctant to acknowledge it. In this respect, Pettersen continues to reflect on the Norwegian Sami situation. She says that there is an unknown number of persons with a clearly defined and unproblematic Sami identity.[30] These persons may consider themselves to be fully Sami, a little Sami, sufficiently Sami or a combination of Sami and another ethnic identity. On the other hand, she continues, an unproblematic Sami identity is not the same as joining the electoral register of the Norwegian Sami Parliament, the *Samediggi*.[31] The estimated total Sami population of Norway varies between 75,000 and 100,000.[32] Similarly, in Sweden estimations vary from 27,000 to 35,000, while only 8,322 persons were registered in the Swedish Sami Parliament electoral roll in 2013.[33]

There may be many different reasons for the varied approaches to identifying and selecting Sami membership in the Nordic countries. One of the biggest differences is that, while the Finnish Sami electoral roll has its legal foundation in the interviews made in the 1960s, the Sami in Sweden and Norway have had the possibility to enter into the roll only since the mid-1990s, when the Swedish and Norwegian Sami Parliaments were established and the first elections were held. The approval for the Norwegian Sami roll has also been very liberal, since there are no cases of declines by the Sami Parliament in Norway and only a few in Sweden.[34] Another reason might be that the Sami are defined differently in Sweden and Norway. 'Saminess' is understood in these countries also through reindeer herding, the traditional livelihood of the Sami, as this was how the numbers of Sami were estimated by the states before the Sami Parliaments existed.[35] For example, according to the Swedish Reindeer Herding Act, section 1, a person with a Sami family background of Sami descent is entitled to use land and water areas for his own living and his reindeer, whereas in Finland, Sami is defined solely as a person registered into the voting roll.

Consortium for Political Research (ECPR), Joint Sessions of Workshops, University of St Gallen, Switzerland 12–17 April 2011) 23.

30   ibid.

31   ibid.

32   Different estimations can be found. For example, see at <http://www.thefreelibrary. com>; <http://nordicway.com>; <www.samediggi.no>; < www.samediggi.se>; <www. samediggi.fi> accessed 20 October 2014.

33   Statistik sameröstlängden <http://www.sametinget.se/6434> accessed 14 November 2014.

34   Government Bill (HE) 167/2014 (n 5).

35   Saamelaiskomitean mietintö (KM 1973:46) 3. On how estimations of Sami population are difficult, since the approach in Nordic countries are so different.

Self-Identification as Sami vs Group Acceptance

What makes a person indigenous? It is often stated that indigenous communities and their individual members draw their identity and form their world-view from specific historical and cultural contexts that include their own beliefs, social organizations, language, customs and knowledge.[36] International law gives some guidelines when defining the beneficiaries of certain conventions and treaties. For example, Article 1 of the International Labour Organization (ILO) Convention No. 169 is often cited when defining indigenous peoples, and it is legally binding on all states that have ratified it. The Convention applies to:

> b) peoples in independent countries who are regarded as indigenous on account of their descent from the populations which inhabited the country, or a geographical region to which the country belongs, at the time of conquest or colonisation or the establishment of present state boundaries and who, irrespective of their legal status, retain some or all of their own social, economic, cultural and political institutions.

Similar definitions or opinions describing the characteristics of indigenous peoples are offered, for example by the Special Rapporteur of the United Nations (UN) Economic and Social Council Sub-Commission on Prevention of Discrimination and Protection of Minorities (1986), the Asian Development Bank (ADB), the World Bank, Professor, the former Chairman and Special Rapporteur on Indigenous Peoples issues Mrs Erica-Irene A Daes, and former UN Special Rapporteur of the Sub-Commission on Prevention of Discrimination and Protection of Minorities, José Martinez-Cobo.[37] As an example, one can refer to Mr M Dodson, Aboriginal and Torres Strait Islander Social Justice Commissioner, who stated: 'There must be [a] scope for self-identification as an individual and acceptance as such by the group. Above all and of crucial and fundamental importance is the historical and ancient connection with lands and territories.'[38] All of these definitions contain

---

36 Innocenti Digest, *Ensuring the Rights of Indigenous Children*. UNICEF, Innocenti Research Centre (2003) 11(2) http://www.unicef-irc.org/media-centre/press-kit/digest11/> accessed 27 May 2014.

37 Asian Development Bank, Definition of Indigenous Peoples <http://www.adb. org/documents/policies/indigenous_peoples/ippp-002.asp> accessed 27 May 2014; World Bank, Policy Brief, Indigenous Peoples, Still among the Poorest of the Poor <http://siteresources.worldbank.org> accessed 27 May 2014; Working paper by the Chairperson-Rapporteur, Mrs Erika-Irene A Daes, on the concept of 'indigenous people' E/CN.4/Sub.2/AC.4/1996/2 10 June 1996; UN ECOSOC (1986); Working definition of indigenous peoples by José R Martinez-Cobo, Study on the Problem of Discrimination against Indigenous Populations at <http://indigenouspeoples.nl/indigenous-peoples/definition-indigenous> accessed 4 June 2014.

38 Report of the Working Group on Indigenous Populations on its thirteenth session. E/CN.4/Sub.2/1995/24, 41–51.

similar characteristics of 'indigenousness'. In short, they all refer to descent, self-identification, culture and connection with land or territory.[39]

The importance of identity, culture and language are also emphasized in many of the Articles of the ILO Convention No 169. Even though Finland has not ratified ILO 169 yet, it has tried to meet many of the provisions of the Convention in the Sami Act of 1995 and also in other Finnish legislation concerning the Sami.[40] The legal application of the Finnish definition of Sami and the challenge therein relates to Sami persons who live in Northern Finland. In this situation, the Sami have descended from the original inhabitants of the area, identify themselves as Sami and have maintained some of their own social, economic, cultural and political institutions, but for one reason or another they have not been accepted to the electoral roll of the Finnish Sami Parliament.[41] Some cases of rejection to the roll are introduced below.

In general, international norms and jurisprudence frame minority and indigenous membership by reference to the overarching principle of 'self-identification',[42] the right of self-identifying minority members to enjoy their culture in community with others. These approaches emphasize individual agency and choice and call on the state to ensure that individuals have reasonable access to the cultural life of the minority to which they 'belong'.[43] On the other hand, Article 33 of the UN Declaration on the Rights of Indigenous Peoples (UNDRIP)[44] emphasizes the right of indigenous peoples to determine their own group identity and membership.[45] This is a change that has been proposed to be included into the new Finnish Sami

---

39   'It is difficult to separate the concept of indigenous peoples' relationship with their lands, territories and resources from that of their cultural differences and values. The relationship with the land and all the living things is at the core of indigenous societies'. Erica-Irene A Daes, 'Prevention and Protection of Indigenous Peoples and Minorities. Indigenous peoples and their relationship to land' (Working paper presented to the Commission on Human Rights, Fifty-third session, 11 June 2001, E/CN.4/Sub.2/2001/21).

40   ibid (10).

41   See more, Erika Sarivaara, 'Statuksettomat saamelaiset Paikantumisia saamelaisuuden rajoilla' [Non-status Sami locations within Sami borderlands] (Doctoral Thesis, Kautokeino Sami Allaskuvla, DIEDUT 2/2012); Tanja Joona *ILO Convention No. 169 in a Nordic Context with Comparative Analysis: An Interdisciplinary Approach* (Juridica Lapponica Series No 37, University of Lapland 2012).

42   ILO Convention 169, Art 1.2, CERD 2008, 274 and ICCPR, Art. 27.

43   ibid (15).

44   United Nations Declaration on the Rights of Indigenous Peoples adopted by the United Nations General Assembly during its 61st session at UN Headquarters in New York City on 13 September 2007.

45   1. Indigenous peoples have the right to determine their own identity or membership in accordance with their customs and traditions. This does not impair the right of indigenous individuals to obtain citizenship of the States in which they live. 2. Indigenous peoples have the right to determine the structures and to select the membership of their institutions in accordance with their own procedures.

Act of 2014.[46] In the Finnish situation, however, it is reasonable to ask what the 'group-acceptance'[47] would mean in practice, since the application of the current legislation has also been problematic – this will be explained shortly below. Even though they fulfil the subjective and objective criteria in the legislation, some persons have not been accepted into the roll.

In contrast to the non-binding nature of the UNDRIP, the UN International Covenant on Civil and Political Rights (ICCPR) carries the weight of a legally binding treaty. Adopted in 1966, Article 27 of the ICCPR applies to ethnic, religious or linguistic minorities located within states party to the treaty, including Finland. The ICCPR provides that those fitting the description must be afforded the right to enjoy their own culture with the other members of the group. The ICCPR is also one of several international rights-based treaties that indigenous peoples have invoked with some success. One of these cases is *Lovelace v. Canada*,[48] brought before the UN Human Rights Committee (HRC) through the treaty's optional protocol. Sandra Lovelace had lost her status as a member of an indigenous community under federal, not tribal, law by marrying a non-member. An Indian man marrying a non-Indian woman, however, would not have lost his Indian status under these provisions. The HRC did not express its views on discrimination on the basis of sex in this situation, because the marriage had occurred before the ICCPR came into force in Canada. The Committee did, however, find that Canada was in violation of Article 27 of the Covenant by continuing to deny Ms Lovelace the opportunity to live on the reserve, the only place where she could practise her culture in a community with other members of the group. Finding no *reasonable* and *objective* justification for denying the right to residence based on Ms Lovelace's marriage to a non-member, the HRC found that Canada had violated the ICCPR.

Another case before the HRC also dealt with ICCPR Article 27. In *Kitok v. Sweden*,[49] an ethnic Sami individual was denied special reindeer herding rights afforded to the Swedish Sami. In Sweden these rights are afforded to the members of a Sami village (a *sameby*), and, since Kitok had moved away from the Sami village, he could not continue the livelihood. In this case, however, The HRC did not find Sweden to have violated Article 27. However, the HRC did expand on the Article with a requirement of states that restrictions on individual membership

---

46   Hallituksen esitys eduskunnalle laeiksi saamelaiskäräjistä annetun lain ja rikoslain 40 luvun ja 11§:n muuttamisesta. Government Bill (HE) 167/2014 vp.

47   This is an English translation for 'ryhmähyväksyntä' in Finnish. The concept is used to describe the membership selection determined by the indigenous peoples (Sami in Finland) themselves.

48   UN Human Rights Committee, *Lovelace v Canada*, Communication No 24/1977, *Selected Decisions under the Optional Protocol*, 2nd–16th Session, UN Doc CCPR/C/OP/1 (30 July 1981) 83, 87.

49   See UN Human Rights Committee, Views of the HRC under Article 5, Paragraph 4 of the Optional Protocol to the ICCPR Concerning Communication No 197/1985, *Kitok v Sweden*, UN GAOR, 43d Session, Supp No 40 (A/43/40) (25 March251987).

decisions should be reasonable, objective, and necessary to ensure the continued existence of the minority as a community.

These decisions by the UN Human Rights Committee show that membership selection had been decided by very small, tight-knit groups who have their own customs and traditions. The problem in the Finnish situation is whether the Sami whose status is in question can be compared to people living on an aboriginal reservation or a Sami village, where the persons who form a tight-knit community are relatives to each other and everyone knows everyone.

In the Finnish case, more than 9,000 Sami persons who live in different parts of Finland and elsewhere in the world are connected to each other by the right to vote in elections of the Finnish Sami Parliament. The question arises whether these persons represent the kind of close community of common shared values and starting points that enable them to decide whether a person in question is a Sami. Even the current Finnish Sami Parliament members have different ideas about who can be considered a Sami. It is a coincidence when a majority is formed of people having shared opinions – a person's right to enjoy minority rights and indigenous membership should not be dependent on such uncertain events.

The Challenge of Membership Governance in Finland

To understand the problematic nature related to the membership governance in Finland, it is reasonable to explain the situation and also to look back at the history. The history of the formulation of the Finnish Sami as a legally recognized indigenous people has its roots in the aftermath of the Second World War and especially during the 1960s. Internationally, this was a time of modern radicalism, and the Sami movement experienced the worldwide awakening of minorities defending their rights. However, the Sami movement was more of a reaction against the post-war custom of trying to forget one's cultural traditions and values by assimilating.[50] The Sami resistance and activism led to formal recognition and, for example, to the establishment of the so-called Sami Delegation, a representative body of the Sami in Finland in 1973. In 1995, the Finnish Sami Parliament replaced the Finnish Sami Delegation with a stronger position in the state law.[51] This chapter will shortly describe how formal indigenous status is granted on a personal level and draws attention to individual human rights in this regard.

The Finnish Sami Parliament's electoral roll is based on interviews conducted in the 1960s by young students.[52] These interviews were conducted only in a very limited area in the northernmost Finland in the current municipalities of Utsjoki,

---

50   Veli-Pekka Lehtola, *The Sámi People, Traditions in Transition* (Kustannus-Puntsi 2002) 58.

51   ibid.

52   See more Juha Joona, 'Kuka kuuluu alkuperäiskansaan – historian vastauksia tämän päivän kysymyksiin' (2013) 4 Lakimies; Juha Joona, *Entisiin Tornion ja Kemin*

Enontekiö, Inari and the northern parts of Kittilä and Sodankylä. As a result, most
of that area became the official area of the Finnish Sami, the *Sapmi*, as the Sami
Home Region with cultural autonomy granted in the Sami Act of Finland. The
present border is in some measure linguistically and ethnically artificial;[53] the
border does not follow the old borders of Lapland (Kemi and Tornio Laplands)
in Finland. This means that a large population of ethnically native Sami remains
inside the old borders in the southern region.[54] According to the present language
and the official Finnish definition of Sami, these people fulfil the Sami criteria.[55]
They live especially in the Tornio River Valley, in the Muonio, Kittilä, Kolari,
Sodankylä, Savukoski and Salla Counties.[56]

The interviews were conducted at the request of the Finnish Department of the
Nordic Sami Council led by a Finnish man by the name of Carl Nickul. The task
was to interview every inhabitant of the Sami region whose parents or grandparents
spoke Sami as their first language; 3,852 people were interviewed.[57] Later, the
language criteria also became the criteria for Sami identity in Finnish law.[58] The
interviews were further analysed in a university master's thesis on statistics by
Erkki Nickul, son of Carl Nickul.[59] The students interviewed local Sami people,
but Erkki Nickul acknowledges some deficiencies in this work: the interviews were
made only in parts of Lapland; not every village was visited; interviewers should
have been more educated; people did not remember their grandfathers' names; and
uncertainty existed in the assessment of language skills. In 1964 Nickul himself
completed the work, at which time, for example, in the case of six people from Inari
the language question was still open. Nickul subsequently answered the language
question on the behalf of these three participants by guessing. As a consequence
of the interviews, these Sami persons formed a part of the basis for the electoral
roll.[60] The composition of the roll might have been very different if the interviews
had been conducted, for example, 10 years earlier or 10 years later, depending on
whom at that particular time happened to be alive. In addition, the interviews were
made to register the *Sami speaking population* and their descendants, not to define
the *indigenous people* in Finland as was done later in the Finnish legislation.[61]

Lapinmaihin kuuluneiden alueiden maa- ja vesioikeuksista (Juridica Lapponica Series No
32, University of Lapland, 2006).

53   Marjut Aikio, 'The Finnish Perspective: Language and Ethnicity' in Dirmid Collin
(ed), *Arctic Languages: An Awakening* (UNESCO 1990).

54   ibid.

55   ibid. See more Sarivaara (n 41).

56   ibid.

57   Erkki Nickul, *Suomen saamelaiset vuonna 1962. Selostus Pohjoismaisen
saamelaisneuvoston suorittamasta väestötutkimuksesta* (Tilastotieteen pro gradu-tutkielma,
Helsinki 1968).

58   Act on Sami Delegation 1973 s 1 para 2.

59   Nickul (n 57).

60   ibid.

61   Suomen perustuslaki (Finnish Constitution) 11.6.1999/731.

The Finnish Sami Parliament, in accordance with section 23–26d of the Act of Sami Parliament, decides who is to be included in the electoral roll. The focus has been on subsection 1, which contains the so-called language criteria. The legal praxis shows that the Finnish Sami Parliament has been quite restrained in its decision-making concerning a person's right to be added to the Sami electoral roll. Some decisions show that proof of relation to language criteria has had no significant meaning.[62] This is considered in more detail below.

The 1995 Act on Sami Parliament states that a person may be a Sami also if he/she is a descendant of a person who is entered as a 'mountain, forest or fishing Lapp'[63] in registers held by either Swedish or Finnish authorities.[64] However, the practical consequences of this amendment have been very small. In 1999, the Finland's Supreme Administrative Court concluded that only a very limited number of people have the right to gain Sami status by this subsection.[65] As mentioned earlier, an electoral board consisting of five persons[66] decides membership, with the possibility of an appeal first to the governmental body of the Finnish Sami Parliament and if rejected, then to the Supreme Administrative Court of Finland.[67] In 1999, 657 persons appealed to the Supreme Administrative Court of Finland on the basis of subsection 2, but only a few were accepted into the register. This ruling made it difficult to raise the issue again. The main argument in this respect was that the indigenous peoples have the right to decide their own membership rules (UNDRIP, Article 33) and that it is to be the Sami who recognize another Sami.

The majority of the politicians in the Finnish Sami Parliament argue that the Sami language and culture will be destroyed if more Sami are let into the roll solely on the basis of subsection 2. In Finland, the basis of a person's 'Saminess' cannot be found from old land and taxation registers, and one or a few forefathers in those registers do not make a person a 'Sami'.[68] It is argued that these persons assimilated into the main population long ago, and they do not have any connections with the

---

62   Joona (n 27).

63   Lapp is an exonym, a name given by outsiders. See more about the concept of Lapp: Kaisa Korpijaakko-Labba, Saamelaisten oikeusasemasta Suomessa. Oikeushistoriallinen tutkimus Länsi-Pohjan maankäyttöoloista ja – oikeuksista ennen 1700-luvun puoliväliä (1989).

64   Act of Sami Parliament 1995, 3.

65   Supreme Administrative Court, KHO 1999:55.

66   In 2011, the members of the electoral board were Pekka Aikio, Marjaana Aikio, Maria Sofia Aikio, Ilmari Laiti ja Juha Magga, all of whom represented the North Sami. New elections will be held on 2015 with new electoral board.

67   Decision by the Supreme Administrative Court of Finland KHO 2003:61.

68   *Näkkäläjärvi: Saamelaismääritelmä on nyt saamelaisyhteisön odotusten mukainen.* <http://yle.fi/uutiset/nakkalajarvi_saamelaismaaritelma_on_nyt_saamelaisyhteison_odotusten_mukainen/690878> At Finnish Broadcasting Company (YLE) 30 October2013 accessed 20 October 2014.

Sami culture. It has been estimated that more than 100,000 people would claim that they are Sami.[69]

The minority[70] at the Finnish Sami Parliament argues the problematic nature related to the language criteria: due to the assimilation policy of the Swedish (Finnish) state and the Lutheran Church, many Sami have been forced to give up of their native language. Therefore, it is now somewhat peculiar that the (same) legislator has set the language as a criterion for 'Saminess'. As time passes, it becomes more and more impossible to find new persons who can fulfil the language criteria, only those who are already included meet the requirement. Future generations will fulfil the criteria only in subsection 3, since the act does not require that a person must speak the Sami language. The confrontation becomes even more distinct when realizing that almost 70 per cent of the Finnish Sami live outside the administrative borders of the Finnish Sami Homeland region, very few of whom speak the Sami languages.

In 2011, the Supreme Administrative Court of Finland changed the application of the Sami Act, but not in favour of the Finnish Sami Parliament.[71] The court considered the appeal of five persons who had not been accepted to the register. The court decided that four of the appellants should be added to the register. Three of them were accepted on the basis of the language criteria, even though they did not speak the Sami language. Their forefathers had been marked as Lapps in the land and taxation register of 1825.[72] One of the claimants provided no evidence of his ancestors' ability to speak the Sami language, but the court emphasized his self-identification as Sami and other cultural characteristics that he was able to present. He was a fisherman from Inari-lake. In this respect, the court changed its view in the context of one person. Of particular interest is that the court referred to Article 1 of international Convention ILO 169 in its reasoning, even though Finland has not ratified the Convention. It also referred to the statements given to

---

69   In the interview by Tapani Leisti at the Finnish Broadcasting Company (YLE), Professor Jaakko Husa estimated that the new (2011) interpretation of the Sami definition by the Supreme Administrative Court would mean that we would soon have 150,000 Sami in Finland. *KHO:n uusi tulkinta saamelaisuudesta kuohuttaa* <http://yle.fi/uutiset/khon_uusi_tulkinta_saamelaisuudesta_kuohuttaa/5436701> accessed 20 October 2014; 'Minä olen saamelainen – ja minä myös' Helsingin Sanomat (Helsinki 1 July 2012) <http://www.hs.fi/paivanlehti/sunnuntai/Min%C3%A4+olen+saamelainen++ja+min%C3%A4+my%C3%B6s/a1341032243214> accessed 21 November 2014.

70   Members of the Finnish Sami Parliament, Mr Pentti Valle, Mrs Anu Avaskari and Mr Antti Sujala, have publicly expressed their dissenting opinion to the majority decisions of the Finnish Sami Parliament concerning the preparation of the new Sami Act of Finland, and especially the Sami definition. Saamelaiskäräjät hyväksyi saamelaiskäräjälain ja saamelaismääritelmän kompromissiratkaisun. <http://yle.fi/uutiset/saamelaiskarajat_hyvaksyi_saamelaiskarajalain_ja_saamelaismaaritelman_kompromissiratkaisun/7325294> accessed at 20 October 2014.

71   Supreme Administrative Court, KHO 26.9.2011 taltio 2711.

72   In the cases of 1999 the Court refused to look back any further than 1875.

Finland by the UN Committee on the Convention on the Elimination of all Forms of Racial Discrimination (CERD).[73] The Finnish Sami Parliament claimed for dissolution of the 2011 judgment, but in March 2013 the Supreme Administrative Court of Finland gave the decision to the Finnish Sami Parliament, in which the court kept in force its ruling of 2011.[74]

There are also persons and families who are considered Sami in Sweden and Norway but who are not accepted to the register in Finland. Members of reindeer herding families, like the families Pokka, Eira, Unga, Suikki and Vasara[75] identify themselves as Sami, but they are not in the Finnish Sami roll, because they were never interviewed or they have not been accepted by the Sami Parliament in Finland.[76]

Examples of the practice of the membership governance by the electoral board and the Sami Parliament of Finland show the arbitrary means of membership selection.[77] The argument of the appellant in 1999, Arto Enojärvi, was denied, and he was not accepted to the electoral roll. Subsequently, Mr Enojärvi moved to Norway, where he was accepted onto the Norwegian Sami electoral roll of the Sami Parliament in Norway. This example suggests that individual Sami are treated very differently within each of the Nordic countries.[78]

In 2003, a new case was brought to the Supreme Administrative Court of Finland.[79] The electoral board of the Finnish Sami Parliament held that person B was mistakenly included in the register in 1999. Nevertheless, person A, a

---

73   Concluding observations of the Committee on the Elimination of Racial Discrimination: Finland, 10.12.2003, CERD/C/63/CO/5; Consideration of reports submitted by states parties under article 9 of the Convention: Finland, 5.3.2009, CERD/C/FIN/CO/19.

74   KHO hylkäsi saamelaiskäräjien purkuhakemukset. Finnish Broadcasting Company. <http://yle.fi/uutiset/kho_hylkasi_saamelaiskarajien_purkuhakemukset/6621852> accessed 20 October 2014.

75   'Saamelaisuus kuuluu minulle' (Saminess belongs to me) *Luoteis-Lappi* (Lapland 28 August 2014) A story about Kalevi Vasara, who has applied to the electoral roll four times every four years. He is born in 1938.

76   See further Supreme Administrative Court 27 September 1999 case 3804; 22 September 1999 case 3182; 27 September 1999 case 3834; 27 September 1999 case 3821, 3804, 3835, 3821–25, 3830, 3831, 3833 and 3760; 5 December 1999 case 3050–55; 27 September 1999 case 3761; 5 December 2001 case 3049.

77   The legal praxis from 2007 shows a decision for demand for rectification to the electoral board of the Finnish Sami Parliament. A person was asking for his right to be marked into the roll as his sister and brother had been. The electoral board declined his demand for rectification, because his approval 'would be involuntary assimilation of indigenous peoples to the main population'. Electoral board of the Sami Parliament of Finland. An excerpt of the minutes 17 April 2007 Dno 113/D.m.3.1.

78   Personal permission given by Arto Enojärvi to use his name in this context. See also his story in the local newspaper 'Saamelainen vain naapurimaassa' (Sami only in neighbouring country, Norway) *Luoteis-Lappi* (Lapland 28 August 2014).

79   Supreme Administrative Court of Finland, KHO 2003: 61.

descendant of person B, was added to the register. This led the court to conclude that person B should also be included in the electoral roll.[80] Sisters and brothers from the same family have also been treated unequally where some have been accepted and others rejected.[81]

It seems that the electoral board approves some persons to the roll for the same reasons that they decline others. The Supreme Administrative Court of Finland's judgment of 2011, as mentioned earlier, allowed one person to enter into the roll according to subsection 2 (Lapp-section) of the act. The Finnish Sami Parliament was unsatisfied with the ruling and claimed dissolution of the judgment. The very same year, however, the Finnish Sami Parliament approved a person to the electoral roll along with his family, according to the same subsection 2. The person was close to the Chairman of the Finnish Sami Parliament; the Chairman had disqualified himself from participating in the decision-making.[82] The Finnish Sami Parliament reasoned that, '… the Sami definition in the law is no longer up to date. It (the electoral roll) excludes persons who are Sami, but who have lost their Sami language due to the strong assimilation policy of the Finnish State …', and he therefore was to be marked into the roll along with his family.[83]

From a human rights perspective, it can be argued that the current situation violates section 6 of the Finnish Constitution, concerning equality before the law, and is therefore unbearable for the individuals who are fighting for their status and identity.

What makes the situation even more controversial is that the definition of a Sami in the Sami Act of Finland does not require that the person must know how to speak a Sami language. It is enough that one of their four grandparents dating back to the 1960s knew that one of his/her (of four) grandparents had Sami as the home language. This means that, if persons consider themselves to be Sami, they are legally recognized as Sami generation after generation, even though they do not necessarily have any connections with the Sami culture. The case law has shown that persons living in Helsinki have formal status as Sami, but, for example, a reindeer herder identifying himself as Sami and descending from four Sami grandparents is not considered a Sami, because the grandparents do not fulfil the language criteria anymore, or they were not interviewed in the 1960s. Naturally, this has caused feelings of injustice among the local [non-status] Sami in Northern Finland.[84]

---

80   ibid.

81   Reijo Eira, 'Sisko tunnustettiin, veljeä ei' (Sister was recognized, brother was not) *Kittilä-lehti* (3 September 2014).

82   See more unpublished document by Heikki J Hyvärinen, Lausunto saamelaiskäräjien vaalilautakunnalle (Statement for the Electoral board of the Sami Parliament 22 December 2011) 19 dealt in the board on 20.12.2011 after which completed.

83   Sami Parliament minutes (31 May 2011).

84   Elina Venesmäki, 'Kiista Lapissa – Kuka saa olla saamelainen?' *Suomen Kuvalehti* (Helsinki No 14 2014).

Recent research by Erika Sarivaara shows that many Finnish Sami who have not been granted entry into the Finnish Sami electoral roll have a strong Sami identity. They live in Lapland, they are descendants of Sami families, they speak Sami and they practise traditional Sami livelihoods. These persons also have a strong will to preserve the Sami culture and language. They simply lack the formal recognition of their Sami identity.[85]

Important questions can be raised in the context of the Finnish non-status Sami. What is the legal status of these persons if they are not included in the electoral roll of the Finnish Sami Parliament? Is their exclusion *reasonably* and *objectively* justified for the sake of the Sami community? They do not have legal protection as indigenous persons, should their cultural self-consciousness be unsupported? Most painful of all, as a result they have difficulties calling themselves Sami. This situation is also causing challenges for families, where one parent is accepted into the roll and the other is rejected.

Conclusion: Defining the Sami Population

In the Finland, Sami indigenousness is commonly understood to be defined through Sami language. This is complicated, as the Sami were previously subject to policies of assimilation, and authorities did not consider the Sami languages worth preserving. The authorities even periodically prohibited teaching Sami language in schools. Therefore, many Sami lost their native tongue. Once the Sami languages were seriously threatened by extinction, the other attributes of Sami identity had to be identified and fostered. Unfortunately, due to assimilation policies, many Sami have mixed feelings about their identity, and they are seeking recognition in formal ways. In Finland, due to the fact that a Sami person is defined under the Sami Act of Finland, the entry into the electoral register of the Finnish Sami Parliament constitutes formal legal recognition.

As explained above, the 1960s interviews conducted in some parts of Finnish Lapland have had consequences that have led to a problematic human rights situation. Furthermore, the restrictive official Finnish Sami politics have caused mixed feelings, and attempts have been made to correct the situation through changes in the Finnish legislation. These changes include emphasizing the acceptance, changes in the formation of the electoral board at the Finnish Sami Parliament, and highlighting the importance of the Sami family and community when determining the status of a Sami person.

The controversy between those who have been entered into the Finnish Sami electoral roll according to the language criteria and those who want to get into the roll according to the Lapp-section is more evident. This is because in practice the forefathers of the 'language-Sami' lived at the beginning of the nineteenth century, exactly at the same time as those persons referred to as Lapps. Moreover,

---

85   See more, ibid to fn 41.

according to the 'language' criteria, future generations are not accepted to the roll based on section 1 but instead on section 3, which provides that at least one of the person's parents *has or could have been* registered as an elector for an election to the Sami Delegation or the Finnish Sami Parliament. Other than the self-identification, this does not require any connection with the Sami culture, lands, livelihoods or language.

To sum up, this chapter has explained the complexity related to Sami identity and its historical roots, according to which the formal indigenous Sami recognition is granted in Finland. An important question that can be raised is this: how should we deal with the dualism? On one hand, the group's right to decide their own membership rules and recognize indigenous peoples' right to self-determination is highlighted. On the other hand, when interpreting this right as including the right to subjugate the membership selection to random preference slanted by political intentions, the rights of an individual are violated according to international law and within the Finnish state's legal system. Naturally, this causes the feeling of injustice amongst the people. Although the attitudes, the legislation and the application of the law can be changed, damage has already been done. However, despite this disagreement regarding official status, many 'non-status' Sami have started to revitalize Sami language, and they have shown a strong will to preserve their indigenous Sami culture.

Chapter 13

To What Extent Can Indigenous Territories be Expropriated?

Mattias Åhrén

Introduction

Over time, international law has taken fundamentally different positions toward indigenous communities' property rights over territories traditionally used.[1]

Classical international law largely emerged to justify European powers placing territories and natural resources in other continents under their hegemony and control.[2] For centuries, international law held that indigenous peoples – due to the 'primitive' nature of their societies and land uses – could hold neither sovereign nor proprietary rights over land.[3]

The contemporary human rights system that emerged following the establishment of the United Nations rests heavily on the right to equality. Such a legal system cannot reasonably uphold an international norm that provides that indigenous peoples are – by the very nature of their societies – incapable of holding

---

1 As elaborated below, the legal ground for indigenous property rights over territories is traditional use. The legal subject therefore, by definition, is the traditional user. In most indigenous cultures, the traditional users are communities within an indigenous people, not the people as such. As Jeremy Webber notes, '[i]t is very rare that indigenous peoples ... hold their entire territory in ... ownership. On the contrary, land is generally held by individuals, families and kinship groups'. He elaborates that '[t]he traditional owners cannot be determined unless one knows, by that [indigenous people's customary law], who is entitled to exercise authority over the lands'. Jeremy Webber, 'The Public-Law Dimension of Indigenous Property Rights' in Nigel Bankes and Timo Koivurova (eds), *The Proposed Nordic Saami Convention National and International Dimensions of Indigenous Property Rights* (Hart Publishing 2013) 83–87. Consequently, this chapter refers to indigenous communities as relevant legal subjects in the context of indigenous property rights over territories.

2 Will Kymlicka, 'Beyond the Indigenous/Minority Dichotomy?' in Stephen Allen and Alexandra Xanthaki (eds), *Reflections on the UN Declaration on the Rights of Indigenous Peoples* (Studies in International Law Vol 30 2011) 183; James Crawford and Martti Koskenniemi, *International Law* (CUP 2012) 15; and Simpson, 'International Law in Diplomatic History' in Crawford and Koskenniemi (ibid) 27.

3 Jérémie Gilbert, *Indigenous Peoples' Land Rights under International Law: From Victims to Actors* (Transnational Publishers 2006) 22–26.

rights over territories. Thus, international law came to recognize, in principle, that indigenous communities hold property rights over territories traditionally used.[4]

Nevertheless, for decades, recognition of this principle did not generally result in the broad acknowledgment of property rights over indigenous territories in practice, essentially because at the time the right to non-discrimination was understood to require only that equal cases be treated equally. States did not need to culturally adjust property right laws to the particular land uses of indigenous communities. More recently, however, the right to equality has taken on a second facet, calling for differential treatment of those who are culturally different. This requires domestic jurisdictions to consider cultural differences between populations within the state when designing property rights regimes.[5] Section 2 elaborates how regional human rights courts and commissions, domestic courts, and UN treaty bodies have responded to this development by repeatedly reaffirming that current international law provides that indigenous communities hold property rights over territories traditionally used.

As a general rule, property right holders have a right to withhold or offer consent to third parties seeking access to their land. Section 3 expands upon how this is also true with regard to indigenous communities' property rights over land established through traditional use. Section 4 then articulates how the exception to the general rule is expropriation; thus, whether resource extraction can legally occur in indigenous territories absent consent largely boils down to whether the territory can be lawfully expropriated. Given the accelerating interest in extracting resources in indigenous territories,[6] whether indigenous lands can be subject to expropriation should reasonably be at the forefront of the indigenous rights regime. Against this background, it is puzzling that this issue has been subject to limited debate. This chapter aims to offer some initial thoughts as to the extent to which indigenous territories can be expropriated.

One reason why analyses on how the expropriation mechanism applies to indigenous territories are scarce may be because of a failure among domestic jurisdictions to consider fully the ramifications of their formal recognition that indigenous communities hold property rights over territories traditionally used. Section 5 contains a practical example from Sweden concerning mining that illustrates this failure. Section 6 wraps up the arguments.

---

4   Anthony Anghie, *Imperialism, Sovereignty and the Making of International Law* (CUP 2006) 111.

5   For an outline of the two facets of equality and the second facet's cardinal importance to the indigenous land rights regime, see Mattias Åhrén, 'International Human Rights Law Relevant to Natural Resource Extraction in Indigenous Territories – An Overview' (2014) 1 Nordic Environmental Law Journal, 21, 23–25, 27–30, with references.

6   Report of the Special Rapporteur on the rights of indigenous peoples, James Anaya; 'Extractive industries and indigenous peoples' A/HRC/24/41 1.

Brief Consideration of Contemporary International Law on Indigenous Communities' Property Rights over Territories Traditionally Used[7]

As mentioned, the claim that indigenous communities hold property rights over territories traditionally used follows from a contemporary understanding of the right to equality. A number of international legal sources, including the UN Declaration on the Rights of Indigenous Peoples (UNDRIP) Article 26, ILO Convention No 169 on Indigenous and Tribal Peoples in Independent Countries (ILO 169) Article 14, and UN treaty body jurisprudence, reflect this development. For instance, the Committee on the Elimination of Racial Discrimination (CERD) calls on states to 'recognize and protect the rights of indigenous peoples to own ... [and] control' their lands and natural resources,[8] a position shared by the Committee on Economic, Social and Cultural Rights (CESC).[9]

The property rights of indigenous communities over territories traditionally used has also been confirmed by a rich jurisprudence emanating from regional and domestic courts. For instance, the Inter-American Court on Human Rights (IACHR) has held that 'traditional possession of their lands by indigenous peoples has equivalent effect ... of state-granted full property title' and further that 'traditional possession entitles indigenous peoples ... to ... official recognition and registration of property title'.[10] The African Commission on Human and Peoples' Rights has echoed this position.[11] The European Court on Human Rights (ECHR) has accepted that indigenous communities' traditional land uses establish property rights, although the Sami reindeer herding communities were not able to prove a violation of the right to property in that particular case.[12] Finally, an

---

7   This chapter provides only a concise overview of the developments that led to the international law's recognition that indigenous communities hold property rights over territories traditionally used. For a more elaborate articulation of this development, see Åhrén (n 5).

8   General Recommendation No 23 and also eg A/56/18(SUPP) 335, CERD/C/64/ CO/9 11, CERD/C/MEX/CO 15, A/51/18/ (SUPP) 304–305, Decision 1 (66), CERD/C/ DEC/NZL/1.27/04/2005 and Decision 1 (68), CERD/USA/DEC/1 (United States).

9   General Comment No 21 36.

10   *Sawhoyamaxa Indigenous Community v Paraguay*, IACHR judgment of 29 March 2006, Series C No 125 (2005) 128. See also eg *Mayagna (Sumo) Community of Awas Tingni v Nicaragua*, Judgment of 31 August 2001, Inter-Am. Ct HR (Ser C) No 79 149–51, *Mary and Carrie Dann v United States*, Case No 11.140, decision on 27 December 2002 130–31, *Maya indigenous communities of the Toledo District v Belize*, Case 12.053, decision on 12 October 2004 and *Yakey Axa Indigenous Community v Paraguay*, IACHR judgment of 1 February 2006, Series C No 141.

11   *Centre for Minority Rights Development (Kenya) and Minority Rights Group International on behalf of Endorois Welfare Council v Kenya*, Comm. 276/2003 (2010) 214–15.

12   *Handölsdalen Sami Village and Others v Sweden*, Appl No 39013/04 (30 March 2010).

ever growing body of domestic jurisprudence confirms the conclusions drawn by the regional human rights institutions, holding that indigenous communities have established in some instances ownership rights and in others usufruct rights through traditional use.[13]

The coherence of international legal sources, coupled with the responses of domestic legal systems to this development, suggest that indigenous communities' property rights over territories traditionally used has crystallized into customary international law.

The General Rule – Indigenous Communities' Right to Offer or Withhold Consent to Third Parties Seeking Access to their Territories

A core element of the right to property is the right to determine who can access the property. As a general rule, property rights in the form of ownership rights and exclusive usufruct rights (below jointly referred to as 'property rights') award the holder the right to deny third parties access to the holder's land without having to provide a justification.[14] This aspect of the right must reasonably also apply to indigenous communities' property. The opposite would be discriminatory. Thus, unsurprisingly, international legal sources affirm that indigenous communities' property rights over territories award them with a right to withhold or offer consent to, for instance, resource extraction on their land.

CERD has repeatedly emphasized that indigenous communities have the right to deny resource extractors access to their traditional territories,[15] as has CESC.[16] The Special Rapporteur on the Rights of Indigenous Peoples (SRIP) concurs. He notes that 'international legal sources of authority ... lead to the general rule that extractive activities should not take place within the territories of indigenous peoples without their ... consent'.[17] Similarly, the Inter-American Commission on Human Rights (IACommHR) has held that 'one of the most central elements of

---

13   See eg *Te Runaga o Wharekuari Rekkohu Inc v Attorney-General* [1993] 2 N.Z.L.R, *Alexkor Ltd & Another v Richtersveld Cmty & Others*, 2003 (5) SA 460 (CC) (S Afr) *Kalahari Game Reserve Case* Misca. No 52 of 2002, of 13 December 2006, *Cal and Others & v Attorney General of Belize and Minister of Natural Resources and Environment*, Claims Nos 171 and 172, Judgment of 18 October 2007, the *Selbu Case*, Rt 2001 s 769, and the Nordmaling Case, NJA 2011 s 109.

14   This general rule follows from the fact that international legal sources establish the exception to the norm. See further Section 4.

15   See eg CERD/C/PER/CO/14–17 14, CERD/C/ECU/CO/19 16, CERD/C/GTM/CO/12–13,11 (a), CERD/C/SUR/CO/12, CERD/C/PHL/CO 22–24, CERD/C/KHM/CO/8–13) 16, and CERD/C/SLV//CO/14–15 19.

16   E/C12/1/add100 12, and E/EC12/Add74 12.

17   Report (n 6) 27.

the protection of indigenous peoples' property rights is ... that states ... ensure a process of fully informed consent on the part of the indigenous community ...'.[18]

In sum, like other property rights holders, indigenous communities are, as a general rule, entitled to offer or withhold consent to resource extraction in their territories. This conclusion follows logically from the right to equality and is reaffirmed by numerous legal sources. Whether resource extraction can occur in indigenous territories absent consent thus depends on the extent of the exceptions to the general rule.

The Exception to the General Rule – Expropriation

Generally on the Expropriation Criteria

Only the most fundamental human rights are absolute.[19] It is generally accepted that, should states be able to govern in a reasonable manner, every infringement of a human right cannot be considered an unlawful violation of that right. Rather, states are allowed legitimately to infringe on most human rights to a certain degree. Such infringements must not, however, be made haphazardly or arbitrarily. Rather, clear criteria should distinguish between a legitimate infringement and an unlawful violation of a human right.

The following elaborates how under international law such infringements, often referred to as expropriation, are allowed only if they are (i) prescribed by law, (ii) fulfil a legitimate aim, and (iii) proportionate. In the context of resource extraction in indigenous territories, the prescribed by law criterion is normally unproblematic.[20] Of greater relevance are the legitimate aim and proportionality criteria.

Generally on the Legitimate Aim and Proportionality Criteria

To fulfil the legitimate aim criterion, the infringement of the property right must be motivated by a legitimate and substantial social need.[21] In non-indigenous contexts, this criterion has been relatively uncontroversial. If a state maintains that expropriation is motivated by a need to meet a legitimate aim, the state's position is normally accepted without much scrutiny. Exceptions may be when it is clear

---

18   *Belize Case* (n 10).

19   Examples are the rights to life, to be free from slavery, and to not be subject to torture.

20   This criterion is normally fulfilled if the state has enacted an expropriation act or comparable legislation that is sufficiently precise and accessible, so that property right holders can foresee the circumstances under which property may be expropriated. See eg *Beyeler v Italy* (2000) 1225 EHRR 88 GC.

21   Additional Protocol 1 to the ECHR, Article 1.

that the expropriation decision has been arbitrary, or when it is evident that the expropriation is motivated by an aim other than that stated.[22]

According to the ECHR, an infringement is proportionate if it 'strike[s] a fair balance between the demands of the general interest of [society as a whole] and the requirements of the protection of ... fundamental rights'. There must further be 'a reasonable relation ... between the means employed and the aim sought to be realised by any measures applied by the state'.[23] The infringement must not leave the property right holder with a 'disproportionate' and 'excessive burden'.[24] In other words, it is not sufficient that expropriation is motivated by a legitimate aim. There are limitations on the sacrifices that a state can require individuals to make for the benefit of society as a whole. The proportionality test aims to strike a fair balance between the interests of the larger society and the interest of the individual not to be deprived of his or her property.

In non-indigenous contexts, whether the proportionality test is met is largely determined by whether market value compensation is provided for the property taken. For instance, in James, the ECHR held that 'compensation terms are material to the assessment whether the contested legislation respects a fair balance between the various interests at stake and ... whether it does not impose a disproportionate burden on the applicants ... [T]he taking of property without payment of an amount reasonably related to its value would normally constitute a disproportionate interference [in the right to property] ...'.[25]

Particularly on the Legitimate Aim Criterion in the Context of Expropriation of Indigenous Territories

As mentioned, conventionally, it has largely been left to states to identify legitimate aims within their jurisdictions without exaggerated in depth outside scrutiny. In keeping with the general rule states will likely claim that at least large-scale resource extraction in indigenous territories meets the legitimate aim criterion. This argument presumably contends that large-scale extraction projects are important to the welfare of society as a whole. However, the SRIP cautions otherwise. He asserts that '[a legitimate aim] is not found in mere commercial interests or revenue-raising objectives, and certainly not when benefits from the extractive activities are primarily for private gain'.[26] The IACHR concurs that one cannot simply assume that resource extraction in indigenous territories meets the legitimate aim criterion, albeit in somewhat more lenient wording. The IACHR accepts that indigenous communities' property rights over territories can

---

22   See eg *James AO v United Kingdom* (1986) 8 EHRR 123.
23   *Draon v France* (2005) 42 EHRR 78, *Sporrong and Lönnroth v Sweden* (1982) 11 EHRR, 69.
24   *James* (n 22) 54–55.
25   *James* (n 22) 54–55.
26   Report (n 6) 35.

be restricted, provided that such restrictions are intended to satisfy an imperative public interest. A mere useful or opportune purpose is, however, not sufficient.[27]

Beyond the positions taken by the SRIP and the IACHR, international legal sources offer limited guidance about when the legitimate aim criterion is fulfilled in the context of resource extraction in indigenous territories. Consequently, it is at this point difficult to establish with any certainty when this criterion has been satisfied. A case may, however, perhaps be made for the position articulated below.

Clearly, one cannot disregard the general rule. When evaluating whether the legitimate aim criterion is fulfilled, one must be mindful that states are normally given considerable leeway in identifying legitimate societal needs. Against this background, at least when resource extraction generates substantial proceeds for the state, either because the state is the resource extractor, or because it receives a substantial share of the proceeds derived from the extraction through royalty or similar schemes, presumably the legitimate aim criterion is met in most instances. This conclusion seems to conform with the ruling by the IACHR and does not contradict the position taken by the SRIP.

The situation may be more complex when the resource extractor is a private entity, and the state does not receive a substantial share of the proceeds from the extraction. As seen, the SRIP takes the position that, in such instances, the legitimate aim criterion is unlikely to be met. To this assertion, governments may retort that large-scale extraction projects may carry substantial benefits to society as a whole beyond generating monetary proceeds to the state. For instance, such projects may create a substantial number of employment opportunities. Governments are likely to argue that job creation is a legitimate aim, in particular in areas affected by high unemployment. Another legitimate aim that governments may put forward is that a large-scale industrial plant, even if privately operated, may result in the construction of infrastructure in the forms of roads, railroads, and electric power grids that, if fully or partly privately financed, generate benefits to the larger society. Presumably, the list of potential legitimate aims can be lengthened.

Domestic courts and regional and international human rights institutions may accept that, among other things, job creation and private sponsorship of infrastructure constitute legitimate aims that justify expropriation of territories traditionally used by indigenous communities, especially if they consider the leeway normally given to states in identifying legitimate societal needs. Such a conclusion seems also to gain support from the ruling by the IACHR. To comply with the IACHR's ruling, the extraction project must presumably genuinely generate substantial benefits for society. A project for private gain that does not generate a large number of jobs and that fails to bring other substantial benefits to society as a whole presumably does not meet the legitimate aim criterion.

---

27   *Yakye Axa* (n 10) 145.

The Proportionality Criterion in the Context of Expropriation of Indigenous Territories

As seen, in non-indigenous contexts, the proportionality test largely boils down to whether market value compensation is provided for the property taken. A property right holder must normally accept expropriation if fully compensated in monetary terms. To some, this might seem to be unfair. However, the rationale is probably to be found in a somewhat stereotypical approach toward how individuals value property.

Certainly, some individuals attach considerable emotional value to a particular land area. Nevertheless, the market value compensation formula that the lawmaker has adopted is probably motivated by an assumption that property is most often not predominantly valued by the holder because of emotional attachment. It is seemingly assumed that, if an individual receives market value compensation for his or her property, expropriation should essentially be acceptable. After all, the compensation received allows the individual to purchase alternate land, equal in quality and value, to the land expropriated. Some may take issue with this reasoning, but it is the position that the law has taken.

Thus, with regard to property rights holders, who largely value their property in monetary terms, or at least are assumed to do so, it is reasonable that the proportionality criterion is met if market value compensation is provided. If such property right holders are awarded something (money) in return for their property that they value (or should value) to the same, or almost same, extent as the property taken, a fair balance between the interest of the property right holder and society as a whole is considered struck.

This is the rationale behind the market value formula being applied in non-indigenous contexts, although some may perceive it to be unfair. But can the same formula reasonably be applied to indigenous territories? Indigenous communities may not value their lands in monetary terms. Rather, one may assume that indigenous communities often value lands and natural resources traditionally used predominantly, or exclusively, because continued access to and control over such territories is fundamental to the continued existence of their cultures, identities, livelihoods and ways of life. For an indigenous community, whose cultural identity is deeply rooted in its traditional livelihoods, subsistence economies, and other forms of traditional land uses, every loss of land implies a blow to the very basis of its cultural identity. Loss of substantial parts of land can significantly threaten the existence of its society, culture and way of life. In addition, contrary to the situation of non-indigenous property right holders, an indigenous community that is deprived of parts of its traditional territory will normally not find alternate land elsewhere. The community may harbour a spiritual and cultural connection to its particular territory, for which there is no substitute. But even if the community is open to compensation in the form of alternate lands suitable for continued pursuit of its traditional livelihoods, other culturally based land activities, and spiritual and cultural practices, such lands will presumably most often not be available.

The different ways in which non-indigenous peoples and indigenous communities value land, is a result of cultural differences. Section 1, above, explains how a contemporary understanding of the right to equality requires states to recognize cultural differences when designing property law and policy. This obligation must reasonably also extend to legislation regulating the circumstances under which property can be expropriated. After all, indigenous communities opposed to resource extraction have a much larger stake in the outcome of such processes than both the extractor and the state.[28] In this context, the ECHR has held that, for an infringement of the right to property to be deemed proportionate, it must be applied in a non-discriminatory manner. The state must not arbitrarily, without objective reason, limit one property right while at the same time leaving a comparable property right unlimited.[29] Consequently, while in non-indigenous contexts the assumption that market value compensation fulfils the proportionality test may conform to international law, the same appears not to be true with regard to indigenous communities. On the contrary, given how significantly differently many indigenous communities value land, compared with non-indigenous peoples, the right to equality seemingly requires that the market value formula not be applied to indigenous territories. As Michael Walzer, among others, notes, criteria for justice vary depending on the different values peoples assign to various things.[30] Similarly, as Isabelle Anguelovski observes, with reference to Schlosberg, to compensate indigenous communities with estimated market value for their traditional land does not recognize their cultural values.[31] To do so violates the evolved understanding of equality.

In sum, because indigenous communities normally do not value their lands predominantly in monetary terms, but rather in cultural and spiritual terms, it is unreasonable to infer that market value compensation necessarily renders expropriation of their territories proportionate. When such communities withhold their consent to resource extraction, one must find other ways to determine proportionality. If the territory is predominantly of cultural and spiritual value to the community, it appears relevant to consider the impact that resource extraction would have on the community's culture, including traditional livelihoods and other culturally based land uses, and spiritual practices.

The SRIP concurs with this line of argument. He states that '[the proportionality criterion] will generally be difficult to meet for extractive industries that are carried

---

28 Emily McAteer, Jamie Caretti and Saleem Ali, 'Shareholder Activism and Corporate Behaviour in Ecuador – A Comparative Study of Two Oil Ventures' in Ciaran O'Farcheallaigh and Saleem Ali (eds), *Earth Matters* (Greenleaf Publishing 2008) 195.

29 *Willis v The United Kingdom* (2002) 35 EHRR 547.

30 Michael Walzer, *Spheres of Justice: A Defense of Pluralism and Equality* (Basic Books 1983).

31 Isabelle Anguelovski, 'Environmental Justice Concerns with Transnational Mining Operations – Exploring the Limitations of Post-crisis Community Dialogues in Peru' in O'Farcheallaigh and Ali et al (n 28) 206.

out within the territories of indigenous peoples without their consent'.[32] Similarly, CERD calls on states to 'ensure that the protection of the rights of indigenous peoples prevails over commercial and economic interests'.[33] The IACHR takes a somewhat more cautious approach, stating that the proportionality criterion is not met if expropriation will deny indigenous traditions and customs and will consequently endanger the cultural survival of the community. It elaborates that indigenous communities always have the right to preserve and protect their special relationship with their territories and to continue to lead their traditional lives.[34]

In sum, indigenous communities' property rights over territories differ from property rights held by others in that, when seeking to expropriate indigenous territories, the proportionality criterion is not met simply because market value compensation is provided. Rather, both reason and existing international legal sources suggest that, in such instances, due consideration should be given to how profoundly important lands and natural resources traditionally used are to indigenous communities' cultures, ways of life, traditional livelihoods, other culturally based land uses, and spiritual and cultural practices. When the negative impacts that a resource extraction project is likely to cause to an indigenous community's territory reaches a certain scale, it apparently fails to meet the fair balance test, as it places a 'disproportionate' and 'excessive burden' on the community. Although the relatively few existing legal sources do not allow a precise determination of where the threshold is or should be, some conclusions may be drawn.

Conclusions

To expropriate an indigenous community's traditional territory lawfully, the resource extraction project must simultaneously meet the legitimate aim and proportionality criteria. This might prove to be a challenge.

Even large-scale resource extraction projects may fail to meet the legitimate aim criterion if motivated by private gain. Publicly operated large-scale resource extraction will, however, presumably normally fulfil a legitimate societal need. Based on existing legal sources, one cannot rule out that also projects motivated by private gain may meet the legitimate aim criterion if they will deliver substantial benefits of other sorts to society, such as mass employment. But in all likelihood, only extraction projects of considerable scale will be held to fulfil a legitimate

---

32 Report (n 6) 36.

33 CERD/C/CHL/CO/15–18, 22–23.

34 *Saramaka People v Suriname*, 2008 Inter-Am Ct HR (ser C) No 185 37. The IACHR employs a test that presents certain communalities with the criteria established by the Human Rights Committee when evaluating whether the right to culture has been violated (Compare *Poma Poma v Peru*, Comm No 1457/2006 7), although the IACHR's comments were delivered in a property rights context.

societal need. Resource extraction projects of lesser importance will presumably find it difficult to pass the legitimate aim test.

If large-scale resource extraction projects meet the legitimate aim criterion, they may find it harder to satisfy the proportionality test. Large-scale resource extraction is likely to consume significant parts of, and inflict considerably damage to, the affected indigenous community's territory. If so, there is an apparent risk that the project will fail to meet the proportionality criterion given the fundamental importance of lands and natural resources to indigenous communities' cultures, livelihoods, and ways of life, in other words to their very identities as indigenous communities. Irrespective of whether an extraction project will generate great wealth to society as a whole, it can hardly be considered proportionate if it will leave a great scar on the society and culture of the indigenous community. The very basis of indigenous communities' societies cannot reasonably be outweighed by monetary gain and job creation. To do so would seem to be a typical example of sacrificing a few for the benefit of society at large to an extent that goes beyond what the proportionality test allows.

In sum, resource extraction projects in indigenous territories that do not consume significant parts of an indigenous community's traditional territory and do not in other ways substantially negatively impact the community, but that genuinely generate considerable benefits to society as a whole, seem to have the best chance to simultaneously meet the legitimate aim and proportionality criteria.

An Illustrative Example; the *Rönnbäcken Case*[35]

Background

Vapsten Sami village pursues traditional Sami reindeer herding in the *County of Västerbotten*, in the centre of the Sami traditional territory in Sweden. The Rönnbäcken area is at the heart of Vapsten's traditional pasture land. Here, a British mining company seeks to establish an open-pit nickel mining system that would consume spring and autumn pasture areas and calving lands of critical importance to Vapsten. Moreover, the mining system would block migration routes without which Vapsten cannot move the reindeer between seasonal pasture areas.

In 2010, the Swedish Mining Inspectorate (*Bergsstaten*) granted a permit to mine in the Rönnbäcken area. Vapsten appealed the decision, but on 22 August 2013, the Swedish government upheld the permit and allowed the company to proceed with its mining plans.

Swedish law acknowledges that Sami traditional use of land for reindeer herding purposes establishes exclusive usufruct rights over territories today shared with the Swedish population and ownership rights to lands where the land use is

---

35 The Rönnbäcken *Case* is also discussed in Kristina Labba's Chapter 11 in this volume.

dominating.[36] The Swedish government has not questioned that Vapsten holds a property right over the area in dispute. Nevertheless, when considering whether to allow the mining project to proceed, the government took no account of Vapsten's property right. Instead, on the basis of balancing provisions in the Environmental Code 1998, it considered only which land utilization is most beneficial to society as a whole; reindeer herding or mining.[37]

Arguments before CERD

Vapsten submitted a complaint to CERD, chiefly arguing a violation of its right to property.[38] The government contested the claim on largely formal grounds, most of which are not relevant to the question of how the government's decision takes account of Vapsten's property right. The argument that is of particular interest here is the government's assertion that Vapsten has not been '*treated less favorably than other parties affected by the government's decision on exploitation concession*'.[39] Therefore, the government submits, there can be no discrimination and, as a consequence, no violation of the right to property.[40] This argument merits examination in some depth.

It is correct that Swedish mining law places all property rights holders in a weak position in relation to prospecting and mining, reflecting Sweden's history as a 'mining nation'. If Swedish authorities grant a concession to mine on private land, a property right holder is normally not in a position to stop the project. No real legitimate aim or proportionality tests are carried out. The former criterion is assumed fulfilled, and proportionality addressed by an authority that calculates the market value of the property lost due to the establishment of the mine. If the property right holder does not accept the calculated market value, the owner can appeal the calculation (but not the decision to establish a mine) to a court of law.[41]

The process can be described as simplified expropriation, as mining is presumed to fulfil the legitimate aim test and the proportionality criterion provided that market value compensation is paid. Consequently, no full scale expropriation procedure is necessary, since the property right holder can appeal the calculated market value to a court of law. Section 4 explains how such a simplified expropriation procedure probably complies with the right to property at least as far as Swedish property

---

36   NJA 1981 s 1 (*Skattefjällsmålet*), and NJA 2011 s 109 (*Nordmalingmålet*).

37   In addition, the government evaluated, but in a sweeping and rudimentary fashion, the scale of the negative impacts of the mining on Vapsten's reindeer herding.

38   The author is legal counsel to Vapsten in the proceedings before CERD.

39   The Swedish government's submission to CERD of 22 January 2014.

40   CERD is not mandated to examine a pure assertion of a violation of a material right that the CERD Convention sets forth. The complaint must be coupled with an arguable claim of discrimination.

41   The Expropriation Act 1972 ch 2 s 4, and the Mining Act 1991 ch 7.

right holders are concerned. But can the same be said with regard to Sami reindeer herding communities?

It is correct that Vapsten is treated in the same way as Swedish title holders in the sense that Vapsten, like the title holders, receives monetary compensation for lands lost.[42] This is presumably why the Swedish government argues that Vapsten is treated equally with other property rights holders affected by the mining. Therefore, the claim seems to be, Vapsten has not been discriminated against. But Vapsten's arguable claim of discrimination is precisely that it *is* treated like Swedish title holders.

That Sami reindeer herding communities have to yield to mining in the same way as Swedish property right holders could at first glance appear as equality. But, as Section 4 explains, a major difference between the two groups is that, while Swedish property right holders may harbour certain emotional attachments to their property, the loss thereof can largely in most instances be offset through market value compensation that allows them to purchase alternate property equal in size and quality. For Sami reindeer herding communities, the situation is quite the opposite. They value pasture areas not in monetary terms, but because continued access to such is a prerequisite for continuously pursuing Sami reindeer herding, the very basis of their cultural identity. If reindeer herding communities are deprived of their pasture areas, there is no alternate pasture to be found. Instead, they are deprived of the basis of their cultural identity, a value that cannot be replaced.

The simplified expropriation employed to the Rönnbäcken area may conform to the law as far as Swedish title holders are concerned. As Section 4 outlines, it is presumably acceptable that they cannot bring the issue of whether the legitimate aim and proportionality criteria are met before a court of law, as long as they are entitled to appeal the calculation of market value to courts. But Vapsten does not value its land in market value terms. Therefore, as Section 4 further explains, by definition, with regard to Vapsten, it cannot be assumed that the legitimate aim test is met, and the proportionality tests cannot be restricted to whether monetary compensation has been provided. As Section 4 articulates, under international law, Vapsten's members' cultural background entitles Vapsten to a full scale evaluation – by a court of law – of whether the legitimate aim and proportionality criteria are indeed fulfilled, or whether the establishment of a mining complex violates Vapsten's property right.[43]

---

42   Ch 2 s 4 of the Expropriation Act and the Mining Act ch 7. The calculation of the amount of compensation is not based on the value of the land as such, but supposedly on the 'market value' of reindeer pasture. But since reindeer pasture is invaluable to Sami reindeer herders, and without value to anyone else, there are no input figures for such a calculation, ie there is no market value. The value of the land as pasture land for Swedish style agriculture is therefore used as substitute.

43   The government's decision can be subject to a 'judicial review' (*rättsprövning*) by the Supreme Administrative Court. The judicial review does not, however, include an

To elaborate on the proportionality test, what should be evaluated is whether a mining complex strikes a *fair balance* between the value of a mine to society as a whole, on one hand, and the negative impacts the mining would have on Vapsten, on the other. To put it differently, it must be determined whether the mine leaves Vapsten with a 'disproportionate' and 'excessive' burden, i.e. whether a mine implies that a few have to sacrifice too much for the benefit of all. To be more precise, what should be considered is whether some hundred jobs created over a period of years is worth the destruction of pasture areas and migration paths of critical importance to a Sami reindeer herding community, placing the very existence of the community, or at least parts of it, at risk. In this evaluation, one needs to consider that the Rönnbäcken area has been reindeer pasture land since time immemorial, and, if destroyed, both present day reindeer herders and future Sami generations will lose the core element of their cultural identity.[44]

The Swedish government may face difficulties substantiating its position that Vapsten has not put forward 'an arguable claim of discrimination'. That Vapsten has been treated the same as 'other parties affected by the … exploitation concession' is not a defence. On the contrary, it is precisely the fact that Sweden treats Vapsten in the same way as Swedish property rights holders, even though their situations are fundamentally different, that raises the question of discrimination. In *DH v Czech Republic*, the ECHR held that laws that on their face appear non-discriminatory may nonetheless still be so if they disproportionately and adversely affect members of a particular group. According to the court, if 'the … legislation as applied in practice at the material time had a disproportionately prejudicial effect [on the group]', this amounts to discrimination.[45] This seems to be the situation at hand. Although Sweden formally treats property rights holders alike, when applied in practice, the Swedish Mining Act has prejudicial effects on Sami reindeer herding communities that constitute structural discrimination against them.

Summary

International law has evolved to proclaim that indigenous communities hold property rights over territories historically used. The right to equality provides that indigenous communities' property rights over land must reasonably contain the same elements as property rights held by others. Consequently, it would appear that, as a general rule, indigenous communities' property rights over territories give them a right to withhold consent to resource extraction on their lands. The exception to the general rule would then be expropriation.

---

evaluation of whether the taking of Vapsten's land amounts to a violation of the right to property.

44	The Rönnbäcken *Case* is still pending before CERD.

45	*DH v Czech Republic* (2008) 47 EHRR 3 207.

Legal sources presently at hand, coupled with reason, suggest that resource extraction projects may face difficulties when seeking to meet simultaneously the two key expropriation criteria, namely the legitimate aim and proportionality tests. It might be hard to argue convincingly that other than large-scale resource extraction fulfils such a pressing societal need that must be present to meet the legitimate aim criterion. Large-scale resource extraction projects may meet the legitimate aim test. But there is an evident risk that resource extraction projects of such proportions carry considerable negative effects on the inflicted indigenous community's culture, livelihoods, other culturally based land uses, way of life, and cultural and spiritual practices, which implicates the proportionality criterion instead. In sum, it would appear that large-scale resource extraction projects that do not consume substantial parts of an indigenous community's traditional territory and that do not in other ways cause considerable harm to the community, have the best chance to meet the legitimate aim and the proportionality criteria at the same time. If expropriation is not an option, the right to property requires that a resource extractor achieve the indigenous community's consent to proceed with the project.

The Rönnbäcken case illustrates how states need to adjust their mining legislation to respect indigenous communities' property rights over territories traditionally used. Sweden takes account of Sami reindeer herding communities' property rights over land in the sense that it awards the communities monetary compensation for lands taken for mining purposes. But the Swedish Mining Act fails to recognize that the right to equality requires differential treatment of those that are culturally different. Consequently, the proportionality test is not met simply because reindeer herding communities receive monetary compensation for their land, since they do not value their lands primarily in monetary terms. Rather, the proportionality test must be based on the fact that Sami reindeer herding communities value their pasture lands, because continued access to such constitutes a prerequisite should they be able to pursue traditional Sami reindeer herding continuously, which is the very basis for their cultural identity.

Chapter 14

The Rapidly Evolving International Status of Indigenous Peoples: The Example of the Sami People in Finland

Leena Heinämäki

Introduction

The doctrines of 'discovery' and 'terra nullius' are examples of international legal concepts that were used to justify the occupation of indigenous territories and the colonization of the populations.[1] This 'classical' state-centred approach is reflected, for instance, in theories of the eighteenth century Swiss legal theorist Vattel, who supported the idea of a separate body of law concerned exclusively with nation states and who averred that states are the legitimate 'subjects' of international law.[2] Out of this approach developed the idea that all other socio-political groupings are merely 'objects' of international law. Accordingly, because states are the only players in this paradigm, only they can create international norms.[3] Within this state-centred

---

1   James Anaya, *Indigenous Peoples in International Law* (2nd edn, Oxford 2004). See also, Mauricio Iván Del Toro Huerta, 'The Contribution of the Jurisprudence of the Inter-American Court of Human Rights to the Configuration of Collective Property Rights of Indigenous Peoples' (2008) Yale Law School, SELA Publications 2–3 <http://www.law. yale.edu/documents/pdf/sela/Del_Toro.pdf> accessed 1 September 2014.

2   Emmerich de Vattel, *The Law of Nations or Principles of the Law of Nature Applied to the Conduct and Affairs of Nations and Sovereigns* (from the French of Monsieur de Vattel, from the new edition, by Joseph Chitty, Philadelphia, 1999, 1883) <http://www. constitution.org/vattel/vattel.htm> accessed 1 September 2014. See generally, Hersch Lauterpacht, 'The Grotian Tradition in International Law' (1946) 23 British Year Book of International Law 29; Martti Koskenniemi, *From Apology to Utopia – The Structure of International Legal Argument* (CUP 2005) 115–21; and Antony Anghie, *Imperialism, Sovereignty and the Making of International Law* (CUP 2004) 42.

3   Gregory Maggio, 'Biodiversity' in L Watters (ed), *Indigenous Peoples, the Environment and Law* (Carolina Academic Press 2004) 45. See, generally, Martti Koskenniemi, *The Gentle Civilized Nations, The Rise and Fall of International Law, 1870–1960* (CUP 2002).

approach to international law, matters concerning indigenous peoples fall within the domestic issues of the states in which the indigenous peoples live.[4]

Yet, it has been recognized both domestically and internationally that many indigenous groups around the world were self-governing nations when the Europeans first arrived. For instance, in Canada, when North America was being colonized by European settlers, France and Great Britain first dealt with the Aboriginal peoples on a nation-to-nation basis and sought to secure their assistance as trading partners and military allies.[5] In 1763, the British Crown issued a Royal Proclamation that, in many ways, has been regarded the most important 'precedent' for Aboriginal rights in Canada. Borrows, for instance, sees the Royal Proclamation as part of a treaty between First Nations and the Crown which positively guaranteed First Nation self-government.[6] Under British colonial rule, however, the authority of Aboriginal governments was gradually eroded.[7] With national legislation and assimilation policies in Canada and in many other parts of the world, the self-governing powers of indigenous peoples were almost completely extinguished or denied by the states.

In Finland, research illustrates that the Sami in Sweden-Finland had an historical right to their lands and waters that was comparable to ownership.[8] In 1673 and 1695, King Carl XI approved the Settlement Bill of Lapland, which allowed non-Lapps to cross the border of Lapland to settle. This is considered to have begun the assimilation and 'integration' of the Finnish Sami.[9] From the

---

4   See, Pablo Gutiérrez Vega, 'The Municipalization of the Legal Status of Indigenous Peoples by Modern (European) International Law' in René Kuppe and Richard Potz (eds), *Law and Anthropology, International Yearbook for Legal Anthropology* (Vol 12 MartinusNijhoff Publishers 2005) 17–54; Mathias Åhren, 'International Human Rights Law Relevant to Natural Resource Extraction in Indigenous Territories, An Overview' (2014) 1 Nordisk Miljörättslig Tidskrift, Nordic Environmental Law Journal Special Issue Extracting Industries in the North: What About Environmental Law and Indigenous Peoples' Law?, Guest Editor Tore Henriksen, 22.

5   Brian Slattery, 'The Hidden Constitution: Aboriginal Rights in Canada' in Menno Boldt and J Anthony Long (eds), *The Quest for Justice, Aboriginal Peoples and Aboriginal Rights* (University of Toronto Press 1985) 115.

6   John Borrows, 'Constitutional Law from a First Nation Perspective: Self-government and the Royal Proclamation' (1994) 28 University of British Columbia Law Review 1–47, 3–4. See also, generally, John Borrows, *Canada's Indigenous Constitution* (University of Toronto Press 2011).

7   Under the British North America Act of 1867 and Indian Act of 1867, the Canadian Federal Government expressed control over Aboriginal peoples and their lands.

8   See, generally, Kaisa Korpijaakko (-Labba), *Saamelaisten oikeusasemasta Ruotsi-Suomessa. Oikeushistoriallinen tutkimus Länsi-Pohjan Lapin maankäyttöoloista ja – oikeuksista ennen 1700-luvun puoliväliä* (Lakimiesliiton kustannus 1989); Tanja Joona and Juha Joona, 'The Historical Basis of Saami Land Rights in Finland and the Application of ILO Convention' (2011) 3 Yearbook of Polar Law 351.

9   Tanja Joona, 'The Subjects of the Draft Nordic Saami Convention' in Nigel Bankes and Timo Koivurova (eds), *The Proposed Nordic Saami Convention, National and*

mid-seventeenth century to late into the twentieth century, the state actively encouraged settlers and others to cultivate areas over which the Sami previously had exclusive use for reindeer herding, fishing and hunting. This led to competition for land and related conflicts and to non-recognition of earlier historical land rights and rights to a traditional way of life.[10]

As will be shown in this chapter, by using the human rights framework, indigenous peoples have succeeded, at least partly, in pressuring state governments to return their lost status of legal subjectivity and self-governance. Focussing solely on the developments in the last decade involving the rights and legal status of indigenous peoples, this chapter aims to show that international human rights law has moved from recognition of indigenous peoples as objects of protection toward the acceptance of indigenous peoples' self-governing powers in the matters that are crucial to preserving their culture and ways of life.

In Finland, the land rights of the Sami have been under political discussion for many decades. At the writing of this chapter, the Finnish government has made a draft proposal to the Parliament finally to ratify the ILO Convention.[11, 12] Finland is currently committed to an even more ambitious process than set out in the ILO Convention by negotiating a Nordic Sami Convention, which, in addition to recognizing directly the right of the Sami to self-determination, guarantees strong rights of the Sami people to their culture, lands and natural resources.

This chapter aims to discuss the main developments in international law that point to relatively rapid evolution in the international legal status of indigenous peoples as objects toward legal subjectivity. Of particular interest is the UN Declaration on the Rights of Indigenous Peoples (UNDRIP) and its endorsement of the right to self-determination and to the free, prior and informed consent (FPIC) of indigenous peoples. Although the main emphasis of this chapter is to analyse the international developments, a further aim is to examine whether and how the state of Finland is currently responding to the evolving international status of indigenous peoples in relation to the Sami people by viewing the Finland's responses to the self-determination question in the Draft Sami Convention and to point out other relevant legal developments related to the status of Sami people in Finland.

International Dimensions of Indigenous Property Rights (Hart Publishing 2013) 255.

10   ibid 256.

11   ILO Convention No 107 Concerning the Protection and Integration of Indigenous and other Tribal and Semi-Tribal Populations in Independent Countries, adopted 26 June 1957, entered into force 2 June 1959, 328 UNTS 247.

12   Government Bill: Hallituksen esitys eduskunnalle itsenäisten maiden alkuperäis- ja heimokansoja koskevan yleissopimuksen hyväksymisestä sekä laiksi yleissopimuksen lainsäädännön alaan kuuluvien määräysten voimaansaattamisesta (20 May 2014) <http://oikeusministerio.fi/material/attachments/om/valmisteilla/lakihankkeet/kielellisetjakulttuurisetoikeudet/lYOmgdMXH/ILO_169_HE_luonnos_200514_liite.pdf> accessed 13 August 2014.

First Era – Recognition and Partnership: Significant International Developments before the UN Declaration

Beginning in 1970, indigenous peoples' representatives, in increasing numbers, began appearing before UN human rights bodies, basing their right claims on generally applicable human rights. In 1982, the Working Group on Indigenous Populations (WGIP) was established by the United Nations Economic and Social Council (ECOSOC).[13] The original mandate of the WGIP was to review developments concerning indigenous peoples and to work toward the development of corresponding international standards.[14] Through the process of drafting a declaration on the rights of indigenous peoples, WGIP engaged states, indigenous peoples and others in a broad multilateral dialogue on the specific content of norms concerning indigenous peoples. This was historically a very important step, since the working group provided an important means for indigenous peoples to promote, for the first time, their own conceptions of their rights within the international arena, enabling them to make proposals and comments.[15] This instrument, prepared by the majority of the states and a great number of indigenous peoples, was finally adopted by the UN General Assembly as the UN Declaration on the Rights of Indigenous Peoples (UNDRIP) two decades later in 2007.[16]

During the 1960s and 1970s the assimilation policies of many countries, which aimed to integrate indigenous peoples into the mainstream population without recognizing their right to specific cultural characteristics, had to make space for the demands of indigenous peoples' movements concerning the right to self-determination and the positive recognition of their cultural integrity. The International Labour Organization's (ILO) first Convention on Indigenous and Tribal Populations of 1957,[17] which utilized a strong integration approach, was replaced by the ILO Convention on indigenous peoples No. 169 of 1989, marking

---

13 Economic and Social Council Resolution 1982/34 <http://ap.ohchr.org/documents/E/ECOSOC/resolutions/E-RES-1982-34.doc> accessed 19 January 2014. The WGIP is an organ of the Sub-Commission on the Promotion and Protection of Human Rights.

14 Human Rights Commission Res 1982/19 (10 March 1982); ESC Res 1982/34 (7 May 1982); UN ESCOR (1982) Supp No 1, 26; UN Doc E/1992/82 (1982) paras 1–2.

15 James Anaya (n 1) 63–64; WGIP was replaced by the Expert Mechanism on the Rights of Indigenous Peoples (EM) in 2007. Human Rights Council Resolution 6/36. Expert Mechanism on the Rights of Indigenous Peoples, 6th Session (14 December 2007) A/HRC/RES/6/36. The mandate of the EM is to provide its thematic expertise in the manner and form requested by the Human Rights Council. It will focus mainly on studies and research-based advice.

16 The United Nations Declaration on the Rights of Indigenous Peoples (7 September 2007) Sixty-first Session, A/61/L.67.

17 ILO Convention No 107 Concerning the Protection and Integration of Indigenous and other Tribal and Semi-Tribal Populations in Independent Countries, adopted 26 June 1957, entered into force 2 June 1959, 328 UNTS 247.

not only a change in the ILO's approach to indigenous peoples but also a shift in the general attitude toward indigenous peoples. The latter Convention is based on respect for indigenous peoples' cultures, their distinct ways of life, and their traditions and customs.

ILO Convention No. 169 contains substantive protection of the cultural integrity of indigenous peoples and in principle recognizes them as political and legal entities that need to be taken into account in making decisions about the matters that concern the group.[18] This idea, however, fell short of full recognition. Indigenous peoples were not able to participate in the creation of the Convention. Secondly, the Convention does not recognize the rights to self-determination and self-governance of indigenous peoples, which means that it still regards indigenous peoples as objects of protection rather than as full subjects of cooperation. Yet, the Convention is meaningful as part of a larger body of developments that can be understood as giving rise to a new customary international law related to the protection of the rights of indigenous peoples to their culture, lands and traditional livelihoods.[19]

The general change in attitudes toward indigenous peoples reflected in the latter ILO Convention can be seen also in the shifting approach of the human rights monitoring bodies. The UN Human Rights Committee (HRC), for instance, has increasingly required positive protection from states, instead of embracing the original passive formulation of Article 27 of the International Covenant on Civil and Political Rights (ICCPR)[20] that requires states only to abstain from 'denying minorities to practice their culture'.[21]

One of the important milestones for the international status of indigenous peoples was the establishment of the Permanent Forum on Indigenous Issues within the ECOSOC, which met for the first time in May 2002.[22] The Forum operates at the highest possible level within the UN system. One of the most important targets

---

18   Russell Lawrence Barsh, 'Indigenous Peoples in the 1990s: From Object to Subject of International Law?' (1994) 33 Harvard Human Rights Journal, reprinted in Laurence Watters (ed), *Indigenous Peoples, the Environment and Law* (Carolina Academic Press 2004) 23.

19   James Anaya, 'Indigenous Peoples' Participatory Rights in Relation to Decisions About Natural Resource Extraction: The More Fundamental Issues of What Rights Indigenous Peoples Have in Land and Resources' (2005) 22 (1) Arizona Journal of International & Comparative Law 9.

20   International Covenant on Civil and Political Rights, adopted 16 December 1966, entered into force 23 March 1976, 999 UNTS 302.

21   Human Rights Committee, General Comment No 23: The Right of Minorities (Art. 27) UN Doc CCPR/C/21/Rev.1/Add. % (8 April 1994). See, generally, Raija Hanski and Martin Scheinin, *Leading Cases of the Human Rights Committee* (Institute for Human Rights, Åbo Akademi University 2003).

22   ECOSOC Res E/RES/2000/22 (28 July 2000) establishing the Permanent Forum; Report of the First Session of the Permanent Forum on Indigenous Issues, UN Doc E/2002/42/Supp 43 (Wilton Littlechild, Rapporteur).

and the main achievement of the Permanent Forum was the successful push for the adoption of the UNDRIP, which had been facing major challenges for more than two decades.

Second Era: UNDRIP, Self-determination and Free, Prior and Informed Consent

The UNDRIP indicates a historical shift in the legal status of indigenous peoples in international law. For the first time, indigenous peoples participated in the drafting process of the actual text with an equal voice with governments.[23] Although the final decision-making was carried out in line with the general practice of international law by a vote of member states in the General Assembly, indigenous peoples, for the very first time in a global context, participated in the making of international law.

It has become commonplace to state that the UNDRIP did not establish any new rights for indigenous peoples but rather codified the existing rights.[24] However, this does not do justice to the ambitious Declaration which celebrates a paradigm shift: not only does it explicitly recognize for the first time the right to self-determination of indigenous peoples, but it also guarantees stronger participatory rights than any earlier instrument, including the free, prior and informed consent (FPIC) in relation to decision-making concerning natural resources and other crucial matters.[25] Although the UNDRIP is not strictly a legally binding instrument,[26] human rights monitoring bodies have already started to apply it as a

---

23   Megan Davis, 'Indigenous Struggle in Standard-Setting: The United Nations Declaration on the Rights of Indigenous Peoples' (2008) 9(2) Melbourne Journal of International Law 1–33, 2.

24   The Ministry of Justice of Finland has also noted that the UN Declaration does not establish new rights. See, Government Bill: Hallituksen esitys eduskunnalle itsenäisten maiden alkuperäis- ja heimokansoja koskevan yleissopimuksen hyväksymisestä sekä laiksi yleissopimuksen lainsäädännön alaan kuuluvien määräysten voimaansaattamisesta (20 May 2014).

25   See Articles 3, 19 and 32 of the UNDRIP.

26   The binding or semi-binding nature of the Declaration is widely discussed amongst international lawyers. It has been argued, at least partly, to already express customary international law or at least generally accepted principles related to indigenous peoples. See, James Anaya, Report of the Special Rapporteur on the rights of indigenous peoples, A/68/317 (14 August 2013) 16–18 <http://daccess-dds-ny.un.org/doc/UNDOC/GEN/N13/427/10/PDF/N1342710.pdf?OpenElement.> accessed 20 August 2014. See also, International Law Association (ILA), 75th conference, resolution No 5/2102, para 2 (5 August 2012); International Law Association, Committee on the Rights of Indigenous Peoples, Final Report (2012).

legal source and as a basis for the rights of indigenous peoples.[27] Additionally, as will be pointed out later, Finland has used UNDRIP as the basis for demonstrating its international obligations concerning indigenous peoples in its legal analysis of the text of the Draft Nordic Sami Convention.

The right to self-determination, as understood in the UNDRIP, does not afford indigenous peoples total freedom to determine their political status since it is also concerned to protect the territorial integrity of sovereign states.[28] Fitzmaurice states that 'the definition of self-determination in the Declaration is considered a compromise between the aspirations of indigenous peoples and the reluctance of states to grant a broadly understood right to self-determination'.[29] Thus, according to the UNDRIP, self-determination does not entail the right to secession. However, the UNDRIP does recognize full self-determination of the economic, social and cultural development of indigenous peoples. The Declaration guarantees the right to self-determination in internal and local matters.[30]

In conclusion, there has been a paradigm shift in the international status of indigenous peoples which continues to evolve. From the original view of indigenous peoples as passive objectives of protection, mainly seeking to guarantee their equal enjoyment of human rights, and from a cautious recognition of their unique culture, many important steps have been taken toward guaranteeing their 'semi-subjectivity', their authoritative position, and their effective participation in the matters that are important to them. A clear shift has taken place from provisions dealing with protection of minorities and the general duty of non-discrimination toward the recognition of indigenous communities as peoples. Both human rights monitoring bodies and biodiversity protection regimes recognize that indigenous peoples should be entitled to special and sui generis protection due to their connection to nature and natural resources.[31] International standards are

---

27   See, *Saramaka People v Suriname*, Inter-American Court of Human Rights, Judgment of 28 November 2007, Series C, No 172. The Supreme Court of Belize made a decision relating to the rights of the Maya community to their lands and resources, applying the Declaration. *Aurelio Cal v Attorney-General of Belize Claim* 121/2007 (18 October 2007) Supreme Court of Belize <http://www.elaw.org/node/1620> accessed 19 January 2014.

28   See UN Doc E/CN.4/Sub2AC.4/1992/3 Add 1 (1992) 5. See Article 46 of the UN Declaration on the Rights of Indigenous Peoples, which explicitly protects the territorial integrity of states.

29   See Malgosia Fitzmaurice, 'The New Developments Regarding the Saami Peoples of the North' (2009) 16 Journal on Minority and Group Rights 67–156, 151. See, generally Stephen Allen and Alexandra Xanthaki (eds), *Reflections on the UN Declaration on the Rights of Indigenous Peoples* (Hart Publishing 2011).

30   Article 4.

31   Indigenous peoples' rights and status have been advanced by Article 8(j) of the Convention on Biological Diversity, (adopted 5 June 1992, entered into force 29 December 1993, 1760 UNTS 79), which recognizes that indigenous peoples' traditional practices contribute to sustainable development and that, therefore, indigenous peoples should

celebrating the beginning of a new era in state-indigenous relations, many parts of which still have to be implemented in domestic and local settings.[32]

The Current Legal Status of FPIC

The concept of the 'free, prior and informed consent' (FPIC) of indigenous peoples is currently a very topical issue internationally, regionally and domestically. As maintained by the study of the Commission on Human Rights, discussion and standard-setting exercises on this topic cover a wide range of bodies and sectors including the safeguard policies of the multilateral development banks and international financial institutions; practices of extractive industries; water and energy development; natural resources management; access to genetic resources and associated traditional knowledge and benefit-sharing arrangements; scientific and medical research; and indigenous cultural heritage.[33]

On a basic level, the concept of FPIC is contained within its phrasing: it is the right of indigenous peoples to make free and informed choices about the development of their culture, lands and resources.[34] The basic idea of FPIC is to make sure that indigenous peoples are not forced, threatened or manipulated, and that their consent is asked and freely given prior to the authorization or commencement of any activities that take place in their traditional lands and that could have significantly negative impacts on them. Ultimately, FPIC signifies that the choices of indigenous peoples to give or withhold consent are respected.[35]

From a legal or technical perspective, however, FPIC is a much contested and confused concept. There are both binding and nonbinding international legal instruments and industry standards that purport to require some form of FPIC.[36]

participate actively in decision-making concerning the environment. See, Peter-Tobias Stoll and Anja von Hahn, 'Indigenous Peoples, Indigenous Knowledge and Indigenous Resources in International Law' in Nazila Ghanea and Alexandra Xanthaki (eds), *Minorities, Peoples and Self-determination* (Martinus Nijhoff Publishers 2005) 3–14.

32   Special Rapporteur James Anaya expresses concerns over the lack of proper implementation of the Declaration in many countries. See, Report of the Special Rapporteur on the rights of indigenous peoples, 2013 (n 26) 15.

33   UN Commission on Human Rights, Sub-Comm on the Promotion and Protection of Human Rights Working Group on Indigenous Populations, Working Paper: Standard-Setting: Legal Commentary on the Concept of Free, Prior and Informed Consent, 57, UN Doc E/CN.4/Sub.2/AC.4/2005/WP.1 (14 July 2005) 3 (prepared by Antoanella-Iulia Motoc and the Tebtebba Foundation).

34   Tara Ward, 'The Right to Free, Prior and Informed Consent: Indigenous Peoples' Participation Rights within International Law' (2011) 10 (2) Northwestern Journal of International Human Rights 54.

35   UN Commission (2005) (n 33).

36   Frank Seier, 'Free, Prior and Informed Consent' under UNDRIP: What Does it Really Mean?' (2011) 1 Right 2 Respect, Business and Human Rights Advisors <http://www. right2respect.com/2011/06/%E2%80%98free-prior-and-informed-consent%E2%80%99-

The right to FPIC should not be seen as a new separate right but as an expansion of the rights of indigenous peoples to participate and to be consulted already well established in human rights law and emerging in international environmental law.[37]

Especially since the adoption of the UNDRIP, the right to FPIC has been directly related to the right of indigenous peoples to self-determination. As maintained by Ward, FPIC and other participation rights are not merely administrative processes, but are an exercise in and expression of the right to self-determination.[38] For Ward FPIC within the UNDRIP seeks to ensure that the right to self-determination is respected and protected by states.[39]

As argued by the report of the UN Commission on Human Rights, self-determination and FPIC, as collective rights, fundamentally entail the exercise of choices by peoples as rights-bearers and legal persons about their economic, social and cultural development. These cannot be weakened by the consultation of individual constituents about their wishes, but rather must enable and guarantee the collective decision-making of the concerned indigenous peoples and their communities through legitimate customary and agreed processes and through their own institutions.[40]

While indigenous rights advocates hold self-determination as the basis for FPIC, in the international human rights jurisprudence, FPIC is legally based on property rights, cultural rights, and the right to non-discrimination.[41] These rights, although recognizing a collective element in the case of indigenous peoples, have an individual rather than a collective basis.[42] The HRC, for instance, only accepts communications from individuals concerning individual human rights. According

---

under-the-un-declaration-on-the-rights-of-indigenous-peoples-what-does-it-really mean/> accessed 19 January 2014.

37   Nagoya Protocol on Access to Genetic Resources and the Fair and Equitable Sharing of Benefits Arising from Their Utilization to the Convention on Biological Diversity, Nagoya (29 October 2010) <http://www.cbd.int/ cop10/doc/> accessed 30 January 2014.

38   Ward (n 34) 55.

39   ibid 58.

40   UN Commission on Human rights (n 33) 12, para 45.

41   Ward (n 34) 56. See, CESCR, Concluding observations on Colombia, UN Doc E/C.12/1/Add.74E/C.12/1/Add.74, para 12; Committee on the Elimination of Racial Discrimination, Eighty-first session, 6–31 August 2012, Consideration of reports submitted by State parties under Article 9 of the Convention, Concluding observation of the Committee on the Elimination of Racial Discrimination, Finland, CERD/C/FIN/CO/20–22, para 13; UN Human Rights Committee, Concluding Observations on Togo (18 April 2011) CCPR/C/TGO/CO/4, para 21.

42   The Inter-American Human Rights system widely recognizes the collective property of indigenous peoples and expands the application of the right to property in cases involving indigenous peoples. See a thorough analysis in Nigel Bankes, 'The Protection of the Rights of Indigenous Peoples to Territory through the Property Rights Provisions of International Regional Human Rights Instruments' (2011) 3 The Yearbook of Polar Law 57–112.

to the case practice of the HRC, it receives only complaints based on individual rights, such as a right of members of a minority group in Article 27, but not a right of self-determination (Art. 1) that is a right of a collective.[43] In 2009, the HRC recognized that the mere consultation of the indigenous community in question may not always satisfy the requirement of Article 27 of ICCPR, when the culture and traditional way of life of indigenous peoples are seriously threatened. In *Poma Poma v. Peru*,[44] for the first time, the HRC stated that mere consultation was not enough; the FPIC of the applicants should have been applied.[45] This case shows how the HRC is ready to expand the interpretation of Article 27. It is noteworthy that the decision was released shortly after the adoption of the UNDRIP. Although the lack of a direct reference in the case to the Declaration has been criticized,[46] it is evident that the Declaration has played a role in this fundamental shift.

The Era of Self-determination and FPIC in the Draft Nordic Sami Convention

In one way, Finland has acted as a pioneer, together with other Nordic states, in advancing the paradigm shift in the international status of Sami people by engaging in the drafting and negotiating process of the Nordic Sami Convention, which began before the final adoption of the UNDRIP. In October 2005, the Expert Group, nominated by the governments of Finland, Norway and Sweden and the respective Sami Parliaments, presented a draft for a Nordic Sami Convention.[47] The Draft Convention, from the outset, recognizes the Sami people as a legal subject and recognizes their right to self-determination.[48] This acknowledgment

---

43   See, *Lubicon Lake Band v Canada*, Communication No 167/1984, CCPR/ C/38/D/167/1884.

44   *Poma Poma v Peru*, Human Rights Committee, Communication No 1457/2006, Doc CCPR/C/95/D/1457/2006 of 27 March 2009.

45   The case concerned a dispute over the exploitation of natural water resources, which caused a direct and negative impact on the indigenous Aymara peoples' traditional means of subsistence – the raising of llamas and alpacas on which the Aymara community depends.

46   See Katja Göcke, 'The Case of Ángela Poma, Poma v Peru before the Human Rights Committee, The Concept of Free, Prior and Informed Consent and the Application of the International Covenant on Civil and Political Rights to the Protection and Promotion of Indigenous Peoples' Rights'(2010) 14 Max Planck Yearbook of United Nations Law 353–57.

47   See an analysis of the Draft Convention; Timo Koivurova, 'The Draft for a Nordic Saami Convention' (2006-07) 6 European Yearbook of Minority Issues 103–36; Timo Koivurova, 'The Draft Nordic Saami Convention: Nations Working Together' (2008) 10 International Community Law Review 279–93.

48   According to the Convention, the Sami people are the indigenous people of Finland, Norway and Sweden. The Sami thus constitute one people living across the

fundamentally changes the status of an indigenous people by making them active actors alongside states, at least in matters that directly concern them.[49]

However, as promising as this may sound, the Finnish Committee nominated by the Ministry of Justice has expressed difficulty in accepting Article 3 of the Draft Convention that refers to the self-determination 'as accorded by international law'.[50] According to the Committee, this formulation contradicts the Finnish Constitution, which does not recognize the self-determination of the Sami but instead guarantees that the Sami, as *an indigenous people*, have the constitutional right to their own language and culture (s17) and the right to cultural and linguistic autonomy (s 121).[51] It is interesting and significant for the purpose of the evolving international status of indigenous peoples that the Finnish Committee uses the UNDRIP to interpret the right to self-determination of indigenous peoples. It concludes that, under the Declaration, the right to self-determination applies only to the internal and local affairs of the indigenous people in question.[52] However, by this statement, the Finnish Committee clearly recognizes the internal aspect of the self-determination of the Sami thereby raising the question of what this internal self-determination means in practical terms.

One crucial aspect of internal self-determination is decision-making power related to natural resources. Article 36 of the Draft Convention states that, 'before public authorities, based on law, grant a permit for prospecting or extraction of minerals or other sub-surface resources, or make decisions concerning utilization

---

national borders. The Expert Group researched the possibility of including the Russian Federation and the Sami people who live in Russia, but concluded, with regret, that it would be too complicated to agree on a strong and effective Sami Convention if the negotiations had to include the Russian Federation. See Mathias Åhren, in Mathias Åhren et al (eds), 'The Nordic Sami Convention: International Human Rights, Self-Determination and other Central Provisions' (2007) 3 (8) Gáldu Cala – Journal of Indigenous Peoples Rights 13.

49   See an analysis of the self-determination articles of the Draft Nordic Sami Convention, Leena Heinämäki, 'The Nordic Saami Convention: The Right of a People to Control Issues of Importance to Them' in Nigel Bankes and Timo Koivurova (eds), *The Proposed Nordic Saami Convention, National and International Dimensions of Indigenous Property Rights* (Hart Publishing 2013) 125–47.

50   The Ministry of Justice of Finland nominated a Committee to evaluate the relationship between the draft and the Finnish Constitution, other legislation and the international commitments of Finland on 8 January 2009 (2009) 18 Työryhmämietintö 16–18. <http://oikeusministerio.fi/fi/index/julkaisut/julkaisuarkisto/200918luonnospohjo ismaiseksisaamelaissopimukseksi/Files/OMTR2009_18_arviomietinto_110_sivua.pdf> accessed 1 September 2014.

51   ibid. See also Finnish Constitution 731/1991.

52   Timo Koivurova, 'Alkuperäiskansojen itsemääräämisoikeus kansainvälisessä oikeudessa' [The right of self-determination of indigenous peoples in international law] in Markku Aarto and Markku Vartiainen, Oikeus kansainvälisessä maailmassa [Law in a changing world] (Edita Publishing Oy, Lapin yliopiston oikeustieteiden tiedekunta [University of Lapland, Faculty of Law] 2008) 249–69, 268.

of other natural resources within such land or water areas that are owned or used by the Sami, negotiations shall be held with the affected Sami, as well as with the Sami parliament, when the matter is such that it falls within Article 16' (matters of major importance). Additionally, Article 36 notes that 'permits for prospecting or extraction of natural resources shall not be granted if the activity would make it impossible or substantially more difficult for the Sami to continue to utilize the areas concerned, and this utilization is essential to the Sami culture, unless so *consented* by the Sami parliament and the affected Sami' (emphasis added).

The Finnish Committee believes that Article 36 would extensively influence Finnish national legislation, thus requiring new legal mechanisms to be established in multiple areas, such as mining and land use. According to the Committee, the proposal may possibly be inconsistent with the non-discrimination obligation of Article 6 of the Finnish Constitution.[53]

Since the Finnish Committee uses the UNDRIP as the basis of Finland's current international commitments, it is important to note that Article 32 of the UNDRIP requires the consent of indigenous peoples prior to the approval of any project affecting their lands or territories. Additionally, Article 19 requires the consent of indigenous peoples before adopting and implementing legislative or administrative measures that may *affect* them. In the Sami Homeland region, this could mean that the Sami Parliament's views should be taken into account in all relevant decision-making that *directly* affects the Sami as an indigenous people.

Although the wording of Article32 – 'states shall consult *in order to obtain* the free, prior and informed consent' – gives states the possibility of modest interpretation, the *Saramaka* case in the Inter-American Court of Human Rights questioned that approach. The Court concluded that the consent (FPIC) of the community in question is needed concerning large-scale exploitation and interference on the lands of indigenous people.[54] Additionally, as mentioned, the HRC has now stated that FPIC is required where the resource exploitation has *substantive* negative impacts on indigenous peoples' enjoyment of their right to enjoy the culture.[55] Thus, by accepting the UNDRIP and the jurisprudence of the HRC without reservations, Finland has already embraced internal self-determination and the right to FPIC of the Sami people. In practice, this should mean that the Sami Parliament should be asked to consent if a third party's planned use of natural resources traditionally owned or used by the Sami makes it significantly more difficult for them to continue to utilize these areas as they have done since 'times immemorial' as an indigenous people.

By interpreting the rights of the Sami to control their most crucial issues as contradicting the non-discrimination requirement of the Constitution, Finland seems to forget that it has already committed itself, via human rights law, to 'affirmative action' (activity vs passivity) to guarantee the equal status of the Sami

---

53   The Ministry of Justice (n 50) 82.

54   *Saramaka People v Suriname* (n 27).

55   Poma Poma (n 44) para 7.5 of the Considerations of the Merits.

in relation to the rest of the population. This matter should be kept in mind in all decision-making concerning the Sami. In 2011, the UN Special Rapporteur James Anaya expressed a concern regarding the failure to apply the right to self-determination of the Sami and the limited ability of the Nordic Sami Parliaments to act independently and to make autonomous decisions over matters that concern the Sami people due to the statutory parameters of their powers and functions.[56]

Other Legal Developments and the Conclusion

The Draft Sami Convention is currently under negotiations that are expected to be finalized by the end of 2016. Thus far, it seems quite clear that Finland is still reluctant to accept any veto rights for the Sami Parliament even in the matters that are the most crucial for the Sami, thus failing to endorse fully their internal self-determination in its practical and actual meaning.

Nevertheless, there is some movement to take the views of the Sami Parliament more seriously and there is a firm effort to reach a common agreement on the crucial matters. This tendency started to emerge some years ago as exemplified in the process to reform the mining legislation. Whereas the old mining legislation was totally silent about the Sami, the new (2011) Mining Act[57] recognizes the Sami 'as an indigenous people' with both substantive and participatory rights related to the mining permission procedures.[58] The right of the Sami to be consulted is also strengthened by the recently proposed modification of the Sami Parliament Act.[59] Section 9 of the current Sami Parliament Act,[60] which regulates the obligation of the state to negotiate with the Sami Parliament in all important measures 'which may directly and in a specific way affect the status of the Sami as an indigenous

---

56   Report of the Special Rapporteur on the situation of human rights and fundamental freedoms of indigenous people, James Anaya, 'The situation of the Sami people in the Sápmi region of Norway, Sweden and Finland' (12 January 2011) para 41 <http://www2.ohchr.org/english/issues/indigenous/rapporteur/docs/Report_SR_SamiPeople.pdf> accessed 1 September 2014.

57   Finnish Mining Act 621/2011. See an analysis on the rights of the Sami people, Timo Koivurova and Anna Petrétei, 'Enacting a New Mining Act in Finland – How were Sami Rights and Interests Taken into Account?' (2014) 1 Nordisk Miljörättslig Tidskrift, Nordic Environmental Law Journal 119–33 <http://nordiskmiljorati.se/onewebmedia/NMT%202014–1.pdf> accessed 1 September 2014.

58   Art. 38.

59   Saamelaiskäräjälakityöryhmän mietintö. Oikeusministeriö, mietintöjä ja lausuntoja 55/2013   <http://oikeusministerio.fi/fi/index/julkaisut/julkaisuarkisto/1382513081296/Files/OMML_55_2013_MIETINTO_196_s.pdf> accessed in 20 August 2014.

60   Sami Parliament Act 974/1995 (amendments up to 1026/2003 included).

people'.[61] The proposed new text talks about the obligation to 'cooperate',[62] indicating a stronger obligation that aims to establish an equal partnership with mutual agreement on the most significant issues for the Sami. However, the Sami Parliament itself suggests that the new provision, while moving in the right direction, fails to embrace the standard of FPIC established in the UNDRIP.[63]

Another proposed legislative change that illustrates the move toward stronger participatory rights of the Sami people is the Act on *Metsähallitus*.[64] In 2013, the Finnish Ministry of Agriculture and Forestry set up a working group to prepare a proposal to be included in the new *Metsähallitus* Act to strengthen the participatory rights of the Sami in the decision-making related to land and water areas in the Sami Homeland region. The proposal of March 2014 suggests that that the plans and projects of the *Metsähallitus* in the Sami Homeland area have to be carried out in a way that they shall not significantly weaken the rights of the Sami, as *an indigenous people*, to practise their traditional livelihoods or otherwise maintain and develop their language and culture. All of the planning must be done in cooperation with the Sami Parliament, which also has the right to petition to the Administrative Court should a plan or a project of the *Metsähallitus* violate the prohibition against weakening Sami culture.[65] These suggestions are definitely positive steps toward embracing the Sami peoples' status as partners and subjects rather than merely objects of protection, and reflects the international paradigm shift.

However, at the international level, the HRC and other human rights monitoring bodies have expressed serious concern over the unsettled land and resource rights of the Sami people. In 2013, the HRC stated in its concluding observations on Finland's country-report that: 'The State party should increase its efforts to revise its legislation to fully guarantee the rights of the Sami people in their traditional land, ensuring respect for the right of Sami communities to engage in free, prior

---

61 Section 9.

62 Saamelaiskäräjälakityöryhmän mietintö (n 59)Yhteistoimintavelvoite (Cooperation requirement) 79.

63 The Statement of the Sami Parliament, Saamelaiskäräjien lausunto saamelaiskäräjälakityöryhmän mietinnöstä, lausuntopyyntö 3/551/2012, 10 <http://www.samediggi.fi/index.php?option=com_content&task=blogcategory&id=247&Itemid=381> accessed in 10 August 2014.

64 Forest Board, governing the state-owned lands. Act on Metsähallitus 1378/2004, English translation available at <http://www.finlex.fi/en/laki/kaannokset/2004/en20041378.pdf> accessed 11 August 2014.

65 Ministry of Forest and Agriculture, Työryhmämuistio MMM (2014) 2 <http://www.mmm.fi/attachments/mmm/julkaisut/tyoryhmamuistiot/2014/t5lQ2u0cf/trm_2_2014_Saamelaisten_osallistumisoikeuksien_lisaaminen_valtion_maa-_ja_vesialueiden_kayttoa_koskevassa_paatoksentekomenettelyssa_saamelaisten_kotiseutualueella_.pdf> accessed 20 August 2014.

and informed participation in policy and development processes that affect them'.[66] It is still important to note that, although the Sami have brought a series of cases to the HRC against Finland, the Committee has not found a *significant* harm to the Sami culture and thus has found no violation of Article 27 of the ICCPR.[67] In this light, it is difficult to know how Finland would have responded had the outcomes been different.

By constantly postponing ratification of ILO Convention No. 169, mainly because of the inability to resolve the land and natural resource rights of the Sami, Finland has so far demonstrated a lack of a real commitment to improve the status of the Sami as an indigenous people with the right to have 'a real say' in those matters that are crucial to them as a group. The most recent news is that Finland has decided to ratify the ILO Convention No. 169 with 'an explanation', according to which it will ratify the Convention without touching upon the land rights issue.[68] This comes as a total surprise and raises the question of how it is possible to do so, since the very reason for postponing ratification for so many years has been the unresolved question of the land rights. Martin Scheinin, an indigenous and Sami rights expert, has noted that legally such 'an explanation' is a reservation that is contrary to international law and the rules of the ILO Convention. He believes that the reservation will have no validity and that, therefore, the ILO Committee will just nullify this 'explanation', meaning that Finland will be bound by the land rights articles.[69] Although expressing its unhappiness with the explanation, the Sami Parliament accepted the proposal. The chair of the Parliament, Klemetti Näkkäläjärvi, commented that, since Finland is ready to ratify the Convention but only on these terms, there was no chance for the Parliament to change anything.[70]

In its rhetoric, Finland has set the Sami rights as a high priority. To follow and implement its own human rights standards, ratification of ILO Convention requires satisfactory and concrete measures regarding the land and natural resource rights of the Sami. Additionally, by accepting the Nordic Sami Convention, Finland could

---

66   UN Human Rights Committee, Concluding observations on Finland, CCPR/C/FIN/CO/6 (22 August 2013) para 16. See also Committee on the Elimination of Racial Discrimination, CERD/C/FIN/CO/20–22 (31 August 2012) para 11, 13 <file:///C:/Users/lheinama/Downloads/CERD%20COBs%20Finland%20PM.pdf> accessed 1 September 2014.

67   See, for instance, *I Länsman et al v Finland*, Communication No 511/1992, UN Doc CCPR/C/52/D/511/1992 (1994) para 9.5 and 9.6.; *J Länsman et al v Finland*, Communication No 671/1995, UN Doc CCPR/C/58/D/671/1995; *A Äärelä and J Näkkäläjärvi v Finland*, Communication No 779/1997, UN Doc CCPR/C/73/D/779/1997; *J and E Länsman et al v Finland*, Communication No 1023/2001, UN Doc CCPR/C/83/D/1023/2001 (2005).

68   12 November 2014 <http://yle.fi/uutiset/saamelaiskarajat_hyvaksyi_hallituksen_ehdotuksen_ilo-sopimuksen_ratifioinnista/7577205> accessed 26 November 2014.

69   12 November 2014 <http://yle.fi/uutiset/scheinin_hallituksen_ilo-ehdotus_ei_poista_saamelaisten_maaoikeuksia/7620371> accessed 26 November 2014.

70   12 November 2014 <http://yle.fi/uutiset/saamelaiskarajat_hyvaksyi_hallituksen_ehdotuksen_ilo-sopimuksen_ratifioinnista/7577205> accessed 26 November 2014.

take a lead in affirming the international status of indigenous peoples as subjects of international law, affirming their strong decision-making powers over the most important matters to develop as an indigenous people with a unique culture that should be seen as enriching the society rather than burdening it.

PART III
Sami Law as a Knowledge Field

Chapter 15

Sami Legal Scholarship: The Making of a Knowledge Field

Eva-Maria Svensson

Introduction

Sami legal scholarship is a fairly young knowledge field in Norwegian, Swedish and Finnish legal scholarship, established as a discipline of its own during the latter part of the twentieth century. The establishment of the discipline can be understood in a context of an international movement with an increasing focus on indigenous people, on minority rights and the principle of non-discrimination. This development is also connected to the political process of reconciliation and the acknowledgment of the rights of the Sami people. The Sami people are an indigenous and minority group in the above-mentioned nation states. The three jurisdictions recognize the specific rights of the Sami people to various degrees. The history of the relationship between the Sami people and the nation states is a history of colonization and conflicts between different interests, mostly concerning the usage of land. According to May-Britt Öhman the colonization of Sapmi is still ongoing and it is aggressive.[1] The knowledge field of Sami legal scholarship is consequently tied to political struggles to recognize Sami rights. It has been stated that the main objective for Sami legal scholarship is to create a strong protection for Sami culture in order to render it sustainable.[2] This emancipatory and empowering objective is a characteristic that the discipline shares with other legal knowledge fields established at the same time, which also address the legal status of certain groups of individuals.[3]

The focus in this chapter will be on Sami legal scholarship as a field of knowledge, which has as its object Sami law (or Sami legal issues), a specific area of law, legal issues and themes. The field is studied with a concept capturing a process of how a knowledge field is formed and transformed,

---

1   <http://www.genus.se/Aktuellt/nyheter/Nyheter/fulltext//samisk-feministisk-kamp-pa-g14.cid1248953> accessed 7 December 2014.

2   Carsten Smith, *Loven Og Livet: Foredrag, Artikler, Taler* (Universitetsforlaget 1996).

3   The political struggle to recognize Sami rights started much earlier. One of the pioneers was Elsa Laula Renberg (1877–1931), a feminist activist important for the Sami political struggle.

i.e. the formation of knowledge.[4] Studies of a knowledge field may focus on different things. One important aim here is to map out how a field is formed and transformed over time and in different contexts, inherent in which are sociological and epistemological questions. Sociological questions are, for example, how a field of knowledge becomes established as a discipline within the academy, how the field is demarcated, performed and communicated, its representation in law schools and in identified research areas. Epistemological questions are, for example, which theories, methods and concepts that are applied.[5] Studies of comprehensive collections of research and research reviews (such as state of the art) can provide knowledge of the content of a field and what kind of theories, methods and concepts are used.[6] The same analytic tool has been used in similar studies of gender legal scholarship.[7] The study of the formation of knowledge in Sami legal scholarship expands the area of inquiry in the legal discipline. Sami legal scholarship has many similarities to gender legal scholarship. They are both critical perspectives on mainstream legal scholarship and thereby challenging the way that the law is constructed as a majority and/or hegemonic legal system. They are also quite recent additions to Nordic legal scholarship, with several challenges and obstacles in their process of being institutionalized. Although both knowledge fields are part of a dynamic international legal scholarship, gender legal scholarship is more established with useful experiences that could be drawn upon in the development of Sami legal scholarship.

One useful perspective from the study of gender legal scholarship is that there are reasons to be self-reflective.[8] At times, we need to reappraise our methods and theories, reflect over priorities, and reconsider if there are some issues that have remained disregarded, all in order to meet contemporary challenges. The need for

---

4 In Swedish *kunskapsbildningsprocess*, see Eva-Maria Svensson, 'Formering och transformering av ett kunskapsfält' in Eva-Maria Svensson, Ulrika Andersson, Hege Bækhus, Monica Burman, Anne Hellum, Stine Jørgensen and Pylkkänen, Anu (eds) *På vei: Kjønn og rett i Norden* (Makadam 2011).

5 Eva-Maria Svensson, 'Contemporary Swedish Feminist Legal Studies: Five Doctoral Theses' (2009) 17 (2) NORA.

6 Such overviews for gender legal studies can be found in Eva-Maria Svensson, *På vei: Kjønn og rett i Norden* (Makadam 2011); Joanne Conaghan, *Feminist Legal Studies Vol I Evolution*, Critical Concepts in Law (Routledge 2009); Joanne Conaghan, *Feminist Legal Studies Vol II Neo/Liberal Encounters*, Critical Concepts in Law (Routledge 2009); Joanne Conaghan, *Feminist Legal Studies Vol III Legal Method, Legal Reason, Legal Change*; Joanne Conaghan, *Feminist Legal Studies Vol IV Challenges and Contestations* (Routledge 2009).

7 Svensson (n 4); Joanne Conaghan, 'The Making of a Field or the Building of a Wall? Feminist Legal Studies and Law, Gender and Sexuality' (2009) 17 Feminist Legal Studies; Svensson (n 5); Anne Bottomley, 'Shock to Thought: An Encounter (of a Third Kind) with Legal Feminism' (2004) 12 Feminist Legal Studies.

8 ibid.

critical scholarship in the field of Sami law has been emphasized repeatedly.[9] In an international context, Gordon Christie has raised the need for theoretical reflections within indigenous law. According to him, few indigenous scholars have broached the relationship among legal theory, indigenous legal scholarship and the question of whether indigenous peoples might not only have particular perspectives from which to critique the law, but also particular theoretical perspectives on the law.[10] This study of the knowledge field is an attempt to reflect on the discipline from this meta-perspective.

This chapter has three objectives. The first is to reflect on sociological aspects of the formatting process and the institutionalization of a specific field of knowledge, Sami legal scholarship. This section begins with the question of how Sami law is defined and how this relates to Sami legal scholarship. The second is to reflect on some epistemological characteristics of the knowledge field. Finally, the third objective is to sketch out some claims for future developments in the field.

The Formatting Process and the Institutionalization of Sami Legal Scholarship

What are Sami Law and Sami Legal Scholarship?

Sami legal scholarship is a knowledge field within Nordic legal scholarship and with specific correlations to international indigenous legal scholarship. The object for this scholarship is *Sami law*. Sami law spans over several areas of law, such as the history of law, constitutional law, public international law, property law, administrative law and environmental law.[11] It has a specific dimension; the legal issues within these areas relate to Sami customs and conceptions shaped in a Sami legal culture, a culture that sometimes is acknowledged as relevant in the national legal system, and at other times is not.

Sami law can be defined in several ways. Susanne Funderud Skogvang presents two definitions in her book *Samerett*. One definition is the legal discipline, in which

---

9   Eivind Torp, 'Samerättslig forskning i Sverige: Pågående forskning och framtida utmaningar' in Peter Sköld (ed) *Människor i norr. Samisk forskning på nya vägar* (Umeå universitet 2008); Susann Funderud Skogvang, *Samerett* (2nd edn, Universitetsforlaget 2009) 60.

10   Christie Gordon, 'Indigenous Legal Theory: Some Initial Considerations' in Benjamin J Richardson, Shin Imai and Kent McNeil (eds), *Indigenous Peoples and the Law: Comparative and Critical Perspectives*, Osgoode Readers (Hart Publishing 2009) 195.

11   These areas are mentioned by Christina Allard in an application for research funding to Norges Forskningsråd *Sámi Rights in a Nordic Context: A Critical Assessment of Legislation and Legal Systems* (SANC) (Forskerprosjekt - SAMISK 2010).

only legal issues special for the Sami group are included. The other definition embraces, in principle, all parts of Norwegian law, in which cultural and linguistic differences between the Sami group and the Norwegian population means that the rules function differently.[12] The discipline as such transcends many of the internal legal disciplinary boundaries.

The themes in focus within the discipline may differ depending on what issues are highlighted as important and problematic in a broader context. It could be claimed that law is always reflective of a social context, but not all legal disciplines recognize this circumstance. In Sami law, this is, however, one of the starting-points. It shares this with other legal disciplines focusing on a specific group identified out of its subordinated status in relation to a specific nation state jurisdiction and to a hegemonic group. As Skogvang puts it, there is a 'sliding transition' between Sami law and Sami politics. One aspect of the acknowledgement of law in this context is that its trans-disciplinarity also applies in relation to disciplines other than law. Sami law (in Norwegian *samerett*) according to the mentioned definition is part of Norwegian law.

The other definition of Sami law (in Norwegian *samisk rett*) is the Sami legal tradition, i.e. the perception of law, legal norms and customs within Sami culture.[13] The difference is easier to notice in Norwegian than in English, *samerett* is a noun and *samisk rett* is an adjective. Sami law in the latter sense has its own legal culture that is distinct from the Norwegian legal system. The Norwegian legal system was developed as a function of the Norwegian nation state as it established itself on territories already populated by the Sami peoples. Parts of Sami law (here, in the adjective sense) have over time been incorporated or accepted in Norwegian law, but is not recognized as forming a distinct legal system.[14] Norway acknowledges only one legal system, the Norwegian, but within its nation state territory exists also a distinct Sami legal culture. The term 'legal culture' can be seen as a colonial word that has been imposed on the Sami nation through a process similar to the forced application of words such as Aboriginal, Native, Indigenous, or Indian as discussed by Patricia A. Monture and Patricia D. McGuire.[15] Sami law is defined as being outside the mainstream legal jurisdiction, and as such not considered to be a legal system but rather a 'legal culture'. Despite the problem with the chosen term, it is used here within citation marks as a signifier of the imposed definition by the nation state. Sami law bears with it this dual meaning (not always explicit or

---

12   Skogvang (n 9) 25. See also Eivind Torp, 'Samerättslig forskning i Sverige-Pågående forskning och framtida utmaningar' in P Sköld (ed), *Människor i norr. Samisk forskning på nya vägar* (Umeå universitet 2008) 84.

13   ibid.

14   ibid 57; Samerettsutvalget, 'NOU 1993:34 Rett til og forvaltning av land og vann i Finnmark' (Norway 1993).

15   Patricia A Monture and Patricia D McGuire (eds), *First Voices an Aboriginal Women's Reader* (Inanna Publications and Education 2009) 1–2.

conscious even in Norwegian languages, despite the possibility of distinguishing it linguistically) and its colonial history.

Law as an object for academic study, both for the professional education and for legal research and scholars, is traditionally (especially in the Nordic context) structured out of specific areas of law. Each area has its own principles, legal sources and academic traditions. During the last part of the twentieth century, another organizational principle has emerged. Instead of taking a special area of law as the starting-point, the structural principle can be an academic or theoretical tradition based on a certain perspective and a specific set of theories and methods. The perspective can be related to a specific group, for example a 'minority group' or 'women', or to a specific epistemology, for example social constructivism or gender/feminist/critical legal studies. This kind of structure is based on a specific field of knowledge instead of a specific area of law. Sami law could also be considered in this perspective, namely as a field of knowledge which encompasses legal themes that vary over time, acknowledging the close relationship between law and politics, specific concepts, theories and methods, and furthermore, looking at certain legal sources, often international treaties, used as arguments to criticize, change or expand domestic law in a certain direction. The term Sami legal scholarship is used signifying the field of knowledge, in order to distinguish it from Sami law, signifying a specific area of law.

The Institutionalization of the Knowledge Field

Sami law developed gradually as a discipline within law at a time when several new disciplines were established in Nordic legal scholarship, starting in the 1970s. Institutional settings, like centres and academic positions, journals, Sami law as a subject within the law programme, publications and doctoral theses are all important in the process of making a knowledge field.[16]

The first university that established Sami law as a specific legal subject was the University of Tromsø (since 2013 UiT The Arctic University of Norway). As pointed out by Øyvind Ravna, the committee that prepared the establishment of a law programme in Tromsø (*Kjønstadutvalget*) highlighted research and education in Sami issues as the specific responsibilities of the university.[17] This specific responsibility contributed to the establishment of the Law Department (*Institutt for Rettsvitenskap*) in 1987. Sami law was one theme in the first issue of the Department's own writing series.[18] It later became a compulsory course in the law programme in 1991, and

---

16   Svensson (n 4).

17   Øyvind Ravna, 'Samerett og samiske rettigheter i Norge' in *Juss i Nord: Hav, fisk og urfolk: En hyllest til Det juridiska fakultet ved Universitetet i Tromsøs 25-årsjubileum* (Gyldendal 2012).

18   Carsten Smith, *Samerett: Gamle rettskilder og ny rettsdisiplin* (Skriftserie / Institutt for Rettsvitenskap University of Tromsø 1987).

also available as an optional course on the master's level. During the launching ceremony of the Department, Carsten Smith referred to the previous lack of interest in Sami legal research among legal scholars and lawyers. According to Smith, it was in this context that the importance of the establishment of Sami law as a discipline and of making it part of the compulsory curriculum in the law programme must be considered.[19] For a few years, Sami and indigenous rights have been prioritized areas at the Faculty of Law and this specific academic environment is probably the largest amongst law schools in Scandinavia.[20] A research group for Sami law was established in 2000.[21] There are no specific academic positions in Sami law in Tromsø, however this is not specific to Sami law, as almost all academic positions are in *Rettsvitenskap* (legal scholarship). There is also a Centre for Sami Studies, with scholars from the humanities, social sciences and education. The only other university in Norway that offers Sami law as an optional subject is the University of Oslo. The Sami University College in Kautokeino instead addresses Sami issues over a broad range, including legal issues.

At the Finnish University of Lapland, Sami-related research is part of every faculty, including the Faculty of Law. The faculty has both research and education in Sami law in accordance with national guidelines for the university, similar to that in Tromsø. Sami law is an optional subject, introduced in 2009. As the only university in the Nordic countries, the University of Lapland has specific academic positions in Sami research, including law. For the moment (November 2014) there are one associate professor and one senior researcher at the Faculty of Social Sciences, and one junior researcher, one fully employed PhD candidate and four other scholars without funding with PhD topics in Sami law at the Law Faculty. These researchers form a research group established in 2009.[22] There is also the national and international hub of information and centre of excellence, the Arctic centre, which conducts multidisciplinary research in changes in the Arctic region.[23] One research group forming a separate unit within this centre is the Northern Institute for Environmental and Minority Law (NIEM), established in 1985. The institute has a special focus on studying the law relating to indigenous peoples in the Arctic and environmental law as it is applied in the Arctic and northern region.[24]

---

19   Ravna (n 16).

20   Hege Brækhus, 'Hvordan gikk det? Det juridiske fakultet i Tromsø under 25 år' in Kirsten Ketscher et al (eds), *Velferd Og Rettferd: Festskrift Til Asbjørn Kjønstad 70 År* (Gyldendal juridisk 2013) 113.

21   <uit.no/om/enhet/artikkel?p_document_id=91269&p_dimension_id=88177> accessed 24 November 2014.

22   Interview with Professor Juha Karhu, Dean at the University of Lapland, 19 November 2014.

23   <http://www.arcticcentre.org/InEnglish/ABOUT-US> accessed 24 November 2014.

24   <http://www.arcticcentre.org/InEnglish/RESEARCH/The-Northern-Institute-for-Environmental-and-Minority-Law> accessed 24 November 2014.

Sami law in Sweden is not established in the same way that it is in Norway and Finland. Courses have been offered in Sami law at Luleå University of Technology and at Mid Sweden University in Östersund, but not currently. There are, however, other departments directed at Sami issues. Umeå University has a Centre for Sami Research (CeSam), coordinating different areas of Sami research, culture, language, history and society, as well as new research initiatives and projects. It aims to be a meeting place for PhD students and researchers from a variety of disciplines at the university.[25]

The only journal fully devoted to Sami legal issues is the *Arctic Review on Law and Politics*, an independent, peer-reviewed journal, initiated by researchers at the University of Tromsø in Norway. It was established to provide a forum for discussing and challenging questions of a legal and political character in an Arctic context. The board of editors come from the eight Arctic countries: Canada, Denmark/Greenland, Finland, Iceland, Russia, Sweden, United States and Norway. The journal publishes articles in the fields of law and politics understood in a wide sense. It encompasses not only research on legal and political sciences, but also such disciplines as economics, sociology, human geography and social anthropology. The aim of the journal is to provide new insights and a deeper understanding of fundamental issues related to the Arctic and the High North and thus become a forum for academic discussion on sustainable development in the North.[26]

The first doctoral thesis in Sami law was defended in 1972 by Sverre Tønnesen.[27] It addressed Sami rights to land in the county of Finnmark in Norway. The second thesis in Sami legal history was published in 1989, by Kaisa Korpijaakko-Labba,[28] and the following on property law in 1999, by Otto Jebens.[29] In the early twenty-first century, several doctoral theses were defended: the theses by Christina Allard[30] in 2006,

---

25　<http://www.cesam.umu.se/english/?languageId=1> accessed 24 November 2014.

26　Øyvind Ravna, 'A New Academic Journal is Born'. (2010) 1 (1) Arctic Review on Law and Politics 1–3.

27　Sverre Tønnesen, *Retten til jorden i Finnmark: Rettsreglene om den såkalte 'statens umatrikulerte grunn': En undersøkelse med særlig sikte på samenes rettigheter.* Skrift nr 3/1972 (Universitetet i Bergen: Institutt for offentlig rett 1972).

28　Kaisa Korpijaakko-Labba, *Saamelaisten oikeusasemasta Ruotsi-Suomessa: oikeushistoriallinen tutkimus Länsi-Pohjan Lapin maankäyttöoloista ja -oikeuksista ennen 1700-luvun puoliväliä* (Lakimiesliiton kustannus 1989). The thesis shed in Swedish five years later; Kaisa Korpijaakko-Labba and Beate-Sofie Nissén-Hyvärinen, *Om samernas rättsliga ställning i Sverige-Finland: En rättshistorisk utredning av markanvändningsförhållanden och rättigheter i Västerbottens lappmark före mitten av 1700-talet* (Juristförbundets förlag 1994).

29　Otto Jebens, *Om eiendomsretten til Grunnen i Indre Finnmark* (Cappelen Akademisk forlag 1999).

30　Christina Allard, *Two Sides of the Coin – Rights and Duties: The Interface between Environmental Law and Saami Law Based on a Comparison with Aoteoaroa/New Zealand and Canada* (Luleå University of Technology 2006).

Øyivind Ravna[31] and Eivind Torp[32] in 2008, Laila Susanne Vars[33] in 2009, Matthias Åhrén[34] and Leena Heinämäki[35] in 2010, Nils-Johan Päiviö[36] in 2011, and Tanja Joona in 2012.[37] The doctoral thesis by Gunnar Eriksen from 2007 was not explicitly on Sami law, but it considered issues at the core of Sami law.[38] Also, the thesis by Ánde Somby[39] in 1999 was influenced by a Sami tradition.

There are comprehensive presentations of Sami law in a few publications serving as textbooks in Norway, Sweden and Finland. The first was published in Norway in 2002 by Susann Funderud Skogvang,[40] the second in Sweden in 2004 by Bertil Bengtsson[41] and the third in Finland in 2010, an anthology edited by Kai T. Kokko.[42] Interestingly, while writing his book, Bengtsson was hesitant to give a comprehensive presentation of Sami law for two reasons. First, the rights of the Sami to a great extent depend on historical circumstances, which had not been fully explored at that time. The second reason was the then ongoing legislative process which was expected to alter the situation for the Sami rights. According to Bengtsson, however, the legislative work was not performed with great enthusiasm.[43]

---

31 Øyvind Ravna, *Rettsutgreiing og bruksordning i reindriftsområder: En undersøkelse med henblikk på bruk av jordskiftelovgivningens virkemidler* (1st edn, Gyldendal akademisk 2008).

32 Eivind Torp, *Renskötselrätten och rätten till naturresurserna: Om Rättslig reglering av mark- och resursanvändningen på renbetesmarken i Sverige* (Universitetet i Tromsø, Det juridiske fakultet 2008).

33 Laila Susanne Vars, *The Sámi People's Right to Self-Determination* (Universitetet i Tromsø, Det juridiske fakultet 2010).

34 Mattias Åhrén, *The Saami Traditional Dress & Beauty Pageants: Indigenous Peoples' Rights of Ownership and Self-Determination over Their Cultures* (Universitetet i Tromsø, Juridisk fakultet 2010).

35 Leena Heinämäki, *The Right to Be a Part of Nature: Indigenous Peoples and the Environment* (University of Lapland 2010).

36 Nils-Johan Päiviö, *Från skattemansrätt till nyttjanderätt: En rättshistorisk studie av utvecklingen av samernas rättigheter från slutet 1500-talet till 1886 års renbeteslag* (Uppsala universitet 2011).

37 Tanja Joona, *Ilo Convention No. 169 in a Nordic Context with Comparative Analysis: An Interdisciplinary Approach* (Juridica Lapponica Series, Lapin yliopistokustannus 2012).

38 Gunnar Eriksen, *Alders tids bruk* (Universitetet i Tromsø, Juridisk fakultet 2007).

39 Ánde Somby, *Juss Som Retorikk* (Tano Aschehoug 1999).

40 Susann Funderud Skogvang, *Samerett: Om samenes rett til en fortid, nåtid og fremtid* (Universitetsforlaget 2002).

41 Bertil Bengtsson, *Samerätt: En översikt* (Norstedts juridik 2004).

42 Kai T Kokko (ed), *Kysymyksiä Saamelaisten Oikeusasemasta* (University of Lappland 2010).

43 Bengtsson (n 41) 12.

Moreover, the Norwegian judges Erik Solem in 1933[44] and Carsten Smith in 1987[45] wrote some earlier publications with a comprehensive aim. Most of what is written in the field is directed toward specific issues. According to Bengtsson, real estate law is at the forefront of Sami law, and reindeer husbandry is included in this field of law.[46] Other specific issues are legal sources for claiming Sami rights, the right to self-determination and cultural rights. One early example of a textbook which has become a central legal text is the first book on reindeer husbandry by Thomas Cramér and Gunnar Prawitz in 1970.[47] In addition to the already mentioned authors Kirsti Strøm Bull has also written extensively within the field.[48]

One characteristic of Sami legal scholarship is its close connection to the jurisdictions of the different nation states, the Finnish, the Norwegian and the Swedish. The obvious explanation for this being that legal issues of concern for the Samis have been dealt with within the nation state context. There are, however, some similarities between the provisions on Sami issues in the three national legal systems, as well as many differences. When establishing a Sami legal knowledge field building on Sami 'legal culture', the nation state jurisdictions can be challenged with arguments not only from the Sami 'legal culture' within the nation state but also from neighbouring nation states with a Sami population. Moreover, international legal documents also strengthen this process of moving from a nation state jurisdiction-based knowledge field to a Sami-cultural-based and global indigenous-people-based legal argumentation. This can also be seen in this publication, in which some of the contributions are not focused on the nation state context.

Arguments based on sources other than those specifically acknowledged as legal sources by the nation state jurisdiction, can be used to strengthen the rights of the Sami people. 'Other sources' in this respect means sources that are recognized as legal sources in another jurisdiction or as not legally binding international document. One example of the latter is the ILO Convention no. 169, which has been ratified in Norway but not in Finland and Sweden. The convention has in fact strengthened the rights of the Sami in Norway, and hence, even if not ratified in the other two countries, it is notable to see how it is used in the work of several scholars.

---

44   Erik Solem, *Lappiske rettstudier*, Institutet for sammenlignende kulturforskning (Serie B, Skrifter, Aschehoug 1933); There is a second edition published in 1970 by Universitetsforlaget.

45   Smith (n 18).

46   Bengtsson (n 41) 12.

47   Tomas Cramér and Gunnar Prawitz, *Studier i Renbeteslagstiftningen* (Norstedt 1970).

48   Two of Bull's books are *Studier i reindriftsrett* (Tano Aschehoug 2007).and *Kystfisket i Finnmark – en rettshistorie* (Universitetsforlaget 2011).

The legal research on Sami issues is today anchored in the international research area of indigenous people's rights. International conventions are ratified in some of the jurisdictions that encompass the Sami 'legal culture'. At the same time, Sami legal knowledge is part of an international knowledge field, loosely held together by international legal sources, such as the ILO Convention 169[49] and the UNDRIP,[50] and by international policies and actions, all forming an international discourse on indigenous people. It is also notable to see how international research on indigenous people is used to an increasing extent, exemplified by the work of James Anaya.[51]

To sum up, it can be said that Sami legal scholarship in the Nordic context has been characterized by its focus on national law, but has increasingly become more Nordic and international. At the same time, it has also shifted in its articulations from a strict focus on black-letter law to becoming more proactive and argumentative as well as more general and theoretical in its approach. This transition process is in itself a good reason to reflect on the knowledge field. As with many other legal knowledge fields transitioned through international, theoretical, methodological changes, and when theories, methods and concepts are exposed to new contexts, new ways of understanding can emerge.

Theories, Methods and Concepts – Characteristics of the Knowledge Field

The Context of Sami Law

The establishment of Sami law within Nordic legal scholarship is, as shown above, quite recent. Yet, legal conflicts between the Sami people, the state, and non-Sami inhabitants, concerning the use of land, have been ongoing since the early colonization of Sapmi several hundred years ago.[52] Why was Sami law not established as a specific discipline earlier? There are several important aspects to consider when reflecting on this question.

One aspect is that law in modern society has been so tied up with the nation state, and it is only recently that the idea of a plurality of law producing subjects has challenged the idea of a monistic legal system.[53] I will come back to this point later.

---

49   The International Labor Organization Convention 169, The Indigenous and Tribal Peoples Convention, 1989.

50   The Declaration on the Rights of Indigenous People adopted by the United Nations General Assembly in 2007.

51   S James Anaya, *Indigenous Peoples in International Law* (2nd edn, OUP 2004).

52   See Chapter 14 by Leena Heinämäki in this edition.

53   See the Chapter 4 by Kjell-Åke Modéer in this edition.

Another aspect is the general turn to acknowledge law as a social phenomenon, i.e. law as contextualized in a broad societal and political context. The turn from a formalistic legal scholarship in the middle of the twentieth century, emphasizing law as a more or less closed normative system, to a realistic approach open for law also as an empirical entity, facilitated the establishment of new legal fields taking as their starting-point the experiences of certain groups being subordinated or excluded from the legislative power. The Sami people share this experience of being in a subordinated position. Not only minorities can be subordinated in relation to formal and informal power to shape the law. The critical position toward law as a system infused with a certain hierarchical order, majority vs minority, resourceful vs impecunious, men vs women, etc., has been the starting-point for several new legal fields, such as Sami law, victimology law, and, women's law (today feminist or gender legal scholarship) just to mention a few.

One common characteristic among those legal fields is the close connection between political and legal claims in the formation process of the field. Political actions and legal reforms on one hand contribute to the formulation of a new academic knowledge field. Scholars within the field are often active in several roles, as political actors or voices, as advocates, or as academic researchers forming a specific legal knowledge field. Over time, these double or triple roles seem to fade out, at least on an individual level. There may be a risk of being accused of being too political and not sufficiently academic. However, with more legislation resulting from political actions and legal reform, the legal status becomes, if not more strengthened, at least possible to address legally and not (only or mostly) politically.

Another common characteristic is the critique of mainstream legal knowledge for not addressing issues that are important for the specific group or for addressing them out of a majority perspective. Such criticism based on the experiences of a specific group might be based on a social epistemology, acknowledging knowledge as social and contextual. Considerations like power, interests and traditions can be articulated and discussed in relation to what knowledge is, what law is, and by identifying the legal sources, and can be made without being trapped in a political or subjective position. Law is always a product of specific power relations, certain acknowledged sources, and these can be subject to reflection and changes. This general epistemological transformation, from an objective epistemology to a social critique, is sometimes referred to as the social turn.[54]

This goes together with a view of law as based on a certain perception of what should be legally regulated and how. How the legal system is constructed is based on several layers of power orders that give certain interests and voices priority above others. The law is tightly connected to the nation state and its representatives. Groups of individuals have been (or are) excluded from influence

---

54   Eva-Maria Svensson, 'Boundary-Work in Legal Scholarship' in Åsa Gunnarsson, Eva-Maria Svensson, Margaret Davies (eds), *Exploiting the Limits of Law: Swedish Feminism and the Challenge to Pessimism* (Ashgate 2007).

formally or have had less influence due to different practical circumstances or due to being a minority group. Sami interests have through history not been the interests of the majority population in the nation states to which Sapmi belongs.[55] Bertil Bengtsson stated quite frankly that 'to support the Sami cause doesn't give any political points; every government, social democrat or bourgeois, seems to watch all legal argumentation which demands greater respect to their rights with uneasiness'.[56]

A third aspect relates to the discussion in the section above on sociological aspects, namely the personal aspect within legal scholarship. The identity and background of the researcher have, generally speaking, an impact on the content of the scholarship. This relationship has been studied and emphasized when it comes to gender studies in general and women's law in particular.[57] Active scholars within a knowledge field impact the process of how knowledge is formed. The situation is not that simple with regard to the establishment of Sami legal scholarship. The establishment of Sami law, led by non-Sami scholars, precede Sami scholars entering the universities. It was only quite recently that the first Sami legal scholars defended their doctoral theses in law.[58] However, the knowledge field is to an increasing degree further developed by Sami academics. But compared to gender legal studies, the situation differs; in gender legal studies there are still almost no men at all.

Law and Politics and the Claim for Rights

The close relationship between law, politics and academic knowledge is apparent within Sami legal scholarship. This does not mean that other legal knowledge fields do not have this close relationship; I certainly think this is the case. However, in Sami legal scholarship, this close relationship is emphasized and used as a point of departure for rights claims. Sami legal scholarship uses the relationship to make political claims and transfer them into legal claims, to perform an argumentation *de lege ferenda* or a legal-political (*rättspolitisk*) argumentation.[59] The field

---

55   Sapmi, the area in the Nordic Hemisphere, is under the jurisdiction of the nation states Norway, Finland, Russia and Sweden.

56   Author's translation. The quotation in Swedish is: 'Att stödja samernas sak ger inte många politiska poäng; varje regering – socialdemokratisk eller borgerlig – tycks se med samma olust på all juridisk argumentation som kräver större hänsyn till deras rättigheter'. Bengtsson (n 41) 13.

57   Svensson (n 4).

58   Jens Edvin Skoghøy, *Factoringpant* (Universitetsforlaget 1990); Ánde Somby, *Juss som retorikk* (Tano Aschehoug 1999).

59   The notions of *de lege ferenda* and legal-political argumentation have several connotations. Here it is used as a broad concept capturing the space for arguing for changes of law based on legitimate normative claims, such as, for example, to improve the situation for a certain group or individual. The argumentation is problematic only in a formalistic perception of law. See a theoretical exposure of the problems in Ota Weinberger,

has developed new ways to promote Sami interests and to guarantee the Sami population rights in several ways. Old and new legal sources, often international treaties, are used as arguments to criticize and change or expand the nation state law in a certain direction, in an interpretative and argumentative style that can be characterized as promoting Sami rights and as engaged scholarship. Like the international field of indigenous legal scholarship, Sami legal scholarship has an emancipatory purpose. Based on a history of colonialism and of being constructed as a minority within a nation state context, the pursuit of justice for Sami people will hopefully be advanced.[60]

The rights that are being claimed have changed over time and differ between the Nordic and the international contexts. Traditionally, the claimed rights for the Sami have been mainly those related to the use of land and, as such, connected to reindeer husbandry and to fishing and hunting. This view is especially emphasized by Bertil Bengtsson, in the book *Samerätt*. When he talks about Sami rights, he generally talks about the rights of the reindeer herding Sami.[61] The content of these rights has been regulated in legislation specifically dealing with the conditions of reindeer husbandry. Throughout history, the conflicting land interests of the Sami, the state and the non-Sami have been regulated in different ways (and resulted in more or less access to the land granted for the Sami.) The access to land has been regulated mainly as usufruct rights but also, to some extent, as property rights. Property rights have in the nation state jurisdictions, in modern times, been the rights that have been the most difficult to modify, but all rights have been questioned from time to time as not based on acknowledged legal sources. I will return to this question of legal sources later. First I will turn to a more general discussion of the concept of right in itself.

The concept of rights in the Nordic context is influenced by a functionalist approach to rights, an approach inherent in Scandinavian legal realism.[62] This tradition has had an important impact upon legal thinking in the Nordic countries. The main issue at hand is that the concept of 'right' is only a word, and that the meaning of the word is interpreted according to certain observable facts and with reference to a concept. In short, the meaning or content of 'rights' has no normative power in itself but rather a directive and informative function. According to this view, the claim for rights can be illusive. Acknowledging a formal right to something does not need to mean anything substantial. The substance of a concept, for example a right to something, is nothing in itself, but rather a word gathering the different elements or functions connected to the concept. This functional approach has been criticized for neglecting the normative aspects of law and for

Law, Institution, and Legal Politics: Fundamental Problems of Legal Theory and Social Philosophy, Law and Philosophy Library (Kluwer 1991).

60   Richardson, Imai and McNeil (n 10) 4.

61   Bengtsson (n 41) 13.

62   Jes Bjarup, 'The Philosophy of Scandinavian Legal Realism' (2005) 18 Ratio Juris.

reducing legal knowledge to empirical knowledge about social-psychological facts.[63] Today, Scandinavian legal realism has lost some of its significance, but it remains important to be aware of its influences on the concept of rights, both in the international human rights discourse as well as in a Nordic setting.

The functionalist approach is still prevalent in mainstream legal scholarship. Traditionally, Sami rights have not been framed as (natural) rights in the sense that they emanate from a human rights discourse. The Nordic approach has instead been to consider regulation as a balancing between conflicting interests in relation to activities related to a Sami livelihood, such as reindeer herding, fishing and hunting, as exemplified in several of the texts in this edition. The content of the right to herd, fish and hunt has been and still is based on real estate law and the criteria defined by this specific field. However, the international framing of indigenous people's rights as rights within the human rights discourse has had an increasing impact in the Nordic context. This is because the concept of rights within the human rights discourse has other connotations. Except being mostly a right for the individual, it is also understood as a right that can be admitted as long as no other individual's right is being breached. This non-relational and non-contextual approach has been criticized within gender legal theory and relational theory.[64]

The transformation of the rights concept is also connected to how the concept of democracy has changed. The perception of democracy has transformed from majority rule to include respect for minorities and anti-discrimination.[65] Notwithstanding the important positive aspects of this transformation for minority groups and for individuals in a subordinated position, there are reasons to be hesitant to abandon the functional approach that focuses on the material context and the balance between different interests. The Nordic welfare state model, characterized by a perception of law as a tool for social change in the context of an active welfare state policy with redistributive ambitions, constructing a society with equal material conditions, has not used the rights concept as its main function. On the contrary, some scholars have highlighted that the dismantling of the welfare state occurs at the same time as the rights discourse gains ground.[66] Distributive equality seems to be replaced by individual rights. One problem is that the latter requires resourceful individuals to take advantage of them.

Taking this into account and paying attention to some possible risks with the rights discourse, the discourse de facto gains importance. More Sami rights

---

63   ibid.

64   Eva-Maria Svensson, *Genus Och Rätt: En Problematisering Av Föreställningen Om Rätten* (Iustus 1997); Jennifer Nedelsky, *Law's Relations: A Relational Theory of Self, Autonomy, and Law* (OUP 2011).

65   See Chapter 4 by Kjell-Åke Modéer in this edition.

66   Anu Pylkkänen and Finska litteratursällskapet, *Trapped in Equality: Women as Legal Persons in the Modernisation of Finnish Law* (Suomalaisen Kirjallisuuden Seura 2009). Åsa Gunnarsson and Eva-Maria Svensson, 'Gender Equality in the Swedish Welfare State' (2012) 1 feminists@law 2.

have emerged over time. Starting with rights (property and usufruct rights of different kinds) to land and livelihoods, rights to language, culture and tradition have become more highlighted over time. In addition, the political right and the right to self-determination have developed more recently in connection with the establishment of specific political institutions, such as the Sami Parliament. Questions of identity, that are issues related to defining who is a Sami and what it means to be a Sami, become more important when the rights are linked to identity instead of function, as for instance reindeer herding or hunting. With an increasing focus on identity and rights linked to identity, the questions of inclusion and exclusion appear. Who can claim the identity of a Sami? What about the right to a traditional livelihood? Can these rights also be claimed by individuals who have left Sapmi and the Sami way of life? Will there be a stratification of the individuals claiming to be identified as a Sami? A transition from a functional approach to a rights approach will surely raise these kinds of questions.[67]

Monism – Pluralism

One theoretical aspect, prevalent explicitly or implicitly in the chapters of this edition, is the question of the relationship between Sami 'legal culture' and the nation state legal system. As argued in the beginning of this chapter, Sami law can be interpreted as either legal issues concerning the Sami people (within the nation state legal system) or as Sami 'legal culture'. The labelling of a legal system and a 'legal culture', respectively, is based on a monistic perception of what law is. According to such perception, law is a legal system that emanates from one specific legislative subject, which, in the Nordic context, is the nation state. Finland, Norway and Sweden have separate legal systems, with some things in common but nevertheless separate and different. How Sami issues are handled within these nation state jurisdictions varies in some respect while it is similar in others.[68] If the nation state legal system is seen as the only legitimate legal system for the specific nation state jurisdiction, than Sami law, that is Sami 'legal culture', cannot be considered a separate legal system. If Sami traditions and Sami perceptions on tradition are to be accepted an adhered to, they must be acknowledged within the legal system of the nation state. This has historically been the main approach in all of the Nordic contexts. It is within the nation state legal system that Sami interests have been acknowledged or not. Legal conflicts and legislative efforts have been perceived in the context of this nation state position. The extent to which Sami claims can be met within the realm of this perspective depends on the willingness of the nation state legal system to acknowledge Sami interests and define how these can be based on legally accepted sources and argumentation. Reform in one jurisdiction can be used as a leverage for arguments in another, however, they cannot be directly applied or gain an automatic relevance in another jurisdiction.

---

67   See Chapter 12 by Tanja Joona in this edition.
68   See Chapter 5 by Christina Allard in this edition.

An alternative way to understand the relation between nation state jurisdiction and Sami 'legal culture' is in a polycentric or pluralistic way. Theories of polycentric law and legal pluralism offer a way to understand law as emerging out of several legal subjects or as a way of acknowledging a situation in which more than one legal system can be both legal and legitimate.[69] Obviously, the nation state is not the only legislative subject. Nation states such as Finland, Norway and Sweden are bound to follow not only legislation adopted by the national Parliament, but also legislation adopted by inter-state legislative subjects and adopted by the states themselves, such as the EU, EFTA, and international bodies, such as the UN and the ILO, just to mention some examples. This polycentric situation, with several legislative subjects, has different impacts. One impact is that one legal source can be used as an argument when interpreting another legal source. In more recent time, international law (legally binding documents, soft law and political agreements or declarations) has become a powerful tool to challenge the nation state legal system and its balancing act between Sami and non-Sami interests.[70]

Legal arguments to strengthen Sami rights could be applied either through a traditional monistic view or a pluralistic or polycentric view. According to traditional monism, legal arguments rely on sources and reasoning traditionally applied in the legal system. International law can, in this context, be used as an interpretative tool and as a normative argument. Arguments concerning a traditional way of life or traditional land use can be made in reference to provisions in international documents calling specifically for an acknowledgement of such cultural manifestations. This line of reasoning is not unfamiliar to Sami legal scholarship, and will be discussed in further detail below under the section on the doctrine of legal sources. The pluralistic approach, on the other hand, implies that it is useful to claim that Sami 'legal culture' is in fact a (Sami) legal system of its own and thereby provide a basis for establishing self-governing institutions in accordance with the idea of self-determination for indigenous people. The presence of a legal system on which the idea of self-determination can be built could strengthen the development of parallel legal systems in the Nordic context. The presence of parallel legal systems is not unusual in an international context. Its impact in the Nordic context ought to be scrutinized. Such development probably has both negative and positive aspects.

Sami Interests Meeting with the Doctrine of Legal Sources

One important aspect of how Sami interests have been acknowledged in the Nordic nation state legal systems is related to *the doctrine of legal sources*. There is, according to Lars Björne, a specific *Nordic* doctrine of legal sources.[71] This view

---

69   See Chapter 4 of Kjell-Åke Modéer in this edition.
70   See Chapter 5 of Christina Allard in this edition.
71   Lars Björne, *Nordisk rättskällelära: Studier i rättskälleläran på 1800-talet* (Skrifter utgivna av institutet för rättshistorisk forskning. Serien 1, Rättshistoriskt Bibliotek,

is accurate on a general level. On the other hand, when considering how strictly the doctrine is followed and the spaces available for dynamic interpretations of the sources, the differences are obvious.[72] I will return to this aspect later. According to Björne, the Nordic countries have shared a common ground in the Ørstedts doctrine of legal sources since the first part of the nineteenth century. In an international context, the doctrine is quite formalistic and closed in relation to what kind of sources could be used to claim different rights. The doctrine of legal sources identifies which sources are considered legal or non-legal by the application of a strict formalistic scheme. The sources acknowledged as legal gains authoritative power within the legal system. Moreover, the doctrine also points out the hierarchy of the legal sources, which legal source has precedence over another. The most important legal source is considered to be the law. The law originates from and is adopted by the nation state Parliament. When interpreting the law, other sources can be relevant according to this doctrine, like *travaux preparatoires*, legal practice (court cases) and custom (as well as usage). Custom is not automatically and always considered a legal source according to the Nordic formalistic doctrine of legal sources. It may be accepted as a legal source, i.e. customary law, if fulfilling certain criteria.[73] As a legal source, it generally has lower authoritative power than law, *travaux preparatoires* and legal practice. However, in a historical perspective, customary law has been considered as a legal source with higher value in the hierarchy.[74] Moreover, customary law is more accepted as a legal source in certain areas of law, such as real estate law and contract law, than in others.

Despite the common doctrine of legal sources in the Nordic context, there are evidently differences between how Sami interests have been acknowledged in the three different jurisdictions as shown in the chapter by Christina Allard. The law concerning Sami interests, such as reindeer herding, fishing and hunting rights, differs as does the ratification of international conventions. The recognition of Sami land rights differs on the grounds of international obligations, national legislation and interpretation of the law. One specific aspect is the acceptance of Sami customs as customary law. As Allard shows, there are differences among the three countries in this respect as well. Perhaps the ratification of the ILO Convention no. 169 explains why the Sami customs have been more successfully accepted in Norway than in the other countries. But Allard also argues for a more general difference in attitude toward Sami. A discussion on the perception of Sami custom is therefore useful.

As already mentioned, not all customs are acknowledged as customary law. In this regard, one of the main conflicts of interest concern Sami issues. Sami

---

Institutet för rättshistorisk forskning: Nordiska bokh 1991) 222.

72   As shown by Christina Allard, Chapter 5 in this book.

73   Aleksander Peczenik, *Vad är rätt?: Om demokrati, rättssäkerhet, etik och juridisk argumentation* (1st edn, Institutet för rättsvetenskaplig forskning/Fritze 1995) 230.

74   Björne (n 71).

customs have not always been accepted as customary law. When are Sami customs recognized as customary law? How has the Sami people's own understanding of their rights to land and water not been congruent with the state's understanding of them? As Eivind Torp mentions in his chapter in this edition, the state officials have long had difficulties translating Sami legal relations (i.e. Sami 'legal culture') into the conceptual language of private law. Torp points out that the conceptual framework of the nation state's legal system does not necessarily fit with the Sami customs. To receive acceptance and acknowledgement, Sami customs must be transformed into the specific framework of the Nordic nation state legal system with its formalistic doctrine of legal sources.

How can a custom be acknowledged as a legal custom and thereby receiving recognition as customary law? What should the custom be based on and how can it be proven? The customs of the Sami people can be perceived in two ways, either as customs under the nation state jurisdiction that may be acknowledged as legal customs (and consequently as customary law), or as legal customs within the Sami 'legal culture'. As said above, Sami 'legal culture' is claimed to be a specific and separate 'legal system' (not with the origin from a nation state but from a specific indigenous group, the Sami) that encompasses Sami customs and perceptions of what law is.[75] These definitional standpoints can have consequences for the structure of the argumentation and for how conflicts are resolved between diverging interests. If a custom is considered to be a legal custom and thereby customary law in the nation state legal system, then the rationality of this system, i.e. the perceptual framework, will determine whether or not it fulfils the requirement to be legally recognized. If a custom is considered a legal custom within a Sami 'legal system', then the argumentation will concern whether the Sami 'legal system' can be recognized. An historical turn from majority nation state jurisdiction and a monistic view on law to minority indigenous self-determination and a pluralistic view on law might go hand in hand with a reform in how Sami rights claims are framed and the extent to which they can be successful.

Bengtsson has argued that the custom of Sami reindeer herding is a legal source, i.e. customary law. It has been acknowledged in the Swedish jurisdiction as a legal source for the legal institute of immemorial prescription. A legal institute is, according to Strömholm, a group of rules with mutual affinity, such as proprietorship and contract.[76] The purpose of an institute is to express the social function of the collection of rules. The difference between legal source and legal institute is consequently that the first is about including and acknowledging some claim based on a specific source within the legal domain, whereas the second is about how to handle the claim based on a source considered legal within the legal system. If a custom is recognized as a legal source (as customary law), it can be captured within an institute affording certain rights to the person (or group) who

75   See the section on what Sami law is with references to Skogvang (n 8).
76   Stig Strömholm, *Rätt, rättskällor och rättstillämpning: En lärobok i allmän rättslära* (5th edn, Norstedts juridik 1996) 164, 178.

has claimed the custom as an authoritative legal source. As such, it can even have precedence before the law, according to Bengtsson with reference to the Taxed mountain case.[77] If case of doubt when interpreting the law, it should be interpreted in accordance with the traditional usage of the land of the Sami people.[78]

History shows that the acknowledgement of Sami customs has not been without complications. It is the legal system of the nation state, in relation to the Sami people and the colonial nation state, which has the privilege to formulate and to define whether a custom should be acknowledged as a legal source, and, if so, under which legal institute a claim could be classified. The conflicts of interest with regard to Sami claims, primarily related to the usage of land, have been handled in different ways over time and in the different Nordic jurisdictions. The claims of the Sami people seem to have been more successful in Norway than in Sweden and Finland. One reason may be the ratification of the ILO Convention no. 169. The convention creates the opportunity to discuss a platform of a more pluralistic understanding of law. If Sami 'legal culture' is recognized as a legal system, and not only as a custom that might be acknowledged as legal within the nation state legal system, it could give Sami interests a better position in relation to the nation state, i.e. Sami claims could be acknowledged as legal, also in the nation state legal system. Together with a strengthening of self-determination and a political structure for self-determination, such as the Sami Parliament, the future of Sami rights, at least with regard to land rights, could be strengthened. This does not mean that the conflicts with other interests disappear; it just means that the position in land claims, etc., for those involved will be more equal.

'Claims' for the Future

In this chapter, I have discussed the formatting process and the institutionalization of Sami legal scholarship. I have also reflected on the context of the field, its emancipatory aim, how the question of a monistic or a pluralistic view on law relates to the field, and the possibility of Sami interests to be transformed to accepted legal sources. In this last section, I will conclude by highlighting some issues that ought to be considered.

The knowledge field is quite young. Nevertheless, an increasingly extensive scholarship has developed in the recent decade. Most of what has been written is related to the issues traditionally and historically perceived as important for the Sami group, namely issues related to land use. As Patricia A Monture and Patricia D McGuire have stated, the land is essential for Sami identity and not only as a source for sustaining a livelihood but also for the existence of Sami culture.[79] Influenced by international developments, the scope of the field of indigenous

---

77 NJA 1981 p 1.
78 Bengtsson (n 41) 88.
79 Monture and McGuire (n 14) 1–2.

legal issues is likely to expand to other issues and has already started to do so. For instance, the oppression that the Sami people have experienced in the twentieth century, with racial studies and forced photography performed by the Swedish Race Biology Institute[80] as well as the systematic silencing of the Sami languages, has not been extensively studied. In addition, questions concerning land conflicts will probably be further considered.

Furthermore, this chapter has explored a claim for a continuous meta-reflection of the field of knowledge. Although Sami issues and interests are the central theme for scholars within the field, I would like to see more reflection on theories, methods and concepts applied in their analysis. Most of what is written on Sami law is written in the Nordic formalistic and pragmatic tradition using the tools offered by mainstream legal scholarship without regard to whether the scholarship, the material or the context is national or international.

I would also like to see more reflections on Sami 'legal culture' and its inherent conflicts. As often follows with a position subordinated to the majority or to the authoritative legal system, the focus for the critique and for certain claims is directed toward 'the other', the mainstream position. I would like to see more of what Sami 'legal culture' can offer and the inherent problems and conflicts that could result from such offerings, such as, for example, between reindeer herders and non-reindeer herders and between men and women within Sami society. If the Sami 'legal culture' is a specific legal system, that system must be open for reflections and critique.

Finally, I recommend that scholars within the field engage in a scholarly discussion on certain basic presumptions, used concepts, theories and methods. For instance, what would adopting a legal pluralistic view mean for the field of Sami law? What would it mean to criticize and to argue for another doctrine of legal sources? What would it mean to study conflicting interests between different Sami legal subjects? These are only some questions, but there are many more. The future for Sami legal scholarship seems to be bright as there is still much to discuss.

---

80   <http://www.do.se/sv/Diskriminerad/Diskrimineringsgrunderna/Etnisk-tillhorighet/Rasism/Sveriges-rasistiska-historia/> accessed 7 December 2014. The investigations carried out by the Swedish Race Biology Institute have been studied by the artist Katarina Pirak Sikku in her Master's thesis at the Umeå Academy of Fine Arts at Umeå University in 2005, see <http://www.genus.se/Aktuellt/nyheter/Nyheter/fulltext//samisk-feministisk-kamp-pa-g14.cid1248953> accessed 7 December 2014.

Index